The Road From Mandalay

A Journey in the Shadow of the East

Richard Rhodes James

authorHOUSE®

AuthorHouse™ *UK Ltd.*
500 Avebury Boulevard
Central Milton Keynes, MK9 2BE
www.authorhouse.co.uk
Phone: 08001974150

© 2007 Richard Rhodes James. All rights reserved.

No part of this book may be reproduced, stored in a retrieval system, or transmitted by any means without the written permission of the author.

First published by AuthorHouse 11/15/2007

ISBN: 978-1-4343-1223-5 (sc)
ISBN: 978-1-4343-1224-2 (hc)

Printed in the United States of America
Bloomington, Indiana

This book is printed on acid-free paper.

In memory of those who bore the burden of Empire.

Also by Richard Rhodes James

Chindit

The Years Between

Table Of Contents

Preface xi
1. Beginnings 1
2. Breaking up 22
3. Into the thirties 43
4. Into the slump 52
5. The march of the years 58
6. Into war 127
7. Battle 155
8. Other lands 169
9. Re-entry 180
10. Echoes of the east 188
11. Shaping the young 196
12. Other people's children 211
13. Words... 226
14. Return to the hills 237
15. Another 245
16. Surprised by Joy 258
17. Into open country 264
18. Back to battle 278
19. Full circle 289
20. And finally 301
Postscript.. 304

Preface

Whose past is worth recording?

This is a question that everyone who has the temerity to offer his or her own life to the public must set their mind to.

I must attempt to answer it.

I am now well into my ninth decade.

Much of what I am recalling is within the memory of few today – it is too long ago - and I believe it is worth recalling. As the title of the book suggests it is the Raj, that essay in Empire that has no parallel in the history of conquest. It may be the last chance to spell out in detail just what it was like those many years ago to be what I might perhaps rather dramatically call the price of empire and describe a life that most today can hardly believe.

It is also probably the last chance to relive the Thirties, that decade so much talked about by those who were not there. What was it like to grow up in those years?

Then there was the war, not many of whose warriors remain, and one which took me back to my roots. After that the post-war years in a world that got no saner, seeking to reach the young and shape them, sharing what I thought was true and hoping I had got it right. And asking you, in what you may feel is an indulgence, to share with me the joys that came my way.

How much do the old remember? Strengthened by letters, some research, help from my family and the traumatic nature of much that I recall, a surprising amount. Memory, some say, can heal wounds. But it can do many other things besides. I hope that what I recall can do a little for you.

"Come, you, back to Mandalay,
Where the old flotilla lay
Can't you 'ear their paddles chunkin' from Rangoon to Mandalay,
Where the flying fishes play
An' the dawn comes up like thunder outer China
'crost the bay"

Rudyard Kipling

1.
Beginnings

I began in Mandalay.

That is a word that does not sit easily in a British passport. Indeed when Burma left the Commonwealth in 1948 I ceased to be a British citizen. I made my way to the Home Office and under the terms of the British Nationality Act 1948 Section 6 (1) on the grounds of ordinary residence in the Unites Kingdom I was registered as a citizen of the United Kingdom and Colonies. They were kind. I had no birth certificate – it had been lost somewhere out east – and only a copy of a page from the baptismal register of St Mary's Church Mandalay dated the 28th of February 1921 to prove my existence.

When I mention the place to my friends they show surprise and then almost without exception start in on Kipling's famous poem. Kipling in fact never went to Mandalay. He only spent a few days in Burma. Mandalay is many miles from the sea and there is no bay over which the sun could come like thunder. And the flying fishes? But all else that he wrote mirrored so much the world that shaped my life.

How did I come to be there?

My father was in the Indian Army. He joined the 89th Punjabis in 1907 and served them with distinction in the First World War winning the Military Cross in Mesopotamia in 1916, and action in 1915 in France at the battle of Loos, a theatre of war for which Indian troops were totally unsuited. He served in Burma from 1909 to 1911 and again from 1917 to 1922. He had a considerable gift for languages, passing exams in Hindustani, Punjabi, Urdu, Kachin, Burmese and colloquial Yunnanese. It was skill in the last, the language of the westernmost province of China that brought him there in 1917. He was seconded for special intelligence duty on the China-Burma border. In those days the Chinese were the bogeymen, the 'yellow peril' whose movements had to be watched. Which he did. And on Sunday 5 August he met my mother at a government lunch party at Maymyo, a hill station. They were married in the following July.

My father, to whom words did not always come readily was said to have proclaimed, "I blight thee my troth."

My mother had reached Burma by the usual circuitous route: born in Burma and then dumped in England aged five, at first looked after by a poor family in the east end of London. This was a strange arrangement. My grandparents had well-to-do relatives living in some style, but it seems that they were not interested, so my mother was farmed out to a very humble home. Her education was minimal - a year at Eastbourne Ladies College, when presumably the money ran out. But she blossomed and her many talents emerged. She was a pupil at the Royal Academy School: studying under Orpen and Ivan Hichens and when not painting developing a fine soprano voice. Her diaries in 1915 show a girl of talent, spirit and a heart in many places, "Struggled away at life. Dashed away at legs…Dawbed away at head….Orpen gave me a lesson in the afternoon and said the head was good…Sargent came round and drew alongside mine, but he mumbled into his beard so that I could hardly hear". "Crept down early and there *was* a letter. Oh joy, very thrilled." And on 20 Sept 1915, "Mother says I am to go out. How exciting." But the rapture was much modified. "I feel it is Burma for certain. O lackaday. They have decided on my coming out. O lordy." She said "I was dragged out." She had a passionate attachment to another student and the parting was hard to contemplate. 31 December. "Oh, my beloved, what will another year bring?" How did her parents know when the time was right? Perhaps she was now mature enough – she was nineteen - and the time was right to start thinking of marriage; Burma held distinct possibilities. Anyway they had been apart too long. So back to Burma, to which she went in 1916 to see her parents after very many years. My mother's first love was killed in France, but that was not uncommon in those days.

It was the meeting of two imperial streams. My father's forebears first went west. Colonel Richard Montague James went to Jamaica with the Penn and Venables Expedition of 1655. There the family made good, growing sugar and prospering. They were said to have acquired a fortune but attempts to find it have failed. A neighbour's slave stock book, showing names and prices, which I have with me, reflects savagely the culture in which my forebears operated. William James, who died in 1720, married Frances Rhodes and these two names were placed side by side, where they have remained. The scene changes. In 1837 my great-grandfather went to South Australia with his two brothers. They built up a large sheep station, but there were disagreements and my great-grandfather returned to England in 1843 to the West Country where the rest of the family had settled. In 1847 he married Mary Lister. They had 13 children, 7 sons and 6 daughters, and he set up a rope factory in Devon. My grandfather William left England for India to grow coffee in the Nilgiri Hills in south India and in 1886 my father was born at Wellington in those lovely rolling hills that remind ex-patriates of their native land. The Jameses had arrived in the east. And my grandfather stayed there, his mind drifting beyond control. It is not known in what place of mental refuge he died, a sadness that it has not been possible to plumb.

With my mother the eastern roots went deeper. Her father was a Swinhoe. In 1779 Henry Swinhoe arrived at Fort William, Calcutta, having gained a writership in the East India Company and he became an attorney of the Supreme Court, "a very distinguished man" according to a gloss in the family records. He had eight children, all baptised at St John's Cathedral, Calcutta, and through them the Swinhoe tentacles spread through India. Hannah married a colonel in the Bengal Army, Laetitia married General Sir William Nott, Sarah married a captain in the 3rd Regiment Native Infantry. Samuel became a general and a son in law in the Bengal Cavalry was killed in the Mutiny at Lucknow. My mother's line descended from the fourth child, Bruce, several of whose fifteen children did not survive childhood.

My mother's mother was a Jones, though like the Jameses she added on another name, Juxon to make it Juxon Jones (They claimed a connection with Bishop Juxon, who stood on the scaffold when Charles I was beheaded.). The Joneses first came to the east in 1840. Henry

Juxon Jones was appointed an assistant surgeon to the East India Company. During the Mutiny he was attached to the Bengal Artillery. In August 1857 he helped to disarm the sepoys of the regiment and marched to Delhi accompanied on that burning journey by his wife. He had fourteen sons and two daughters. One of these daughters, Annie Stirling, was my grandmother.

Her husband, Rodway Swinhoe, was a barrister. He started work in Calcutta in 1887 and moved to Burma in 1888. In 1889 he married the bride who had been waiting patiently for him in England and after a rather precarious start he built up a large practice in Upper Burma. A man of wide culture, he made a considerable impression both on the small colony of British and on the Burmese, for whose way of life he had a deep appreciation. He took a party of Burmese to the Empire Exhibition in London in 1926. What he did not have, which became apparent from time to time, was the capacity to handle money.

My parents spent their honeymoon at Pagan, the city of a thousand pagodas. And then with barely a pause my father went north on the Kuki Punitive Expedition. A young policeman had refused to take a bribe. This was taken as an insult and he was attacked with a poisoned arrow, and there must be punishment. My mother, just returned from her honeymoon, saw him in hospital, a very frail figure. It was a start to a married life that was, like her own character, seldom orthodox.

On reading Orwell's *Burmese Days* I saw the other side of the picture, the real country and what he saw as the imperial minuet of a governing race. And I wondered if my parents knew what the people among whom the British moved with such assurance really thought of them. I have often wondered this. When I mentioned his name to my mother she deployed the venom that came so easily to her when she recognised an enemy; enemies got short shrift. The country which saw my beginning was one she never really understood.

But it did not contain my first memories. There was too little of me to remember anything, as we moved from Burma soon after I was born.

I am told that we returned to England in 1922 in a hospital ship *Assaye* with my father very ill, and took refuge with aunts in Sidmouth. There were always aunts. Faded photographs show them assembled in groups, with a row of small children in front.

My first memory came in 1924 in India when becoming three I was starting to register. Down the drive of our bungalow came a cart pulled by bullocks and on it a large dead crocodile. It was said that when the crocodile was killed they found inside it a woman and her jewellery. There were many crocodiles in the river. Some of our family went there for a picnic. As they ate lunch they saw a crocodile rise out of the water, seize a goat, draw it under the water, surface with it and beat it savagely to pieces. Suddenly the picnic was no longer enjoyable and the party packed and left. Rumour had it that crocodiles came up and took unattended children from the bank of the river. There was also a fleeting memory of a wedding, and in growing but confused expectation I asked, "When will the train arrive?"

My father had left the Indian Army proper as he could not afford to bring up a family on Army pay and he had joined a semi-civilian branch called the Cantonment Department whose job it was to administer the British Army settlements; which he did with a quiet regard for all. The colonel of his regiment was so incensed by my father's decision that he threatened to expunge any reference to him in the regiment's records. My father is unlikely to have been moved by this. And so we found ourselves in Jhansi. This was a city in the extreme south west corner of the United Provinces, now Uttar Pradesh, and about 250 miles south east of Delhi. To the east and west lie the hills of Shivpuri and Bundelkhand, a broken landscape of sudden hills where Kipling sited his Jungle Books and where many years later I plodded ceaselessly in pursuit of military skill and endurance.

In 1924 it was for us an evil place. Certainly its history did it no favours. Early in June 1857 the 12th Native Infantry murdered all but one of their officers, released the convicts from the jail, set fire to the bungalows and marched on the small fort where the rest of the Europeans in Jhansi had taken refuge. The Europeans fired the fort's guns and decided to surrender on the condition that the mutineers allowed them safe conduct out of the fort. It was a vain hope. Early in the morning of 8 June the mutineers surrounded the fort and succeeded in gaining entry. They took prisoner all the European officers and their women and children, took them outside the city walls and murdered every one of them.

Retribution came in April 1858. The British broke in and wholesale murder followed. It was said that that the rebels who could not escape threw their women and children down the wells and jumped down themselves. About 5000 are believed to have been killed. The final slaughter took place outside the city at a place that came to be called Retribution Hill.

There was no murder in 1924 but some suffering. The climate was fearsome. One optimistic brochure declared, "Though Jhansi is not entirely a healthy district, the climate is not an insalubrious one." But one British officer said of it, "I don't think there are many stations worse than Jhansi". It was designated a third class station and at least one regiment was sent there as a punishment for previous misdemeanours.

There was one pleasure to remember in much gloom. We went to Chatterpore, 80 miles away to stay with the maharajah, about whom EM Foster wrote his little gem *The hill of Devi*. He wrote it in 1921. Was it the same maharajah of whom he wrote, "A most unusual character – mystical and sensual, silly and shrewd"? My parents remember a very tired, oldish little man, who fetched us each afternoon for a drive. And I said one day with more confidence than knowledge, "This is like an English road," which pleased him a lot.

But heat and illness closed in on us. My sister, Iris, went down with dysentery and was close to death. There was a serious and intimate difficulty. Her nappy had to be removed before the specimen could be sent to the laboratory, and by the time it arrived it was cold and the doctors could not carry out the diagnosis to determine whether it was bacillary or amoebic dysentery; the cure for these two types were quite different. My mother offered up a strange but fervent prayer – that she herself should succumb so that the specimen could provide the answer. Her prayers were answered. She contracted the disease and the doctors reported, "A classic case of amoebic dysentery". And my sister was saved. Much credit was also due to the magnificent matron, Miss Maclean, whose two sisters started that great English institution, Universal Aunts. Iris also had an emaciated leg, the result of polio contracted two years before which encased her leg in iron and left her with a life-long limp.

Then we called it infantile paralysis and my mother found it a kind of shame. I myself contracted dysentery but not badly.

For Iris there were other hazards. She had serious trouble with one of her feet, due (so it was believed) to inattention at the hospital where she lay ill. The railway surgeon, a man of proven skill, said, "I must operate". The resident military surgeon, the senior doctor on the station, a man of less proven skill and of touchy disposition said, "No. That is my job. I will operate." My mother, fearing the latter's knife, said, "I want a second opinion." The civil surgeon, called in to give his advice, said, "Don't operate." But he explained afterwards in an aside to my mother that he had said this because he did not think that the military surgeon was competent to carry out the operation. Eventually my mother had the operation performed in Simla away from the quarrels of Jhansi. This more or less broke our finances and on returning to Jhansi she was greeted cheerily by one of the other wives, "Aren't you in a debtor's prison?" We seemed quite close. And she discovered that she was expecting another child. Thirty nine years later I entered Jhansi Military Hospital with a severe dose of malaria.

We were in crisis. We badly needed to recuperate but could not afford another trip to a hill station. Even my mother was shaken. In desperation my father wrote to his boss and pleaded with him for a better place. His request was granted and we left the hell of Jhansi for the much fairer airs of Mhow in February 1925.

Mhow was the last staging post. "It is raised 1800 feet above the heat of the plain, ten miles south of Indore and 327 miles from Bombay. It lies on the Grand Trunk Road which runs between Bombay and north India. The cantonment shares in the temperate climate of the plateau, having an average rainfall of 30 inches. The climate is a healthy one." There were two units stationed there: the Royal Artillery and the West Yorks. And behind our bungalow was a dusty plateau called One Tree Hill. It was a splendid parade ground and here on the great occasions of the year the Army paraded. The King's Birthday was the greatest of these. Glittering lines of soldiery, inspection, march past and a salvo of guns with the families watching from the sidelines. We watched and were proud, leaving to others questions that would gather strength as the years went by.

And our bungalow was a grand one, Number One Bungalow, The Mall. It was occupied by another officer who was going on leave and who said we could have it until his return. But he had not reckoned, like other people to their cost, on my mother. She said, "I am not moving", and there followed a skirmish typical of British India. My father's superior said kindly to my mother. "This is not going to affect your husband's promotion". The juxtaposition of sahib and memsahib was meat and drink to Kipling. All those plain tales.

We stayed and drew breath and enjoyed a measure of ease assisted by a staff that read: 1 bearer (personal servant), 2 khitmagars (butlers), 2 syces (grooms) 1 khansamah (cook), 1 khansamah's mate, 1 masalchi (washer up) 2 malis (gardeners), 1 dhobi (laundryman), 1 bhisti (water carrier, Kipling's Gunga Din), 1 sweeper, 1 chowkidar (guard), 1 ayah (nursemaid), 1 Anglo-Indian nannie.

This was a carefully graded regiment. The khitmagar commanded the household, a kind of major-domo, chief steward and warrant officer. He hovered by the table resplendent in white with a turban and a cummerbund in the colours of the sahib's service. At the bottom of the heap were the sweeper and the bhisit. The sweeper, a low cast Indian, emptied the contents of the lavatory pan, at the shout of command, either an imperious "Sweeper", or the universal cry for servants in India, "Koi hai" – "Anyone there?"

The sanitation of the Raj was most underdeveloped. I cannot remember either as a child or as an adult staying in a house that had flush sanitation. And scarcely ever running hot water. The bhisti, on hearing the shout "Bhisti, garm pani", would stagger over with a large skinful of hot water. It was a strange contrast: grand endless social occasions, and thunderboxes.

The syce was the aristocrat of the outside servants. There were always horses; almost anyone could afford one or two servants. And we had 2 horses, 1 pony and donkeys. We hunted. Colonel Selby-Lownes, the commander of the Royal Artillery unit, was a powerful hunting figure in England and had imported foxhounds. With these we pursued jackals over the rather arid countryside. Bill and I rode the donkeys. On one occasion my donkey lowered its head to eat a thistle and I slid down on to the sharpness.

Sometimes we had to ride with care. One day my mother was riding with Mrs Thomas across the plain near our house when they heard some loud bangs. A young officer hastened up to them and cried urgently, "Madam, we are firing live rounds."

They hastened away.

Among the battery of servants one stood apart, the bearer, the sahib's personal servant. He was the family retainer. If you found a good one, you hung on to him. Mohammed Baksh had been with my father for eight years. Bearers would wait for their sahibs when they returned from leave and would greet them at the railway station or even at the dockside. At the beginning of the Second World War, when retired officers were recalled, the word got round in the mysterious way that it does in the east and there were all the bearers waiting – and also the money-lenders waiting to collect some very old debts.

My mother managed the rest of our bevy of servants - memsahibs were basically managers - which she found no difficulty in being. Authority came easily. But she also cared. If children were sick, she visited. The son of Mohammed Baksh was very ill and he came to ask for help. My mother took some milk and brandy. "Heat up the milk", she said and applied some wool to the small boy's chest. She retired to bed, wondering. Next morning she went down to the compound to see what had happened. The child was well. Mohammed Baksh went on his knees and grabbed my mother's ankles in a touching act of worship and thanks. On one occasion she visited the dhobi's wife who just had their third child. "Where is the baby?" she asked. "I have thrown it away." "What?" "What is the use of three daughters?"

During our time at Mhow, a baby clinic was opened. The opening was performed by a member of the Cantonment Board. He ended his inaugural speech with the following words by quoting an English poet, "learn to labour and to wait", a quotation so apposite that my mother, whose sense of humour was never far away, was hard put to it to receive it in silence.

And we had a new baby. Monty was born on the 17th of August. There were now four of us. That seemed a good round number. But you can never tell.

We had our last free run as a family, playing in the dust with young Indians, speaking their language with an ease that escaped our parents and believing that life was fun.

We played with the servants' children in the monsoon and on one appalling occasion Bill pushed the dhobi's child into the well. The dhobi jumped in and rescued him and had the difficult task of showing to the master race that he was displeased.

Snakes were around, and in the rainy season they made their way into houses. A local hospital was researching into snake venom and they asked us to catch any snakes we saw. Thus the sighting of a snake was the occasion for a large-scale hunt with a number of servants trying to catch the writhing creature and force it into a large glass jar for onward transit. One day we saw a cobra coiled up in the bath; the bathroom was always a dangerous place for snakes. A wardrobe fell on me one day when I disturbed its centre of gravity, but without harm and my mother, seeing my fortitude when I emerged from under it, called me Nelson. A steamroller arrived to assist in the mending of the road that ran past our garden and Bill and I sat insecurely by its long raked steering wheel, the metal hot and the air heavy with tar. It was a happy flow of little things. And another fragment of memory, though not a fragrance. Walking by a field of chillies, grasping a bunch and putting it into my mouth. I learnt.

But in the midst of play there was often danger. One day my mother took Mrs Scrimgeour for a drive. She had just had a baby and needed a day out. As they approached their planned destination my mother jammed on the brakes of the car. A strong smell came to them across the water. My mother said, "This smells like the lion house in the zoo. I'm not stopping." She turned round and drove quickly away. On the same day Dr Pritchett Taylor was shooting at that spot. A bird fell and he walked towards it, keeping his eyes on the place where it had fallen. He trod on a tiger and tried to fight it off; he was severely mauled. Somehow he got back and was operated on but he died a few days later.

There was one affliction powerful enough to extinguish all boundaries. That was rabies. One of the British soldiers died of rabies at Jhansi. The sister nursing him said to my mother, "I never want to see anything like that again." It was a danger lurking in every cantonment in the strange dogs that roamed along the roads and around the houses – and in one's own pet. The sudden snarl of a family dog could bring terror to a household. On one occasion one of our dogs came up to my mother and nuzzled her arm just a little aggressively. My mother ran off and plunged her arm into carbolic, to clean it and see if the skin had been broken. There was a cure for rabies but it had to be immediate and it was painful; many and massive jabs.

When the weather grew hot we put our beds outside. It was delicious to wake to the cool small wind of the day, secure inside our mosquito nets. Safe? The chowkidar prowled around and the only other sound was the howl of the jackal, whose baleful cry we translated into the words, "I smell the body of a dead Hindu", words which on reflection I hope the Indians did not hear. Adults flitted across our world, mostly soldiers and their wives. My mother liked entertaining and well dressed ladies and gentlemen would alight from their tongas, the two wheeled pony traps that were India's taxis. The courteous chatter of those who knew each other well and still had so much to say came through to our rooms as the ayah and the nanny put us to bed. It was an open society and appeared to have no enemies.

Remembering these days, my brother Bill adds a sad note. "When I look back the strongest feeling I have is being deprived of affection. Mum and Dad were apparently always involved in cantonment life. The club, hunting, entertaining, bridge. We went to children's parties with the ayah; we went riding with the syce. I cannot remember ever being read to at bedtime, or even being said goodnight to. Our parents were elsewhere attending to their social functions. One night we heard the distant strains of the national anthem coming from the club. We rose slowly from our beds and under our mosquito nets stood shakily to attention, little people caught in the loyalties of our race." When he was stung by a scorpion a servant pushed him to hospital. Such thoughts do not easily dissolve over the years.

Our parents had other things on their mind. They were looking ahead. My father was due for his long leave, six months, and this was The Leave after which the family would start to break into pieces. For reasons that parents said over to themselves many times, the children must go to school in England. That is, they must be left behind. Indian education was unsatisfactory; the climate was debilitating; the growing up was artificial and above all the children might become too 'Indian', the fatal sing-song that might cast doubts on one's lineage. The arguments were seldom articulated, but were always understood. The shadow was taken for granted. But when should the separation start? In our family the spread of ages was a problem. My elder brother, Bill, was clearly almost old enough to be left in England, and equally clearly Monty would stay with my parents for quite a while more. With Iris and myself the issue was not quite so clear. My father only had home leave at rare intervals. To take us straight away would be too soon; to wait until the next home leave might be too late. It would he hard for Bill to be left by himself in England. The arithmetic of separation is quite tricky.

My parents devised a plan. My father was able to get a long leave of something over six months. Either he had accumulated some extra leave or the authorities had kindly given him extra at this critical moment of our family life. We would go to Italy and collect the money my father had been sending back – 200 rupees a month to Thomas Cook in Genoa and then go for a long holiday in Switzerland. After that we would proceed to England where my mother would stay to see us settled in. It seemed a good plan.

We said goodbye to Mhow and the British who spent most of their time saying goodbye and to all our servants, who lined up and whispered polite farewell greetings to us, and we hoped that they would find good employment. They in their turn wrote touching farewells and expressed hopes of future patronage. One Badri Kali wrote, "I dare say you have safely landed and reached your happy land. After having enjoyed a happy family life and regaining health and vigour I would be at your service. Forget me not." The Raj was a very useful employer. We handed over the bungalow for the next military occupant and boarded the train, catching our last glimpses of the Indian countryside as it passed slowly by. There was a slight panic at Bombay as we could not find our Anglo-Indian nanny's passport and then we boarded the Lloyd Trestino ship, the *Genova*. When, if ever, would we see India again?

For our parents it was a voyage like those many that had come before; meeting other fragments of the Raj and catching up on them; those going home on leave, those retiring, all with memories and aspirations and all with tales to tell - a society like this lives on anecdotes. For us children it was a splendid mobile play area and not too many thoughts of what lay ahead. We arrived at Genoa on the 24th of December 1926. Yes. It was Christmas Eve. My father went along to Thomas Cook to collect the money that was to take us to Switzerland. He received a considerable shock. "There seems to have been some mistake", said the man behind the counter. "A technical error. The arrangement with Lloyds Bank has been misunderstood. I have forty pounds for you."

We were stranded. What should we do? My parents conferred. It must have been a tense conference. They emerged with a plan. We would stay in Italy, which was much cheaper. "There's a nice pension at Osopodeletti", said someone. My parents went there by train to have a look. It was dreadful. My father, who seldom committed himself to emphatic statements, said, "We can't". But we knew that each year Aunt May went to the Hotel Angleterre at Bordighera which was along the Riviera coast not far from Nice. We set off from Genoa between seven and eight in the evening and arrived at Bordighera just before midnight with seven suitcases and bedding rolls. Christmas Eve. Would there be room at the inn? The girl who received us at the hotel looked astonished as we staggered into the foyer, waifs from the east. Yes. There were two rooms. She gave us hot milk and fresh rolls and butter. My mother consulted further with her. She said, "Can we have sweets from Father Christmas?" Somehow, they must give us Christmas. No, there were no sweets but we could have some nuts. So Father Christmas late that night dispensed nuts and liras. On the following morning our beds were awash with nuts, but we had had our Christmas awakening.

Amazingly we found a relative, Nelly Watkins, at the hotel. She was not unnaturally rather surprised to see us. Maiden ladies wintering in Italy do not expect to see a large family of relatives surface on Christmas morning from previously unoccupied beds. But the hotel was too expensive and we would have to look elsewhere. There was a Miss Daly, an English lady domiciled in Bordighera. She had a ground floor flat in the Casa Giovanelli. Perhaps we might like it. So we collected our luggage, paid our dues and proceeded up the steep hill that lay behind the town. We sat down and took stock. And then we went outside and surveyed the scene. It was a remarkable one. Far below, beyond the roofs of Bordighera lay the Mediterranean, behind us the steep slopes of the Maritime Alps. Along the coast the road wound its way, barely gaining a foothold between sea and mountains, to the west to Ventimiglia and across the border to Menton, Monte Carlo, Monaco, Nice, and to the east to San Remo. In the immediate foreground in the little garden of the Casa Giovanelli a row of tangerine trees took us by surprise.

This paradise had some shadows. Signor Giovanelli wanted for some reason to get rid of us. We would not be moved. So he cut our water off for two or three weeks. We fetched our water from the English couple who lived above us, Mr and Mrs Groundsell, who became known to us not surprisingly as Mr and Mrs Chickweed. He was the organist at the English church where wintering and domiciled Britons worshipped. Eventually we went to the local podesta and made a complaint on health grounds and Signor Giovanelli was brought to heel.

We took trips to Ventimiglia and Nice and saw what I have always thought was the unacceptable face of France. By the sea Frenchmen practised their shooting skills by releasing pigeons from small boxes and shooting them as they emerged. This is not, we thought, how civilised people should behave. But we also saw the Blue Train go by, taking with it so many fantasies; dreams of speed and luxury. Italy gave us two faces. One was the State. Mussolini had recently come into power and the trains were said to run on time; and heavily booted soldiers gathered and swaggered and sang a patriotic song, starting, "Mussolini prima vera", the tune still lingering in my head. The other face was the people. In the shops British paid more for their goods than Italians. It was a gentle form of discrimination, and we found them though sometimes devious warm and friendly and with a kind of cheerful improvidence. I have often thought what a strange disguise fascism was.

At one stage there was an idea that we should spend the early summer in the mountains at Grasse. My parents were told of a Russian émigré who ran hotels at San Remo and Grasse and had a house at Grasse that we might rent. So they walked down to San Remo and entered the émigré's house. Down the stairs came a woman in black with gorgeous ear-rings. She talked to my father with her back to my mother. Being the taker of most family decisions my mother was affronted. Does your house have a garden?" my father asked. "Garden?" came the sharp reply, "I am used to a park". At that a quaintly dressed man entered, who said he was a Count, and then the lady's husband, who said, "My wife is the Princess Obolensky in her own right and I am the Governor of Odessa." My mother had had enough and decided to go. The

Russians pressed them, but my parents left and returned to Bordighera to announce to us that we would be staying where we were.

It was not all pleasure. Unexpectedly there was a small school of British children. I think we learnt little but enjoyed each others' company. But it was mostly a kind of heaven. Winter started to turn to spring and we witnessed a staggering rebirth. The steep mountainsides burst into colour, tumbling in a multi-coloured cascade to the sea. We packed our lunch and set off up the steep paths that lay behind our flat. The paths were cobbled so as to allow the mules to gain a foothold and we used to see them toeing their way carefully up the sharp slopes. We sat pleasurably weary by the track and munched our sandwiches gazing around and wondering so many things. And then back to the Casa Giovanelli to talk with the Groundsells or to listen to the lady in the neighbouring flat who had operatic ambitions and used to practise her scales most of the day.

Heaven had to have an end. It was June and it was time to go. We said goodbye to the Groudsells and Signor Giovanelli. We packed our seven suitcases and bedding rolls. Our father was to bring on the luggage and we were to go ahead. When he arrived at the station the official was horrified at the mounds of luggage and said, "Too much!" and threw his arms about him. My father did not say a word but with a quiet deliberation he drew from his coat pocket one by one the seven railway tickets; our Anglo-Indian nanny had been an unseen presence. We travelled to Paris by night, sitting up all the way, hunched against the dawn. At Paris we changed trains, as one always did. We sat forlornly on the platform at a bleak hour waiting for our next train. A

French porter saw us and with the daring gallantry of the French he drew my mother into conversation.

"Where has Madame come from?"

"From India."

"And is she returning there?"

"No. Only my husband."

"Oh. So dangerous. Your husband will meet so many other ladies. But Madame is charming"

We crossed the Channel and met England. It closed in around us as we steamed from Dover to London and to the house in Earl's Court Road where we were to stay for a month.

We were home.

2.
Breaking up

It was 1927. Aged 8, 6, 5 and 2, we were returning to a country that we had never known.

The dust had gone and the wide blue skies and the open spaces and the shrill intonations of Hindustani and the sense of being at the top of things and the slow measured pace of life and the indefinable smells that were the breath of the East, and the sense of mystery that drives so many people there today. There was a greenness, as there had been in Italy, but it was a kind that could not rest. There was little dust, but there was dirt, as I found as I ran my finger along the railings. It was a hurrying world. In this strange, cool, busy new land our parents had to settle us, deciding many things and hoping that they had got it right. My mother's forthright certainties admirably suited this situation. My father could only agree, a gracious and gentle man. For them the complicated decision-making process had started, as the leaving was about to be set in place, and it pursued them down the years. We never knew whether they agonised or lost sleep over it. We received their decisions and asked no questions, sometimes wondering whether things could have been arranged differently. The one common factor was separation.

For now there were four decisions to take: find a roof over our heads when we arrived, take a holiday, locate relatives and finally choose a place to live. The first was Earls Court Road. I never knew how this came about. But I recollect being taken by our nanny to Kensington Gardens and gazing at model yachts in the Round Pond. There were the other nannies, all white, who glided by pushing stately prams that rocked gently on their huge springs, stopping to talk to fellow nannies or wait for some of their older charges, giving them just the freedom that their own convenience could stand. On one occasion I decided to try to find my own way home. I got lost and after alarms I was rescued by the police. We sought our own people and a holiday and fortunately they were in the same place.

My father's forebears had settled in Devon, attaining a genteel affluence in the area between Honiton, Chard and Sidmouth. One had operated a rope factory, another had ridden hard round his parish as a hunting vicar, and now Aunt Irene was living in a lovely house near Sidmouth. It was our first seaside holiday and after the sudden confines of London it was a marvellous release. I still remember those rock pools over which we scrambled and into which we peered hoping that our nets would find a harvest. Wet with the waves we munched sandwiches and were content. I remember too peaches growing up the side of Aunt Irene's house. It was an interlude that we needed.

Then where to live. It was a challenge. It was, as it always would be, a temporary home. My mother would stay a year to see us settled and then return to her husband in India. There must be schools nearby and hopefully relatives. Our choice fell on Berkhamsted. It seemed to have little against it. It was near London and there were schools. I am not sure where the nearest relative was. It was splendidly ordinary. And we rented 11 Boxwell Road, the top house on a steep hill. Berkhamsted seemed to have been made of hills and we climbed much. It also had the Grand Union Canal. We walked along its bank watching horses pulling the long boats and at each bridge and lock dextrously disengaging and re-engaging their burdens. There were blackberries to be picked on the common. It was a life lived at a pace that we would have liked. But there was much to be done.

Education. That was why we had returned to England. It had to be private because it had after the first stages to be boarding, and anyway the class to which we believed we belonged would never have considered state education; the class distinctions were firmly drawn. What I have always wondered at was how our parents afforded to send us all to private schools. My father had left the army proper for a better paid branch, and in those days a pound went a long way, but educating us must still have been a huge undertaking.

Beginnings are important, and we made a good one. Dear Miss Whitaker ran a kindergarten and we were happy to be there. We read and counted and made all sorts of things out of raffia and put on a performance of Beowulf with school benches as the only scenery. And we moulded in plastercine the Norman castle, the remains of which look over the town from across the line of the London Midland and Scottish Railway. My view of history has ever been fashioned by two splendid books: *The early cave dwellers* and *The early tree dwellers*. I long to believe that they were accurate, but I am not confident. When

I left Miss Whitaker wrote me a remarkable reference saying that she was confident that I was destined for great things; which confirmed me in the belief that it is encouragers that keep the world going. A world of Miss Whitakers would be a happy place. Our farewells to her were as poignant as only such young farewells can be. The girls wept; the boys sniffled. The parents were sad and hoped that the future would be as happy.

My father left very soon after arriving at Berkhamsted. He would return in three years. It was the first gap. To console my mother for that first parting, Elsie, a girl we employed, brought her a cup of coffee. Elsie was willing but only fairly competent. I seem to remember that we had to tell her how to poach an egg. But she operated the mangle with gusto and was of good cheer. In those days you had to be quite poor to be without a servant, and I have recollections in the days ahead of boy friends sitting in the corner of the kitchen trying within the confines that they faced to advance a friendship.

After Miss Whitaker's more thought. Bill went for a term to Hillsea College in Portsmouth recommended by some India friends. He arrived back at the end of the first term in good spirits but with one fatal flaw. He offered my parents a recitation, "There's a deathly 'ush in the close tonight. Ply up, ply up and ply the gyme." My parents shuddered and removed him summarily. That would never do. But there was a prep school near at hand, The Hall, the junior department of Berkhamsted School where we both went. Memories linger uncertainly, trivia jostling for position. I remember giving up second helpings of pudding for Lent and generating a loathing for blackberry jam and struggling into an Eton collar. This was proper school.

Iris went elsewhere, the first of a series of schools that were to reveal her high intelligence and to confuse her sense of direction, each move hard to explain and difficult to endure. The most unfortunate move was to take her away, for reasons that are not easy to understand, from the one school where she found real happiness. It was a piece of mismanagement that my mother never really acknowledged. Its price became evident as the years went by. When she was sixty Iris discovered that she had been offered the chance of a scholarship to Oxford. My mother, who had her own values, tore up the letter.

Bill and I went to board and had our first nights away from home, training to be apart, learning to wake and discover that we were not at home. The moment had to come, the moment of parting, the Big Goodbye. It was a September evening. I had gone to bed and sought sleep, which did not come. My mother came and we chatted for quite a time. Then she said, "Goodnight" and left. Tears kept back for so long – perhaps too long – came pouring out.

Why did she just say, "Goodnight"? Why didn't she say, "I'm leaving you now and I won't see you for two years?" Was that the best she could do? The person who always seemed to have so much to say had said far too little. I didn't understand. I knew this moment was coming; I had known it for years, but I didn't expect it to come like this. That moment I have lived a thousand times.

The weeks that followed told me that I must harden my heart and I did my best. The school helped by filling my days. That, I think, is all it did. And under supervision I wrote. "My dear mother, I hope you are getting on well. I am surprised at what a tremendous amount of people go on board at Port Said, and a tremendous amount of oil they need for the homeward journey." Quite mature words. Were they my own? The pattern of the voyages was born. As my parents journeyed we had to try to catch them at the various ports of call and they in turn would take the chance to send letters from their stopping places. Keeping in touch was what mattered above all else. The ships they chose were usually from the Anchor Line. They lacked the grandeur of the P and O but were a good deal cheaper, and this mattered when balancing a rather complex budget.

Mr Frost, the ageing headmaster in whose charge we were left, was an uncertain hand on the tiller. On making his farewells he had alarmed my mother by kissing her, attended by the heavily peroxided matron to whom he was clearly attached. It was not a good start.

But the next question loomed: where would we go in the holidays? It was a critical question that could make or break our wellbeing, and it was being faced for the first time. It was an important moment. Relatives were the first port of call and were on standby, but ours were also linked with the east and were not immediately available. So we went to Mrs Cowan, a kindly widow who lived in Watford and to make ends meet ran a small school and took people in. She took us all in. It is not easy to be a home to strangers who wished their parents were around, but she did her best. One memory remains. One morning as we woke she said, "There was a fire last night and the fire engine came, but I didn't have to wake you."

But she had an unexpected problem on her hands. We arrived back for the Easter holidays of 1929 in a disgraceful state. Unwashed, unkempt, huge toenails growing into our feet; or so we were told. Telegrams were sent to India, and Mrs Cowan wrote to Mr Frost, who wrote abusively in return. Another decision time had arrived. My mother said she wished to take her sons away for gross negligence and an abusive letter. Mr Flecker, the head of the senior school, asked her to reconsider. "Please change your mind. Will consider a transfer to Mr Baker's house". This was the house for older boys, which my mother thought unsuitable. There was no going back.

More decisions, and from a great distance. The network came into action.

Friends told of another school that had done them well. And so in the summer of 1929 we landed at the place which would give my brother and me years that we needed; it nourished us and fashioned us. It was more than a necessary base. It was a life. There is a passage in one of the great novels of those years, JBPriestley's *The Good Companions* published in 1929 in which he conjured up one such school. "If you are a parent in India, is it not worth cutting things down a little, depriving yourself of a few holidays in the hills, we will say, merely to know that your boy is in such hands as these." Boarding schools were where the children of the Raj were left.

Stratton Park lay on the outskirts of the village of Great Brickhill on the low hills to the south east of Bletchley. Down in the valley the trains thundered from Euston to the north west, trailing white plumes. A couple of miles to the north east the A5 turns gently at Little Brickhill where the Romans had taken fresh bearings for the next stretch of Watling Street. Stratton Park had a grandeur that I had not met before. You entered through imposing wrought iron gates, curving round a magnificent clump of beech trees, where we were told that Cromwell had once stabled his horses. The house, a Georgian building, was almost a stately home. Today the National Trust might have taken a look at it if they could have filled it with good things.

For us it was a grand background to much learning and not a little play. Today it no it longer stands. The owner, an eccentric baronet, pulled it down in 1933. I asked his son, who now helps to maintain Bletchley Park, that very different place where we undid enemy ciphers, why he had done this. He said it was because his father was expecting war. He was clearly looking further ahead than most of us. In front was an estate of sixty five acres. It was the space we needed. The school fashioned a five hole golf course and we swung experimentally. Once I stood too close to the swinger and received the iron club on the side of my head. I was not too successful. "I am not going in for the golf competition after all, because I lose too many balls." But in this area I had a strange success. Every so often the whole school was let loose on a neighbouring golf course; it must have been a very accommodating club. We hacked our way round seeking a prize. This went not to the boy with the lowest score but the boy with the score identical to the one in a sealed envelope. My score was the magic 92. It was less commendable than it sounds; it was a nine hole course.

We did with nature what we wanted. We trapped moles and admired their glossy coats. We collected every bird's egg we could lay our hands on and we blew out their yolks and added them to our collection. The Canada Goose we prized most. We bred rabbits and sadly allowed some of them to starve. We climbed the great beech trees, groping higher until we quaked and could go no higher. There were no safety regulations and some went into very high places. Those who could looked down on those who couldn't. There were many chestnut trees and their conkers we gathered and with them we did battle every autumn. To succeed conkers must be hard, and the best way to harden them was to put them under your mattress. Those willing to wait for success would do this for a whole year and they then were said to possess 'seasoners'. There was one tree with exceptional conkers, but this was reserved for the prefects who had various ways of marking out their authority. This could be a dangerous license, but I cannot recollect it being abused. They were clearly superior but seldom offensively so. But we could all enjoy the ground, lying around in mid summer in our floppy hats, training the sun through a magnifying glass on to bits of paper that suddenly burst into flames, and manufacturing coloured potions: elder leaves for the rich green and pine cones for a reddy brown. These were areas of freedom to pit against the other restraints of those days. How free were we?

The constraints were clear. Serious misdemeanour brought the cane, and Mr Clouston wielded it without hesitation if he felt it was deserved. I lined up once for this treatment and the boy in front, awaiting the same treatment, pleaded for mercy. Mr Clouston replied, "All play and no work makes Jack a dull shirk." Less serious offences were rewarded with Order Marks. From time to time an Order Mark Holiday was decreed and we were given the freedom proportionate to the marks we had received. On one occasion I was the only one to have received the maximum marks, and in the afternoon I was the only one constrained. It was a loneliness I had not anticipated.

Games were a serious business and we were good at them. Rugger was the final test of our young manhood. Other schools less finely tuned to the sport we trampled underfoot. There was one school that we frequently massacred. On one occasion the score at half time was so embarrassing that we received instructions not to score again. Shortly afterwards Bill was heading for the line. Recalling his orders he stopped in his tracks and allowed his pursuers to catch him up and floor him. Our cup of joy was full when we beat the Dragon School and Mr Clouston took the team to see an international match. In away matches we would wait eagerly by the drive as the transport returned. Success meant a wave of scarves from the windows; defeat a silent ride and solemn people disembarking. It mattered dreadfully.

We slept in dormitories named after great commanders: Drake, Marlborough, Bruce, Wellington, Nelson, Collingwood. Here we rested every day after lunch and here at night after the lights had gone out and the staff who had seen us to bed had left us we told stories, starting tales, challenging others to take up the narrative and bring us new adventures. We got into strange places, and out of them with not one but several bounds. It was a secret fun that drew us together and even the shyest could from the safety of his bed add a few words and take strength. It was a magic way out of a closed world.

We pitted ourselves against each other. "What does your father do?" Much lay on the answer. Fathers gave us our place; mothers we kept to ourselves. There was one special case. Taylor, a boy rougher than I had hoped, said to me, "My father teaches sheet metal working in Letchworth, and my mother went to prison". I could not take the conversation further, but long afterwards I discovered that his mother was Annie Kenny, a leading suffragette, who had been put inside for defying the law in aid of women's right to vote. There was no shame. "My mother," said Gardner, "breeds hens and shows them."

"What kind"? "Sicilian buttercups."

There was Peter Casement who was the nephew of Sir Roger, an Irish patriot whom we executed for treason. He was always quarrelling. I remember quoting to myself a misquotation of a line of English poetry, "One by one the casements scratch." Lawrence was the spit image of TE Lawrence, of Arabia, and he must have been a kin. John Hammersley became one of our most distinguished mathematicians, and even then showed a remarkable flair for numbers. Kenneth Martin, was another outstanding mathematician whom we nicknamed for no apparent reason, 'poached egg in pyjamas.' His home address was The Presbyterian War Memorial Hostel, Belfast, and with precocious snobbery I thought: that's a humble dwelling place. There were no fewer than six Johnsons. Johnsons 5 and 6, brothers, who had connections with our family, both perished in the war piloting bombers. And there were the Bournes, a legendary family of Etonian and Oxford oarsmen. Anthony got a scholarship to Eton and we rejoiced with a day's holiday. After being a prisoner of war he returned and rowed for Oxford. There was an aura of distinction about him. I was in awe when I saw the letter addressed to his mother, Lady Hester Bourne. There was another boy who became the deputy head of a national daily. He was very clever, but his cleverness alarmed those in charge. His father had died of a brainstorm and they feared it might be in the family. Somehow his mental development must not be allowed to proceed too fast. I don't know how the school set about solving this problem, but he retained his normality which was coloured only by a somewhat odd diction. One boy's mother had lost her reason and was confined in an asylum where she had been for two years. It was a tragic matrimonial cul-de-sac. AP

Herbert was to bring in a Marriage Bill to find ways of release, ideas which he described in his book *Holy Deadlock*. I have often wondered if the father found the freedom he was seeking. And there was a bully, Maclaren, who oppressed anyone younger and who for obvious reasons was called Ears. We had a gallant lineage in our midst. Pat McSwiney's grandfather had won the DSO in a distant conflict, his father had won the DSO and MC in the First World War and Pat was to win the same two decorations in the Second World War; he was one of nature's commanders. A relative of his was the Mayor of Cork who starved himself to death in the Troubles. We did not guess futures; we were too busy establishing ourselves in a present and hoping we were somebody. And there was Hall. He had a fearful stammer; words queued to come out, and they had to wait their turn. And he had a much older sister for whom I fell, to the discreet amusement of his parents. I became known for a time as Young Woodley, after a play of that time in which a young boy falls for his housemaster's wife. How fast was I growing up? There were also those who seemed lost. One such came up to me and said, "Will you be my friend this term?" A boarding prep school without friends is a sombre place.

The headmaster, Mr Clouston, was a savage figure, or that is how it appeared to us. He was old and dark featured and had a deeply lined face that resembled the furrows on the face of WH Auden. When his temper was roused we quaked. I was once unwise enough to translate the French word 'minuit' as 'minute', which seemed a reasonable suggestion. It was not. He gave my ear a sharp tweak. "He was an evil man", said Aunt M, but I was unwilling to believe her. I think he wanted the best but was unwilling to wait until it was achieved. And he had a past to contend with. His first wife had died tragically; I believe she fell down the stairs that led to the front rooms of the house.

His second wife was French, very young, beautiful and utterly charming. She softened the many hard outlines in our life and did much to reassure parents that there was humanity somewhere. A smile from her brought a blush of pleasure to cheeks that too often reddened for other reasons. But at the same time she taught with rigour and demanded that every week we must learn scores of French words. Knowledge has seldom had lovelier contours. In the war she served with gallantry in the Resistance in France.

Mr Clouston had his own reassurance to give to parents. He was a patrician. He had been a master of foxhounds and liked his shooting. He invited his friends to shoot the neighbouring woods and sometimes we were brought in to beat, wading through the damp undergrowth and being shouted at to keep into line and in the lunch break seeing piles of beautiful birds, the Amherst pheasant catching the eye. "Some people went beating out pheasants. In the morning we got twenty and in the afternoon we got 7½ brace." On special occasions senior prefects were allowed to handle guns and one day a man turned up to show us how to cast flies. We were being taught how to be gentlemen, some of us finding it harder than others. All this certainly attracted gentry to the school. It was a kind of product plus.

They had a son, Rudolf. He was a thug. Hugely muscular, he was one of the foremost amateur boxers in the land. He would invite other pugilists to the school and set up a ring in the school grounds and we would watch them bash each other, persuaded that it was a noble art. He also coached us in boxing, his proximity unnerving us. He ran off with a servant girl and joined Oswald Moseley's Blackshirts. Moseley had started as one of Labour's brightest hope, but his sharp mind became disillusioned at the way things were going and he became a kind of Hitler, a screaming anti-Semite, his fist throwing a challenge to any form of democracy. He marched through the east end of London spreading hatred and generating serious riots, showing to anyone who cared to notice that the ideas then fermenting in Germany were foreign to the great majority of us. His meetings were ferocious affairs. We followed these ugly scenes in the papers. Rudolf joined his bodyguard, ready to treat brutally any who threatened to disturb his meetings. He died during the war from a disease contracted abroad.

And the staff. Prep school staffs are a kind of educational fruit salad; all shapes and sizes; and ages. And Stratton Park had its share. There were one or two who had grown old in the service of the very young and still had much to teach them. They were gold dust. We sat at their feet and learnt things that still surprise us. That they were very old and just went on and on did not surprise us. We saw wisdom of a special kind and saw how lucky we were. When the scholarships came we saw why. There is a subset here: women who pour into their charges a love that has had no other outlet and have found in little boys a family that they never cease to delight in. Miss Ewen was such a one. I reach beyond university and public school and see who it was who first showed me that to learn was the most exciting thing you could do. Giving passion to truth, she took us with her. There were others who found it a not too demanding a post at a time when jobs were not always easy to come by. Mr Pilner and Miss Cave were such as these. And when they grew closer together we watched with delight, sorrowing with them when the three-wheeler they were travelling in overturned and Miss Cave arrived in the classroom rather battered, and happy when they married. Mr Bax was a relation of the composer and Mr Briers was clearly marking time. He served with distinction in the Second World War. There are others who seek refuge in prep schools because they want something that does not demand too much; a quiet life. Of these there are some who find that they cannot cope. Mr Hall was such a one. We called him Jabberwocky and we destroyed him.

And finally, there are those whom the reader was hoping I might not mention, the people who should never have been allowed near small boys. We had one such, Mr W. What he did in that school I am unwilling to say, and I have told no one. What he did to many of us, if it had been exposed, would have given him a very long prison sentence. In those days prep schools were an underworld in which too much was hidden. Fortunately Mr W left after not too long a stay and we could learn in safety. I do not think that we were really damaged, though perhaps today an army of counsellors would be at the ready. What was Mr W's future? He had joined the Territorial Army in the Duke of Wellington's Regiment, and we were told that he had been dismissed 'for bad language'. I have been reading between the lines ever since.

In all this there was a world that I could call my own and I needed a kingdom quite badly. It was the library. Words, which have been my companion all my life, started here. I devoured Conan Doyle, PG Wodehouse, Baroness Orczy, the moving and tragic Owd Bob, a rattling yarn of the prairies *Jack the young ranchman*, John Buchan, and Bulldog Drummond. Percy F Westerman, Henty and *Fights for the flag*, and Biggles. It was a great moment when I met WE Johns at the Schoolboys Exhibition and got his signature. Impelled by him and by the tales of the great airmen of the First World War – Mannock, Bishop, McCudden, Moorhouse, I constructed wooden models of the Sopwith Camel and the SE5. I borrowed from the library as soon as it arrived *Fighting planes and aces*. We were in need of aces. This world I could inhabit on my own terms. There was one wound. Reading *The hound of the Baskervilles* gave me fearful dreams and Miss Ewen had to come into my dormitory and comfort me. The pretence of manhood can be easily breached.

And boyhood needed its special food. Mine was "The Modern Boy" a magazine which to my mind had no equal, outstripping even "The Boys Own Paper". Captain Justice strode across its pages and with power beyond my imagining conquered all before him. Every so often a gift was enclosed and delight multiplied. From the bits that fell from it I assembled a glider. It hardly flew but it was my creation. In our little world the post generated its own tensions and if the magazine did not arrive the sky darkened. We had ways of generating our own post and 'sending up' for things. Business was in a bad way and free samples were being offered on a lavish scale. And there were the cigarette cards which you could collect without having to smoke, and to have a complete set of famous cricketers or Household Hints was to bring joy when we needed it. One cigarette company, desperate for custom, printed flags on what looked like silk. Had I kept all these I could have interested Sothebys.

I fashioned my letters, written on Sunday afternoons, closely supervised and carefully formed. They contained the trivia of our world, little happenings, many on the field of play, and the names of friends, and glances at the staff. "There is a new master and a new mistress. The new master never sits down, he is always walking." and requests, asking for things. "I am wanting a camera very badly. Nearly all the boys have got cameras. So why shouldn't I have?" A Box Brownie arrived. "Thank you very very much for your awfully nice Brownie No1 camera you so kindly sent me." I could show it to my friends. And sometimes the assurance that parents needed. "I am awfully happy at Stratton Park." The censor over my shoulder would like that. But sometimes they went further afield. "We heard the service in Westminster Abbey because the king is better again."

George V had been very seriously ill. He shared his family's passion for cigarettes and it did him no good at all. He had been taken ill in the previous November with acute septicaemia and was operated on in December. We followed his progress closely and anxiously. Churches were kept open day and night. In February he was allowed his first cigarette for 2½ months and was well enough to move from Buckingham Palace to Craigwell House near Bognor and in April a generous donation started a thanksgiving fund for the king's convalescence. In May he left Craigwell House for Windsor Castle. On the 12th of June he resumed his duties. On the seventh of July there were services of thanksgiving for the king's recovery, though his wound was still unhealed. There was national rejoicing, and Bognor added 'Regis' proudly to its name. Harold Nicholson wrote, "The king was a bad patient and an even worse convalescent". But he was a king we revered.

Sometimes events came our way. In October I wrote, "At the window of the sickroom we saw an airship called R101 on its first flight and the next day they said all about it in the newspapers." And

Bill wrote, "The R101 came over the school and it came in front of our window so that we could see it from our beds, which was rather nice." It was indeed, a mammoth cigar that seemed to fill the sky and which turned gently as it came over us. Were we a landmark, we asked ourselves. Its first flight was October the fourteenth and on November the eight on its fifth flight it carried 82 people, the largest number ever carried by a British aircraft. We were in bed because chicken pox had swept through the school, a rest we first enjoyed and then with the impatience of the convalescent fretted against.

The skies started to darken. I had written in one of my many letters of expectation, "Won't it be lovely when you Daddy and Monty come home from India. There is only four more terms to wait for you to come back from India. Won't Monty be pleased to see Iris, Billy and I because he hasn't seen us for such a long time". But one November afternoon I was summoned from my bed where I was resting. It was Miss Warren. She was a relative of the headmaster, a quiet, polite rather faded lady who was kind to all.

I entered her room. "Richard. I have something to tell you. Your brother Monty, who has been very ill, has gone to be with Jesus." I said nothing and returned to my bed. I can remember only a great emptiness. What was I supposed to think? A brother gone. Looking back one can see it rather dramatically perhaps as the price of the East. Then it was a sadness we took on board, our feelings carefully corralled.

Iris heard the news in a way that still haunts me. She was summoned by the headmistress, of whom she was terrified. What had she done wrong? What fierce reprimand awaited her? She did not receive one, and her relief was such that she left the Presence with a broad grin on her face. She was alright. She had not been reprimanded. Values can seldom have been more cruelly confused.

The year that was ending so sadly for me had its own bad moments. July had been a month of disasters. 24 lost in a submarine, 8 killed in a pit explosion, 15 burnt to death at a hospital fete at Gillingham. And on the last day of the year 70 children died in a panic in a Paisley cinema.

But the most spectacular disaster was on the 23rd of October when the bottom fell out of America, a day on which 19,226,400 shares were sold on the New York Stock Exchange, a paper loss of $26,000 billion, equal to the entire wartime increase in the American national debt. Seldom has hope been so dramatically punctured, dreams turned to nightmares, riches to dust. A contemporary wrote, "The landslide from the mad, irresponsible world of the 20's began in America in 1929." We saw the headlines and the staff told us what they meant. We waited to see what echoes would reach us. Our post-war boom had faded but seemed to be gathering a little momentum, although there were still almost 1½ million unemployed. Now that seemed doomed. The Indian Army suddenly seemed a firmer platform than jobs that most Stratton Park fathers were employed in.

How did my parents react to the declaration of the Viceroy of India, Lord Irwin, at the end of October, "It is implicit in the declaration of 1917 that the natural issue of India's constitution as there contemplated, is the attainment of Dominion Status."? For the more hard-line British Irwin was always a little suspect, too ready to give away. His willingness to talk with Gandhi was disquieting. And there was something of an outcry. My mother would have had a few sharp words to say. My father, at ease with Indians, must have been content with Irwin's words. Following the politics of India was to become a nail-biting business. The attempt to assassinate the Viceroy on the 23rd of December made things no easier.

Before the year ended it was decision time again. Mrs Cowan, who had cared for us as best she could, was ill. We had to find another place to spend the Christmas of 1929, and quickly. Messages flowed over many miles and a choice was made. We found ourselves in the vicarage of Potten End, a village near Berkhamsted. The ageing vicar 'took in' children to augment his stipend. We do not know why we should land here, but at this distance mistakes are possible. This was one of them. It was a bleak place. To maximise his income the vicar had taken in as many children as he could, and he spent little on their food. Chicken pox broke out. There were bikes which we rode and fell off. On one occasion, which I am horrified to recall, we skidded our bikes on a green on Berkhamsted golf course, being shouted off by reasonably irate golfers. And we wandered, counting the days and thinking: where do we go from here? I have one curious recollection. On the lavatory wall was pinned the Collect which ended, "And the busy world is hushed, the fever of life is over and our work is done. Then grant us thy rest." This seemed rather an early sunset, but it set the tone for a place that had an air of total unreality and a hint of menace: was this the shape of holidays to come?

Into this no-mans-land my mother arrived, by herself. It was the first of many returns, but it had a poignancy none of the others had. She made no mention to us of Monty and just carried on. We could fault her for many things, but never for courage. What she did do was to take us round to see old friends and on each occasion describe in detail the last few days of Monty's life. She shared sorrow with those who did not have to weep and we sat and listened. She was telling us without us having to cry.

There was one weeping. I had been sent to bed for making a nuisance of myself. My mother came up to see me, saw my tears and believing that I was mourning Monty, broke down and wept. It was a rare sight of her in distress. I do not think her defences came down again.

And so the year ended, a year that I cannot ever forget. And we were ready to launch on that era on which so many have pronounced - the Thirties...

3.
Into the thirties

Indeed few decades have had so many judgements thrust upon them.

J.Laver, "After the fruitless twenties, the guilt-ridden thirties. After the party, the hangover, and what a headache it was." "The frantic, frivolous, frustrated, puzzled, frantic period of Between the Wars."

C Trewin, "The turbulent thirties."

Ronald Blythe, "The Age of Illusion."

C Day Lewis, "A tricky darkening decade … the brooding light before a thunderstorm."

Robin Skelton, editor of The Thirties Poetry. "Even before they were quite over, the thirties took on the appearance of a myth."

David Gascoigne, "And so, goodbye, grim thirties."

M.Garland, "The indecisive decade."

WH Auden, whose words commanded these years, "A low, dishonest decade."

Colin Brooks, "It was the devil's decade. It came in like a ravening wolf and went out like a roaring lion."

John Gore, "The fateful thirties"

Were they as bad as this? Were they a myth? Had guilt devoured judgement? Was there too much looking back? We were to find out their quality as the years unravelled and ponder the comment of one writer "Too many historians have dismissed the 1930's, as wasted years."

We had a living to do. We looked in, burdened by a fragmented life, but we also looked out and saw things happening. We passed judgement, as the young do, but I think our judgements were no more flawed than those of many who misread the times and those who misdirected them. Those who never knew them, but who may be required to pass exams on them may be interested to know what happened

Through these years, whatever the world was doing, came the sound of music. It was the golden age of British dance bands and we listened and sang with them: Ray Noble, Lew Stone, Roy Fox, Ambrose, Jack Hylton, Jack Payne, Henry Hall, Harry Roy, Carol Gibbons, Billy Cotton, Maurice Winnick, Ted Heath, Geraldo, Jack Jackson each with their signature tune; serried ranks of brass into which the crooners inserted their soft beguiling tones. Their words brought a warmth that was not always with us. So 1930 brought, *"Happy days are here again"*, *"On the sunny side of the street"*, *"Who's been polishing the sun, wiping all the clouds away?"*

In fact the decade came in with severe gales, sleet and snow. The economic situation was worsening. By the end of March over 1,600,000 were unemployed, higher than for eight years. What had hit America was beginning to hit us and in the Budget, "In the interests of financial probity Mr Snowden proposed to wipe out the deficit of £14,500,000." As we later realised, the Chancellor could not have embarked on a more destructive policy. There was a good deal of stumbling in those years.

My family entered the thirties drawing breath. We were together again, sadly incomplete but with somewhere to go that we could call a home. My parents never owned a house; they were too stretched in running a family to afford one. They were life-long renters and we became used to following them from place to place, hoping for something good and never being entirely disappointed. The first place – this was the beginning of the life cycle – was the well ordered seaside town of Littlehampton, a place with a measure of gentility but no great pretensions. We rented a house that belonged to a coal merchant who also ran a taxi service, and for some reason he had a caravan in the garden where he did some of his business. And I wrote perplexed, "It is a funny idea of Mrs Harris to have the bus coming right into the garden." And with perplexity trivia. "Mummy, I hope you enjoy mending your punctures." We hired a 'help', who came to work accompanied by her small daughter. Things didn't go as well as they should. Money started to disappear and we called in the police. They advised us to mark our money and the help was found out. She left. We did not regret her parting, but we felt for the little girl who apparently had the making of a dancer.

In Littlehampton we saw our first talkie, and faces became voices, some more successfully than others. The cinema was where you went every week, at least once. In a rather drab world they were luxurious places where beautiful girls showed you to your seat and organs rose out of the floor. This year cinemas were opening at a rate of two a week.

What did it matter if the world seemed to be heading for bankruptcy if you could see Madeleine Carroll, Claudette Colbert. When Marlene Dietrich appeared fantasies took off and the present could be postponed. And of course there was Greta Garbo, whose silences held us.

On the 6th of April our father returned. We had overcome our first gap. He was to return again in 1934 and 1938. And that is how we found ourselves sitting on the beach in that scorching August, a heat wave. It burst on us on the 26th when the temperature reached 87, the 27th 90 and on the 28th 92. It was a recollection of heat that I have never forgotten, though the scorching mid nineteen seventies on the sands of Norfolk should have reminded me that from time to time our country fries. As most heat waves did, it ended in a massive thunderstorm, and we ran for the beach hut. The cousins had gathered homing in on their kind, all of them connected with India. But, as I recollect, the other two Dads were in India and we could play host. Photographs testify that we did that, an extended, perhaps an over-extended, family being happy together while they could. We swam; we biked, we were as carefree as we could be.

Along the coast lay Hove, the genteel face of Brighton and there Sussex played their cricket. We spent many days there and saw men who are now historic figures. Duleepsinghi, who was surely the most graceful batsman there has ever been; his leg glances remain in my memory. In the previous summer he had had an astonishing run: inningses that read as follows: 202, 118, 112, 115, 246. And Maurice Tate, a burly figure who bowled his heart out and from time to time slogged to revive a flagging innings and we cheered a very popular figure; on one occasion receiving a ball from the Australian slow bowler

Grimmett which just missed his stumps he turned round and blew a kiss to the bowler. They were both in the MCC team in Australia, at the end of 1929 which won four of its five tests, a tour which contained massive totals and two double centuries from Hammond. Hove was a friendly place with a family feeling, the Parkses and the Langridges and Bert Wensley and others entertaining us and longing to win the Championship, which they did not achieve until 2003. The Australians were in England and Bradman was supreme. We read with wonder: 1st Test 131, 2nd Test 254, 3rd Test 334, 5th Test 232. But Duleepsinghi my hero also did wonders. 173 in the 3rd Test and 333 against Northants, a county that came bottom so monotonously that I wondered whether it was really a first class county. I noted in one of my letters, "In the test against Australia two niggers (a word that my spellchecker fortunately does not recognise) playing for Sussex made the highest score." Were we racist? There was a boy called Mayer at Stratton Park. He was a Jew and we were always conscious of this. In the competitive society of a prep school differences could not be ignored. Did we persecute him? It is very likely.

My father no doubt did his best to forget India. But there it was a momentous year. The Indians were flexing their muscles for independence. Gandhi, that holy fox, started his campaign to shake the foundations of the Raj. In March he undertook a 200 mile march to the sea, where taking the salt water he fingered it, and said, "I am making salt. I defy you to tax me." The symbolism struck home. The British must be defied. They were. Two words appeared that would command the grammar of those times – civil disobedience. Gandhi said: disobey, but do it peacefully. It was a masterstroke. Beating peaceful people hurts only the beaters. The British looked both foolish and cruel.

The authorities had only one answer to this. On the fifth of May they imprisoned Gandhi. Disturbances increased and the gaols filled up. But Irwin was always looking for a better way. He freed Gandhi and on the 12th of November he started a roundtable conference, in the course of which it was agreed in principle to separate Burma from India. The Annual Home Register said, "Irwin strengthened his remarkable hold on the respect and esteem of the Indian public". The British in India took sides. At dinner parties the name of Irwin caused many words to fly, and at home Churchill, whose brain never functioned reasonably on India – his mindset was that of an unreconstructed imperialist, was apoplectic. It is interesting to note that when a biography of Irwin, then Lord Halifax, came out it was entitled *Holy Fox*; like speaking to like.

This was my parents' world. The Empire still mattered but for most of us there were other things to cling to. In years badly in need of heroics the aviators enthralled us and from those years I date my passion for aviation. For me this is what made the Thirties less ordinary; achievements at a time when such were hard to come by. It was the age of the record breakers. The first half of 1930 belonged to Amy Johnson. This remarkable lady, an inexpert but determined flier, took our hearts. On the fifth of May she took off for Australia in her Gypsy Moth, on the 11th she reached Karachi. Many adventures followed. She force-landed at Jhansi and said with words that echoed, "Jhansi was hotter than I had ever imagined a place on earth could be." She force-landed at Insein 5 miles north of Rangoon, she force-landed in Java on the 24th and she landed at Darwin 20 days from England, beating Bert Hinkler's record by two days. Finally she crashed while landing at Brisbane. Someone said of her flying skills: she didn't land, she just arrived. She could barely contain the fame that came her way.

In this year Frank Whittle took up his first patent on a jet engine. And four years later the Under Secretary of State for Air, made the following remarkable statement. "Scientific investigations have given no indication that this method can be a serious competitor to the airscrew-engine combination. We do not consider that we should be justified in spending any time or money on it ourselves."

The Germans harboured no such doubts.

This was the year of airships. The Graf Zeppelin and the R100 had both flown the Atlantic and our latest and largest, the R101, the one we had seen from our beds at Stratton Park, was due to fly to Karachi as an imperial technical gesture. Politics got dangerously confused with engineering. The omens were not good. Already not long before the flight it was declared ready to fly, "but only just". It was twenty three tons heavier than predicted and it had 11½ tons less lift. It was sliced in half and a new bag inserted. In a trial flight the air cooler broke down. The Certificate of Airworthiness was issued without an inspector's report. The speed test must be done during the Indian flight. The catalogue of errors has been fearfully narrated by Nevil Shute, the novelist and aeronautical engineer who helped to design the R100.

The R101 set off from Cardington in Bedfordshire at 1840 on the 4th of October with 54 passengers and a crew of 42, a generous ratio. By 1845 it had reached Elstree. Lord Thomson, the Secretary of State for air, who was on board, sent a message, "She is as safe as a house – except for a millionth chance". An eyewitness from the ground said,

"The airship was very low on an absolutely horrible night." At 1916 it had travelled 24½ miles at an average speed of 36.75 miles an hour. At 1930 the passengers dined. Number 5 engine was out of action for three hours. It crossed the English coast at 2135. The Dungeness lifeboat was warned to keep a lookout in case it came down in the sea. At 2400 the passengers retired to bed. At 0209 there was a sudden squall. The airship suddenly dived twice, and then struck the ground near the town of Beauvais. In seven hours it had done 248 miles. There had been a failure of the fabric, which had split its outer cover, and a fatal decision to cut power. 54 died including Lord Thomson and Sir Sefton Branker, the Director of Civil Aviation. Five engineers and one wireless operator survived.

At Stratton Park we saw the pictures. In The Daily Express, the huge craft lying broken on the hillside like a great mortally wounded whale. The funeral of the dead was a grand national occasion, The bodies were brought back to Cardington and more than half a million turned out to watch the funeral procession from Westminster Hall to Euston Station; the two miles took an hour. The country reeled and those connected with the airship were asked to explain quite a lot. Airships clearly had little future. The R100 was retired in the following year. Two spectacular crashes in the USA in 1933 and 1936 brought the whole ambitious enterprise to a blazing halt.

For us 1930 ended quietly.

My father left for India on the ninth of December; he would return in 1934.

We had laid the foundations for our future, overcoming sorrow and hoping that the years ahead would give us a life. We accepted the patterns that lay before us and were thankful that our parents cared, even though at a distance. And in a country that was growing poorer and hoped it knew where it was going we were well provided for. In a decade of limited horizons I suppose we fitted in.

4.
Into the slump

1931 was a dark year. Johnson 6 came up to me one day, as we were sucking our malt in the morning break and said, "We shouldn't call this the economic depression. We should call it the economising craze." It was a very apt comment. The British economy was in a dreadful plight. The National Register said, "The year 1931 witnessed the most tumultuous economic crisis the modern world has known." And Britain felt its full force. We had come back on to the Gold Standard with the pound given a value far above what it was worth and at those prices few countries wanted our goods. On the 10th of January 20,000 Bolton weavers came out on strike. The owners were unable to sell their goods to countries which could now make their own, and the workers were fearful of wage cuts. In June the unemployment total reached 2,664,889.

What should we do? We should apparently economise. The Geddes Committee wielded its famous Axe. Many salaries must be cut - and that included my father's. In March the May Committee was set up with a similar remit. It reported in August and it had the same dreary message. Public Expenditure must be reduced, in particular Unemployment Benefit; the Prime Minister agreed to a 10% cut

Johnson 6 had used a powerful and accurate word. It was crazy. JM Keynes was waiting in the wings to tell us all in words that gradually and reluctantly sank in that our leaders were mad. He was to tangle with the governor of the Bank of England, Sir Montague Norman, in evidence to the Macmillan Committee and tell him how misguided he was. Forget the balancing of budgets. If you take money out of people's pockets who can buy anything? Supply without demand is a recipe for disaster. There was a continuing confusion between the housekeeping of the family and the housekeeping of the state. Many years later I was explaining this to sixth formers. Then I was seeing it all happen and believing, as most of us did, that we were being heroic.

Our leaders realised that they were lost. The decision to cut Unemployment Benefit was so obviously a desperate last resort and with the unemployment queues multiplying we were heading further into the dark. Ramsay Macdonald, who had struggled on with an inadequate majority, resigned on the 24th of August. What would happen now? The answer was – something remarkable. I remember opening the Illustrated London News and seeing a group photograph of our new masters, and above it the inscription *None for the party. All for the state.* Macdonald had decided to form a National Government, all three parties combined to rescue the country. And here they were. Labour: Macdonald, Snowden, Thomas, Lord Sankey. Conservative: Baldwin, Chamberlain, Hoare. Liberal: Lord Reading, Sir Herbert Samuel. The grave faces of men who hoped that they could find a way out of the abyss stared at us with the solemnity that matched the times. They had got in by a massive majority of 502; 65 members were elected unopposed. To us as we read the words and saw the pictures it was splendid; all pulling together. To the Labour Party it was a disaster. They were split and the great majority of Macdonald's former colleagues refused 'almost contemptuously' to cooperate with him. To them it was black treachery.

In September Philip Snowden fashioned his first budget for the National Government. It was the same all over again. The budget tax proposals included cuts in the salaries of ministers, MP's, judges and state school teachers and in the Unemployment Benefit of 10%. There was an orgy of sacrifice. The king offered to forgo £50,000 of his income, the Prince of Wales £10,000. Some old age pensioners returned their pension books, war pensioners offered to forgo their pensions for three years, National Savings Certificates and 5% War Bonds were returned cancelled. How brave, we thought. Now was the time for all good men to come to the aid of the party. But the trouble continued. On the 21st of September there was a run on the pound and the Bank of England was obliged to sell gold, and it decided to come off the Gold Standard freeing Sterling to show its real value. The sailors of the Fleet, infuriated by the drop in their pay and the appalling conditions under which they operated, mutinied at Invergordon.

Not everything was gloom. Men in aeroplanes and in fast cars raised our spirits; gallantry was still around and we watched each on the newsreels, Gaumont British or Pathe Gazette. These were the curtain raisers to the two films that followed. One face that we saw many times was Malcolm Campbell, who had a life devoted wholly to speed. On the 5th of February he raised the world land speed record to 246.575 mph on Daytona Beach, and he continued, with a persistence that we never ceased to admire, to go faster year by year. The aviators were always striving. It was Australia; how quickly could we get there? In April CWA Scott in 9 days, 3 hours, 40 minutes, in August, Jim Mollison, who was to have a tumultuous marriage with Amy Johnson, 8 days 20 hours 19 minutes. And on July the first Post and Gatty arrived at New York having been round the world in 9 days. Where would it stop?

At school we constructed crystal wireless sets, a cat's whisker reconnoitring the crystal until a sound came through. And on these sets we heard the roar of aeroplanes. It was the Schneider Trophy, a competition between a few nations round a tight circuit in the Channel. The craft were seaplanes with huge engines and a body that was later to form the shape of the Spitfire. We won the competition with monotonous regularity; until 1931 when the enterprise ran out of money. Would the state help? No, said Macdonald, and the Chancellor, Philip Snowden said he wanted to get rid of "The pernicious rivalry between nations." The ironies behind this statement never really reached us. We just thought he was just being feeble. Anyway, Lady Lucy Houston, the widow of a millionaire ship owner, offered £100,000, which Macdonald accepted. The French withdrew, an Italian pilot was killed and France and Italy asked for a postponement. We refused and continued to prepare. The roar we heard on our crystal sets was Flight Lieutenant Boothman, who won the race unhampered by competitors at 340.08 mph. Shortly afterwards another member of our team Flight Lieutenant Stainforth broke the world speed record with 379,08 mph and then 407.5 mph. At the end of the year Britain held the world speed records for aeroplanes, motor cars, motor boats, motor cycles and boats with outboard motors. Significant? Maybe not, but it helped to give a nation struggling with its fabric a measure of pride and for the young it was great.

I was passionate about horses and followed their fortunes, assisted by a member of the Stratton Park ground staff who hinted darkly that Lochiel would win the Derby. It did not. In fact it was Cameronian piloted by Freddie Fox. It had already won the Two Thousand Guineas and it was hotly tipped to complete the classic treble with the St Leger, a race that had much more prominence than it has today, and I longed for it to do so. Alas it failed. In those years we watched Gordon Richards attain total mastery in the saddle; no other jockey got near him. He had the supreme advantage of being able to ride light without weakening himself. And owners wished that they could match the Aga Khan who became closely acquainted with the winner's enclosure. In one astonishing St Leger in the following year his horses came 1st, 2nd, 4th and 5th and he had three Derby winners. He was a genial and popular figure, the acceptable face of Islam, which anyway was offering no threats. Sophisticated interests for small boys? No. It was food and drink to me as I looked for colour. And I needed colour to light up the days.

Few noticed that a Mrs Simpson had been presented at court.

It was time for my mother to return to India; it was father's turn to have her. I cannot remember any trauma; perhaps we had accepted the cycle of our years. As my mother made her way east I found myself writing to my father, "I should think Mummie has nearly reached Bombay by now." "I got a letter from Mummie and she said that she had had very good weather indeed." My mother's letters were affectionately gossipy, my father's carefully constructed and containing useful information and later some literary references. He tended to treat me as someone worth informing. My letters to him, which I have by me as I write, are also constructed with care. The to-ing and fro-ing of our parents comes out in a letter I wrote in March to my mother. "I am not writing to Daddy as it is rather unconvenient writing to two people in one letter when they are not in the same place". The logic of this is not easy to follow, but it was an excuse to limit my correspondence.

Anyway, by the end of the year my parents were together abroad and the family would need to be redeployed.

5.
The march of the years

1932.

The framework of care was being fashioned, an operation managed from a distance. The backbone and the first choice was the aunts, that stalwart band always ready to give shelter, and a happy alternative to the holiday homes that children of the Raj had sometimes to seek shelter in. My father had two sisters and to them we turned and found a generous welcome. Aunt Evelyn was married to a member of the Indian Civil Service, Aunt Hilda to an officer in the Indian Navy. We seemed tied to the east. It was a kind of irony that they, who might have been with their husbands, provided shelter for us whose mother preferred to join her husband. Bill had a school friend who could fill gaps. And behind all was Granny, my mother's mother, who was more than a shelter. She was our anchor of affection, the one we loved. She filled a huge gap.

So Christmas found us all in Guildford with Aunt Evelyn. The welcome was warm, but the house was cold, and it is not easy to share festivities without having many gifts to offer. Dear Granny sent us some presents to hand round. "How very kind", said Aunt Evelyn. We couldn't say, "Well actually..." It was hard to be generous by proxy, the trappings of a rather second-hand life. We sang carols round the neighbouring houses and doors were opened because there was no television to watch. We went to church with the formality of those days moderated for the children; and after the service we were introduced to people we did not know. Aunt Evelyn said, "You must meet the Turings. They have a very clever son, Alan." They did indeed, and he helped to win the war by breaking the enemy codes and in order to do so constructing what was probably the world's first computer.

There was no war in sight as we moved into 1932, but there some premonitions. One rather odd one perhaps whose meaning meant nothing to us, yet. In January the Simpsons were invited to spend the weekend at Fort Belvedere. But more seriously, in Germany the National Socialist Party became by far the largest party. Germany was rearming beyond Versailles. The League of Nations pronounced gloom. "It is not inapt to describe 1932 as the *annus terribilis*". A disarmament Conference in February achieved little. In Britain unemployment was moving towards 3 million. What should we do? The answer came in the pattern of those days. On the 4th of February a general tariff of 10% was levied on all goods entering the country. It was hoped among other things to encourage greater efficiency. This was a special brand of nonsense. Its main effect was to export our unemployment to other countries. As other countries did the same the effect was to plunge the world economy into a deeper pit. Trade was reduced to less than 50% of its 1924 volume. My own horizon was rather more limited. On the 24th of January, back at Stratton Park, I wrote to my parents "Hay

2 has got some guinea pigs and they have just had babies." Did Hay 1 have any share of the litter?

There was some meeting of horizons. If we could not judge the mood of the times, we could follow men and women of action. In March Jim Mollison, an intrepid playboy, flew to Cape Town in 4 days 17½ hours. Waiting for him there was Amy Johnson. They married in July. We thought what a lovely partnership. It was in fact a disaster; Jim was one of life's bad husbands. But he was a good flier. In August he made a remarkable flight across the Atlantic, the first solo flight east to west. In November Amy beat Jim's record to the Cape by 10 hours. Later they were to fly together. Campbell was still at it. 25 February, 253.97 mph in his beloved Bluebird. On the water Kaye Don reached 120 mph.

On the cricket field Yorkshire (Hobbes and Sutcliffe) scored 555 for one wicket against Essex and I pondered the Essex bowling averages. The tests were against All India whom we brushed aside, though very wet weather did not help. In India there was much trouble. Those who wanted to get rid of us launched the third civil disobedience campaign. By the end of the year 67,000 people had been sentenced. There was terrorism in Bengal and two infantry brigades were sent there to perform what was to become a regular part of the army's duties: 'in aid of the civil power.'

Cambridge won the boat race by 5 lengths for the ninth successive year. For one who always supported Oxford these were hard times and in the competitive society of Stratton Park I had a fight on my hands.

While all this was going on our family had to be redeployed. There was a further shuffling of the pack. The Grays at Guildford could not take us and we had to go elsewhere. Solutions had to be found. And one solution proved to be disastrous. Iris went to Aunt M., my mother's sister. She was a very unstable lady – deranged would be a more accurate description - and her family showed the results. Her daughter spent much of her childhood in a mental home and having married a fine young man who was unaware of her condition, finally took her life. The son was expelled from two schools, married several times and after a short prison sentence fled the country to escape from a tangled life but has found peace at last in Germany. The father, a splendid colonel in the Gurkhas, was unable to stand the strain and died of a heart attack. Staying with her Iris found a kind of hell which she was unwilling to describe in detail. Years later she asked our mother, "Why did you send me there"? There was no suitable answer; separation sometimes gets too complicated.

That spring found Bill and me on a farm on the borders of Essex and Cambridgeshire. There was a boy at Stratton Park called Scales, friendly but not over-talented. They would take us in. His father ran a farm near Great Chesterford, not many miles from Cambridge. It was 200 acres, mostly barley and rented from St John's College, Cambridge. Those were hard times for farmers. They had prospered in the First World War, but the lavish promises made to them were unfulfilled, little money was forthcoming and the countryside had a threadbare look. Mr Scales, or Uncle George as we were told to call him, was a kindly man who regretted the times but never seemed to fret. Mrs Scales was a sterner figure who brought us to heel when our behaviour displeased her.

Uncle George took the trouble to explain all that he did and from time to time allowed us to help, leading the horses and busying ourselves with small things. He had both horses and tractors; farming was at an interesting stage of transition. There were two farmhands; Jack who looked after the horses and Fred who tended the tractor. I visited them a few years ago in the tied cottage that they still occupied and we talked about those far off times. And they were lonely times. Kindness can go so far, but we reached its limits. Bill wrote not long ago. "The sense of deprivation was felt particularly when we came home and spent our holidays with various strangers. We were then always visitors and therefore of secondary status. We had no one to turn to when troubled. I think of myself as a 'watcher', standing behind all the time; being left out."

We wandered about the farm. At one moment of dereliction I knelt in the farmyard and prayed, hoping for light. It was a grey time. I was given an air gun and shot any birds that came my way. I remember with shame getting a blue tit in my sights and seeing it fall. I constructed a nest to trap vermin but found in the gin a partridge badly injured. As a treat we were taken to Cambridge to a variety show where a man turned water into beer and handed it round, and it was good to laugh together.

There was one place I liked to go. A few miles down below lay Duxford aerodrome, a grass field where fighter planes operated. I went there and saw our latest fighters, Bristol Bulldogs biplanes that dropped down over the hedge and pulled up in a few yards. Aeroplanes have always enthralled me and I was content to lie down on the grass and forget. I now live a few miles from there and can go to see the displays of the planes of the heroic days, the Spitfires and the Hurricanes. But when younger people are gasping I am remembering a boy who found delight in British Bulldogs. I cannot remember where Iris went. It was like that. The fragments were beginning to appear.

In August 2006 I returned to the farm, hoping to gather up the memories of seventy three years. The fields stood as they were. They no longer yielded barley, because the bottom had fallen out of the barley market, and now it was wheat, newly shorn and awaiting the next stage in the farmer's cycle. There was the hilltop crowned by trees, from which I had gazed down on Duxford. There was the yard, in which I had fallen to my knees in desolation and the farm buildings inside which I had messed about and tried to make things. I approached the house, seeking for some traces of what had been. I saw just desolation. The farm had been taken over by Elizabeth, the daughter of the couple who had sheltered me. She had died three years ago. The present owner was now in Canada and had delegated the management of the farm to a relative who was doing his best . That best could not extend to the house, which stood derelict, a shell filled with the jumble of past living, comfort become chaos. The garden in front of the house was no more and the tennis court, where I had tried to show that I could do things, was a wasteland. I walked away wondering if the ruin I had just seen reflected in a kind of way the inner desolation of those former days.

Spring turned into summer. On the first of May, Cockroft and Walton split the atom at the Cavendish Laboratory in Cambridge. This was such a staggering event that even at Stratton Park we heard about it and tried to understand. Like so many events in the thirties it contained the seeds of the future, and ever since then hindsight has been in full cry.

The summer holidays. Where should we go? The family split up each of us finding a separate home. Bill and Iris went elsewhere. I found myself with the Grays again and they took me to the Dorset coast. It was Studland, a comfortable seaside resort just clear of the hubbub of Swanage and looking across the wide expanses of Poole Harbour. The Grays had 'taken rooms' with Mrs Belchamber. It is striking how those who lived in some state in imperial bungalows had to transform their lifestyle when they came home. It was a tight fit in Mrs Belchamber's. I shared a bed with Alan, who was lost in a submarine in the War. He was a good companion. A man we had never met before took us out each day to trawl for mackerel. We asked no questions; it was an age less beset with suspicion. On one occasion we caught a mackerel that had been wounded by a swordfish and soon afterwards the baby swordfish that had done the damage. We went to the end of Goathorn Pier in Poole Harbour and lowered our lines, but found nothing at the other end. It was just fun doing things together and being a kind of family. And we sang *"Sweet Sue, just you"*, *"Dinah"*, *"Let's put out the lights and go to sleep"*; heady stuff for an eleven year old. Bing Crosby was now in full cry and we loved his gravelly groans.

There was another interest that helped to light up the years; motor racing. This was Formula 1 in very different clothes. Not safety-sealed computers but chunks of metal steered by men who sat surrounded by nothing but the fresh air. As the thirties opened the Italians were still in charge, the Alfa Romeos headed by what I have always believed was the greatest driver there has ever been, Tazio Nuvolari. The Germans, the power of their machines echoing their ambition to dominate, were breathing down his neck, but for a few remarkable years he held them at bay, and we followed and hoped he would hold his own. We were delighted when in 1932 he won at Monaco, but a Mercedes win in the following month showed what was coming.

What was coming to our family was something altogether surprising.

1933

My mother wrote early in 1933 and said, "You are going to have another brother or sister". Amazing. A gap of eight years. A classic question posed itself: was this a consolation or an accident? Only partly aware of the mysteries of conception I thought: that is quite a surprise, and perhaps it will make up for Monty, and having a baby around there will be some more things to be done. The birth took place on the tenth of April, at Murree, a hill station in what is now Pakistan. It was a difficult birth; there was talk of forceps and Robert's eyesight was affected. His life was going to be an unusual one and bring the family to the edges of distinction.

There were others surprises in store. I wrote in a letter otherwise confined to the description of cricket matches, and the unlikely remark "I began slogging", "The school is going to move to near Hertford". The owner wanted to pull the lovely house down. In effect he pulled the school down. There was nothing to match its peerless setting, but we would have to go. I would have one year at its new site before moving on.

There was one remark in a letter that showed us a bit of the world. "The whole school is contributing to the poor in Bletchley". There were plenty of them around. In January the Prince of Wales, who became known as a man concerned for the poor, made an Appeal of Unemployment, "I have in mind a common attempt to discover how empty hours may be turned to good account". In February there was a debate on the government's economic policy. Chamberlain's speech in which he said we must "keep pegging on until better times arrived" had a chilly reception. There were other ideas. In March Keynes wrote a series of articles in The Times. The vocabulary of economics was beginning to change. 'Wise spending' was being talked about rather than 'economy'. What would Johnson 6 make of this?

We were growing uneasy about Europe. On the fifth of March the National Socialists assumed power in Germany with 44% of the polls and on the 30th Parliament debated the outrages that we were beginning to hear about, especially a vicious anti-Semitism. At Stratton Park we had our own unarticulated view on Jews, but this was something quite different. The League of Nations was perplexed. The National Register noted, "1933 might not unfairly be described as the most critical and the most crowded in the history of the League of Nations". There was much talk about disarmament. It was the main topic at the opening address in Parliament in November. The Lords replied "The House views with great disquiet the present inadequacy of the provision made for the air defence of the British Isles." Did we notice – it was certainly big news - that on the ninth of February the Oxford Union passed a resolution "that the house will in no circumstances fight for its King and country" by 275 votes to 153.

We were fumbling and Ramsay Macdonald was becoming senile. He visited Italy and it was commented, "Mr MacDonald expressed himself in a tortuous manner which made it very difficult for his hearers to gather what he had actually achieved". Did this register with us? Maybe. I wrote, "On Tuesday our new parson, Mr Moxon, gave a lecture on Germany." What *did* he say?

Our own plans were becoming rather uncertain. There was a polio scare in the summer. In those days polio was an unconquered affliction and from time to time a measure of panic arose. The Scaleses said they could not take us and we would have to make other arrangements. Plan B was brought into operation. Part of the summer I would go to Studland with the Grays. Here there was a shadow. In July Uncle Jack, the father of the family, a senior Indian civil servant, died in India of a streptococcal infection. The news reached the family in England by cable. There was no question of flying out, so I don't know quite what arrangements were made, but I asked whether in the circumstances the trip to Studland was on. The Grays had suffered a previous tragedy, a daughter drowned in a skating accident, and they were to suffer another. They said bravely that the holiday was on. And we went again to that pleasant beach and tried to enjoy ourselves, which I believe we did, although Alan while leaping into a pile of sand landed on a jagged tin and had to be stitched up. Fortunately the summer of 1933 was one of the driest, sunniest and warmest on record, and we could all recharge. And we could sing the songs which today would be in the charts, *Brother, can you spare a dime? Some body stole my gal, Home, home on the range where the deer and the buffalo play, where there's seldom heard a discouraging word and the skies are not cloudy all day.* My father used to jib at this last song. "Impossible weather. Nonsense."

For the rest of the summer there was an interesting variation. Dear Granny, our great stand by stepped into the breach; which today grannies spend most of their time doing. Early widowed she lived in a top flat overlooking Church Street, Kensington, surrounded by the beautiful bric a brac of Burma where she had spent most of her life. Passionately literary – she once took me to a meeting of the Poetry Society of which she was a life-long member – and artistic and with her attachment to the Empire, a member of the Overseas League. She was always ready. It was very good to know that she was there. So she took us to the seaside at Seaford and gave us a family holiday of a special kind. Iris said they were some of the happiest days of her life; she needed happiness.

CS Lewis wrote a memoir which he entitled *Surprised by Joy* as he found a faith. I was taken by surprise as I attended a children's beach mission on the sands of Seaford where I found the seeds of joy which blossomed later. I continue to be surprised. And I continue to thank a dear grandmother. It took a Granny to give us a sense of togetherness and to give me the avenue to truth.

There was the usual spate of records in the air; here were the heroes. Jim Mollison to South America, the record non-stop flight of 5,340 miles. And to show that there were always records for the taking, the record for inverted flying, when an Italian flew upside down for 42 minutes 37 seconds, beaten later in the air by an American who stayed upside down for 1 hour 46 minutes 59 seconds. Italy was determined to do something spectacular and in July a fleet of twenty four seaplanes set off across the Atlantic under Admiral Balbo. They returned in August with only two missing. Italy cheered and Mussolini swelled. There was one flight that did not go quite as it intended. The Mollisons set off together to cross the Atlantic. The first attempt of their heavily laden plane to take off from Pendine Sands in Wales failed. But they finally got into the air. They ran out of fuel within sight of their destination and crashed at Bridgeport. A battered couple were given a heroes' welcome. It might not have been a great marriage, but they were quite a pair. We found plenty of skies to watch.

Cambridge won the Boat Race for the tenth successive year and the event was beginning to lose its excitement. But on the home front there was expectation. My mother was due to return, with Robert. In India things were looking up. "A remarkable psychological change in India's politics brought greater quietude towards the close of 1933 than for many years". By the end of the year the numbers imprisoned had dropped to less than 3000 (from over 14,000). This did not prevent Gandhi being rearrested on the first of August, but law and order had been reasserted.

My mother arrived back with Robert in the autumn and it was strange to have a baby in our midst; the years had got confused. My mother had to pick up the threads, which were becoming a little more complex. Bill had moved on to public school, Iris was assimilating herself to her latest school, and there was Robert. Where to live? The answer was 17 Pembridge Gardens in Bayswater. It is a mystery how my parents could afford to house us in a private hotel, but then their finances were always a mystery which we made no attempt to plumb. It was back to Kensington Gardens and the Round Pond, but this time not a little boy lost, but a twelve year old pushing a pram. The elegant Norland Nannies were still there, gossiping and pushing and shepherding and I may well have lowered the tone a bit. I remember misjudging a corner and landing Robert with a bump against some railings and I felt privileged when the policeman on duty stopped the traffic so that I could cross.

Christmas was a well organised event with merriment running to schedule. We shopped in Whiteleys, my grandmother's favourite shop, and Hamleys where we could dream dreams and drop hints. And we skated at the Queen's Ice Rink which was close by. But a few days before Christmas tragedy struck France. On the 23rd of December two trains on the Strasbourg - Nancy line collided in the fog. 220 were killed and 300 injured. The photographs in the papers showed the carnage. In our hotel was an inventor and word went round that he was in the process of inventing a device that could have stopped this fearful event. I wondered if his big chance had come and he could make a fortune by marketing his device. We never found out, but as he seemed a man of limited resources I hoped that his moment had come.

From the other side of the world a crisis was brewing of a very British kind. Bodyline. The English cricket team that was touring Australia was facing a challenge – how to get the wicket of the ultimate run machine, Bradman. Under their iron captain, Douglas Jardine, they devised a strategy so crude that one blushes to recollect it. Larwood, a whirlwind bowler, was instructed to bowl at the batsman's body. In an attempt to shield himself from serious injury the batsman would fend off the ball into the hands of short leg who was waiting there for just such a shot. It worked. Larwood took seventeen wickets and England won the series by four matches to one. But there was uproar. At one match the police had to be called in, and there was talk about whether Australia should break off relations with England: the Empire was striking back. The MCC passed a resolution, "That any form of bowling which is obviously a direct attack by a bowler upon the batsman would be an offence against the spirit of the game." Hearing this in England our disgust at the tactics was severely moderated by satisfaction at its results. But we had to find more orthodox ways of getting the great man out. We awaited the arrival of the Australian team in the summer of 1934.

The year passing had one pleasantly unusual event. An AA Scout driving along the shores of Loch Ness thought he saw a monster. He had started something.

1934

1934 was a year to remember, though it started badly with intense fog in London and many deaths. It was the pea soup that today we seem to have put to flight. Roads were more dangerous than they have ever been since. In that year 7343 died, a figure hardly equalled in the post war years with far more traffic. Hore-Belisha the publicity-conscious Minister of Transport bemoaned 'the mass murder on the roads', much of which was pedestrians, and so we had the Belisha beacons, lollipops to see us across the road. Safety became a kind of fun, and Hore-Belisha the butt of harmless pantomime jokes. This colourful man saved lives.

But for our family the year had another joy. Dad was home on leave. We had moved again, to a delightful house in the village of Blackheath a few miles south of Guildford. It was owned by a rather eccentric colonel who would peer through the hedge from time to time to see what was going on. What was going on was a happy gathering of the family, with one extra member, drawing breath. But perhaps not quite enough drawing. My mother wanted to visit old India friends and we spent much of our time driving into her past. Bill and I wanted to complain, and we muttered to ourselves, but our mother was not someone whom one could complain against, so we resigned ourselves to motoring too often and meeting and chattering with people we did not know, the Raj touching base and eager to sustain a framework; they were, to quote a very recent phrase, 'one of us'. The East was a close society. With my father's arrival, the driving moderated; his quiet protests sometimes prevailed. We bought a bull-nosed Morris for twelve pounds, a huge beast that roared when it was working but sometimes sulked and had to be persuaded to move. On one occasion it was unwilling to leave a ferry. As we were the leading car the other drivers had to be patient. If my recollection is correct we were more patient then; the roads required it. But it was open, a 'tourer' and it was fun. And for my father it brought him closer to England.

The Australians were in England, and we followed their progress with care, hoping for more success. Bodyline was out – the previous tour in Australia had exposed it - and the MCC made the following statement, "That the type of bowling regarded as a direct attack by the bowler upon the batsman, and therefore unjust, consists, in persistent and systematic bowling of fast, short-pitched balls at the batsman standing clear of the wicket." In those days the batsmen had no protective armour other than a box.

The first test Australia won by 238 runs, aided critically by the bowling of O'Reilly and Grimmett, the latter being crafty and slow. The second test went to England by an innings and 38 runs. They made 440 with centuries by Leyland and Ames. The third test was a draw, a match of massive scores, England 627 for 9 and 123 for 0, Australia

491 and 66 for 1. The fourth match England were very lucky to draw. Australia made 584 with the unbeatable Bradman 304. The series was thus all square. Under the rules then prevailing the last match would be timeless, played until there was a result. It proved to be a remarkable contest.

It was at the Oval, as all last tests were, and I went with my father to watch. This was an important togetherness. And what did we see? Australia batting, Bradman and Ponsford, all through a scorching day. And the score sheet read: Ponsford 266 Bradman 244. It was an extraordinary display; a run machine without parallel that even achieved a kind of monotony. It was good to have been there and to have seen the great man in action. The Australian total was 701. King George proclaimed "His Majesty feels sure that such a brilliant display of batting will appeal to all lovers of cricket and ever be remembered in the history of this great sport." England could not climb such a mountain. They made 321 and then facing an Australian innings of 327 they limped to 145. The result, a victory for Australia by 562 runs, a margin that, believe it not, was to be surpassed by a significant margin in a few years. Why were runs so easy to come by?

On another field of play was a situation that we would not recognise today. At Wimbledon Perry won the men's singles, as he would in the next two years and Dorothy Round won the women's singles. And we retained the Davis Cup by beating the USA. Perry and Bunny Austin were an unbeatable combination. What has happened to these skills? On the Thames it was business as usual. Cambridge won by 4½ lengths, and I was beginning to despair. And at Aintree the greatest steeplechaser ever, Golden Miller, won the Grand National in record time. In India the year was rather mottled. In the political field there was recovery and adjustment and preparation for a great constitutional advance. But an earthquake in Bihar and Nepal killed over 10,000.

For me it was the parting of the ways. Goodbye to Stratton Park, where I had made a kind of home and been taught to learn and to endeavour. It was time to move up, thankful for what the past had given me and hoping that the sky ahead was bright. We said goodbye at the site we had moved to, a place that pleased us but lacked the majestic sweep of Great Brickhill. The school was destined not to last the war. It was a tense goodbye. Mr Clouston seemed affronted by our ancient car, which must have lowered the tone of the place a bit, and he wanted me to stay on; perhaps he was wondering if he could fill all his beds. So we shook hands and after some gruff exchanges we roared off. Five multi-coloured years ended by a grunt. Such, as Shakespeare might have said, is the breath of headmasters. Some goodbyes are better than others.

Where next? It was a most unlikely venue, far to the north.

Stratton Park had, by a process I never discovered, established a link with Sedbergh. Where? It is not a name to drop when discussing one's education; not many seem to have heard of it. But it is placed in such a magical part of England that those passing through it for the first time often exclaim, "What a wonderful place. Why haven't I heard of it before."? One reason is that Sedbergh refuses to place itself on the tourist map. It is not the Dales where many come to relive James Herriot, nor is it the Lakes which can have no peer in our land. It is between these two and the fells which rise majestically above it take their name from a tiny hamlet, Howgill, that few ever visit. It is a place through which you go to get somewhere else. You can come to it from the east up Wensleydale or from the west from Kendal just eleven miles away. From either direction to arrive is to wonder, and to look at hills that are like none other: smooth and sweeping and accessible to all. It is becoming known. The M6 lies close to it and from the service station south of intersection 38 the hills come splendidly into view and hold the eye in surprise. It has been squeezed into the National Park and has its visitors' centre and urges people to come and visit, which they do.

The Sedbergh I came to in September 1934 and which Bill had started at a year before was as it had been for very many years, a town with a rough Pennine feel to it surrounded by hills that few ever trod over – except the farmers who grazed their sheep and the boys of Sedbergh School. The school is not famous, but it is very old. It was founded in 1525 and re-founded under Edward VI, one of the 53 grammar schools as part of a vision to spread learning to barbarous places. It had practically expired in the nineteenth century but had been revived by men of resolve.

The 1930's were offering a fresh challenge as the depression that had struck the north was emptying the pockets of parents. There was a dramatic illustration of this during that first term. On the fifth of October a party of miners set off from Jarrow, which had an unemployment rate of 67.8%. Their aim was to march to London to present their plight to the government. The papers showed pictures of men huddled against the rain with boots that were wearing out and a kind of despair on their faces. They were led by a fiery little Labour redhead, Ellen Wilkinson. Wherever they went they were received with acclaim and were offered food and shelter. But after they had been on the road for a week they received a message from the Cabinet that such marches were wholly undesirable and that they would not receive a delegation. They reached London on the first of November. And that was that.

JB Priestly wrote in 1934 a striking account of the land in *English Journey*. And in it he proclaimed. "It is all very puzzling. Was Jarrow still in England or not? Had we excluded Lancashire and the north east coast? Were we no longer on speaking terms with cotton weavers and miners and platers and riveters? Why had nothing been done about these decaying towns and their workless people?" I was going to this blighted north but where it showed its other lovely face. But how did one reach it? By the means that most people used – by train. At Euston Station parents saying goodbye and boys uneasily trying to end conversations that were becoming hard to sustain. Hopes and fears and for new boys varying degrees of emptiness. And then, off. The LMS reserved carriage drew out of the station, and the names unwound: Berkhamsted, and in the fields hoardings advertising Carters Little Liver Pills and a glimpse of the Ovaltine factory and a fleeting view at my past, Rugby, Stafford where engineering was stumbling, Crewe where so many railway lines decided to meet, Warrington, Wigan where Orwell told us of its squalor and its pier, Preston, Lancaster a glimpse of the sea. Carnforth, Oxenholme, names that are not easily erased from memory because they stand for that different world. We usually changed at Oxenholme, and later saw the Coronation Scot roar through. Sometimes we changed at Carnforth where trains gathered strength and additional power for the challenge of Shap, or Tebay, where railway, road and river forced their way through the hills, and then by a line that no longer runs across viaducts that now stand silent and from which we could see the river Lune winding its way.

And then I was at Sedbergh. This was a new land. It bore no resemblance to any I had seen before. The hills surrounded it, a huge but never threatening embrace, a backdrop that no other school possessed: to the north Winder, Crook, Sickers and Knott, a row of smooth round sentinels, and behind them The Calf presiding over the surrounding tops and to the east Baugh Fell and many other high places which I looked up at and wondered if I could conquer. There were no fences or barred gates; the land was yours to wander over.

There were two places of worship at Sedbergh: the school chapel and the rugby football ground. This game, in which the school achieved a pre-eminence, flavoured our life and to achieve there, at whatever level, was to succeed. To fail was a blight. In that first term terrible news reached Sedbergh: we had been beaten by Ampleforth. A pall fell over the hills; a record run of success had been broken and we were distraught. I hope that the fact that they were Catholic did not cast an extra shadow. Into this area of excellence Bill fitted well; he was an exceptionally gifted player and I was able, as I struggled to gain a footing in the school, to have some reflected glory. I wrote in that first term, "A terrific lot is expected of me being Billy's brother."

Sedbergh has always been regarded as a tough school. Certainly the school motto *Dura virum nutrix*, 'the hard nurse of men', suggests this. The first appointment of the day was a cold bath and the weather was often very Pennine. One of the dormitories in my boarding house where the wind and snow came straight off the hills we called Siberia. But I think it was the setting and the myths attached to them, such as that you had to run up the neighbouring fell before breakfast that gave it this reputation. Life was hard, but I think that was true of most boarding schools in the thirties, as the anguished memoirs of those years have shown. There were rigours unaffected by the mountains. Yes. The day started with cold baths and the juniors had to dry on the landing outside the bathroom, in winter a very cold business. The 'fags', those totemic figures of English boarding education, had to take turn to shout out the time so that the prefects, allowed warmth, would know when to get out and dry themselves and prepare for the prep which preceded breakfast. On one occasion I muddled the times and there were some last minute panics and my name was mud. "My duties consist of sweeping out the Senior Study and preparing brews". This meant handing a hot drink to a prefect as he lay in his bath after games. Once the brew I had prepared was not hot enough, and there was a roar from the bath. Good clean fun, or a touch of barbarism?

And games were always the touchstone of success. Entering this new world was a struggle, but Sedbergh became for me a place in which striving was always worth while and with no fixed home a solid base in which to try to do the best I could. Struggling up those hills, which were yours for the taking, was a kind of liberation and an acting out of the endeavour that I felt I needed for success. Anyone can run.

I prepared to enter that unique social unit, the boarding house. I was to direct one of these for a number of years, striving to care for other people's children, and here I saw it from the other end, and I learnt much. The boarding house is a unit of intense loyalties, seeking to create an identity in a world in which belonging is not easy. It is a living together and trying to get on. It is a close-quarters life where who and what you are is not easy to disguise. It is a world of thrusting male egos trying to establish a firm base. And if you fail, life can be quite hard. And always: our house must be the best; it must win. It was a loyalty that gave life a satisfactory focus.

With so much at stake what matters is who is in charge. He is the one in whose charge you are, who can create more directly than any other member of the staff the quality of your life. Reflecting from both ends of the hierarchy I continue to feel uneasy about how much depends on this one man, and how critical it is to find the right men for the job. I hear that it is now not always easy to find these men. I have more to say later, to describe the time when I was one of these men. I was very lucky. We were in the hands of Ivan Christopherson, known to us as Christo and to his colleagues for obvious reasons as Monty. He was unmarried, but he was not incomplete. He was firm and understanding and could laugh and knew what was going on. When I heard what was going on in some other houses where lesser men were in charge I was very thankful, and began to understand that the house is at least as important as the school.

The other critical point is one's peers. If you are going to be herded together in rather close quarters your co-herdees are very important. There is some connection here, as I was to find out. A good housemaster is more likely to attract good boys if he is networking well. I was exceptionally fortunate. Thirteen of us arrived that September, several from Stratton Park, and many of them achieved distinction. I have recently read the obituaries of three of them in The Times: a highly decorated warrior, a foreign correspondent of remarkable quality and one of our top mathematicians. It is interesting that the foreign correspondent, a person of great charm and culture who might have been out of place among the mountains, described his years at Sedbergh as extremely happy ones.

It was certainly a very busy life. With the press of a big new world, with cold baths, a prefect whose shoes I had to clean and whose commands I had to obey, a hierarchy that it was fatal to attempt to scorn, a rush to do many things fast and be in many places, a constant worry whether I was doing anything right, drawing breath was a bit of a luxury. The houseroom where we spent our days echoed with the latest songs; not pop, but either dance bands and crooners or small groups of rather hectic instrumentalists with not a guitar in sight, though there was George Formby with his ukulele singing songs of chirpy rudeness. Nat Gonella was a favourite and such rather mad ditties as *I'm nuts about screwy music.* And the inimitable Fats Waller who growled over his piano *Your feet's too big* and *I'm going to sit right down and write myself a letter in make believe it came from you.* For something gentler there was Reginald Dixon at the organ of the Tower Ballroom Blackpool, and Charlie Kunz who played the piano with a lilt that rather engaged us. As today, there had to be noise. To youth the final obscenity is silence.

But we were still able to catch glimpses of the world outside. On the 22nd of September there was a terrible tragedy. Gresford Colliery near Wrexham exploded and 260 died. My addiction to aeroplanes drew my attention elsewhere and continued to do so. On the 20th of October 20 planes took off on a most unusual enterprise: a race from Mildenhall in Suffolk to Melbourne for the MacRobertson Trophy financed by a biscuit millionaire, to celebrate the centenary of Melbourne. Planes of all kinds took part suitably handicapped, and we watched to see what would happen. The result was remarkable. The winner, as expected, was the Comet, a purpose built racer which completed the journey in 2 days 23 hours and 18 seconds. But second was a DC2, a fledgling airliner and third a DH Moth, a small biplane that Amy Johnson used for her record flights. Courage came in many sizes. The Mollisons in their de Haviland Comet led easily to Karachi but they lost their way and their engine seized up. Their relationship did the same.

And then something for the heart. On the 29th of November the Duke of Kent married Princess Marina, a Greek lady who took our affection in a very special way, though I think the public was not really aware of the kind of husband she had taken on. The Archbishop of Canterbury, who was willing to pronounce on most things, declared, "Never in history, may we dare to say, has a marriage been attended by so vast a company of witnesses. For by a new and marvellous invention of science countless multitudes in every variety of place and home are joining in the service." We had got beyond crystal sets, and the wireless, now well into its stride, delivered in a precision of tone that we now find hard to take seriously what was happening in the world.

And the tunes that the world was singing that year; *Over my shoulder, Smoke gets in your eyes, The Isle of Capri, The object of my affection,* but above all what I sang as I ran over those new high places, and which was top of the pops *Little man you've had a busy day.* This was the tale of a tired little boy ready for bed, perhaps more suitable for mothers than for a growing boy, but a considerable solace for one trying to find his way.

1935

While I was getting on terms with my own world, the world outside was making conflicting noises. The Annual Register proclaimed hopefully, "When the year 1935 opened the international sky was clearer than it had been for some time." But like the opening of an English day this carried few reliable indications about what was to follow. Anthony Eden said with less assurance, "1935 will be the most challenging year in post-war history. It will show whether we can make the League – the collective system – effective, or whether nations are determined to pursue a selfish course." It was to show an awful lot.

Important things were happening. In January Lloyd George, a man with no power but with a tireless mind, came up with a "New Deal", a plan for massive state assistance for industry. There should be a great Prosperity Loan. The end of 'economising'?

The government did not listen. It was going to increase its spending, but in another direction – defence. Germany was rearming and was introducing conscription. We could not stand by. A dozen new RAF squadrons were to be created. At the time we did not realise what a critical decision this was.

As we came into summer, our attention was drawn to a very happy event. The King and Queen were celebrating their Silver Jubilee, and the country was to show how well it organised ceremony. London prepared and spent the then enormous sum of one million pounds on the occasion. We made ready to celebrate. The family camped in Granny's flat, with whose floor we were to become well acquainted, and we took up our position on the Mall to wait for some hours. With us was Pat McSwiney, the school friend who was to be a warrior. He was staying with us as his mother was dangerously ill; she died not long afterwards. It was the sixth of May and the weather was perfect. At 10.30am the procession left Buckingham Palace and then passed along Constitution Hill, Piccadilly, the Strand, St Paul's to a congregation of 2,000. There the Archbishop proclaimed, "Beneath the troubled surface there has been in the life of the nation the deep underflow of a spirit of unity, confidence and steadfast strength. That spirit has found a centre in the throne." The procession returned by the Embankment, Admiralty Arch and the Mall. We thought we had done well to be in the front row, but as so often happens rows of soldiers and policemen came in at the last moment and we had to peer. It was still a beautiful sight, the open carriage and a monarch glad to be among his people. With some difficulty we found a taxi and made our way to Granny's flat where we collapsed agreeably and said what a wonderful day it had been. The royal pair came on to the balcony of Buckingham Palace. There were shouts of "We want the Prince", but the Prince did not appear, an absence into which one can read almost anything.

And in the evening the king broadcast a message of thanks. "As I passed this morning through cheering multitudes to and from St Paul's Cathedral, as I thought there of all that these twenty five years have brought to me and to my country and empire, how could I fail to be deeply moved…I dedicate myself anew to your service for the years that may still be given me." Soon after dark he pressed an electric button to start a chain of 2,000 beacons. He was stunned by the warmth with which his people greeted him. "I never knew they thought that about me." London was en fête for a week; three ceremonial drives, a reception at St James's Palace for the Diplomatic Corps, humble addresses in

Parliament and an address of greeting in Westminster Hall read by the Lord Chancellor. The Prime Minister. "He is the king of his people." The Lords "Your majesty's own personality has made the throne not merely a symbol, but a loved and living reality." There were jubilee RAF reviews at Mildenhall and Duxford. We had moved from Bristol Bulldogs to Gloster Gauntlets, edging slowly towards a force that would be able to defend our shores.

So that first summer term started in a flood of celebration. And also in a change of government. Macdonald retired, not to acclaim but in a sad dimming of his powers and leaving a party that was still living through the shame of his treachery. It was now Baldwin, who got alongside us and with a skill that he hid from us, persuaded us that we were in good hands. How effective he was still exercises the minds of those who try to make sense of those times. The men he chose stood for the pluses and minuses of those years: Simon, Hoare, Eden. We got to know them and we became uncertain of them.

And India took a big step forward. On the 20th of June the India Bill passed its second reading 'easily the longest bill ever placed before Parliament', 323 pages of it. It created eleven autonomous provinces, each with a directly elected legislative assembly, reserving to the central government defence, foreign relations and, rather oddly, ecclesiastical affairs. Attlee, who was to know that country well, said it had the right to dominion status. Churchill, who had opposed every clause with a ferocity that cast increasing doubts on his political judgement, calmed down and agreed to 'bury the hatchet'.

But India had other things on its mind. On the second of June Quetta, a town high up on the Persian border of what is now Pakistan, where Iris had been born in 1922, suffered a horrific earthquake. About 40,000 died, including 250 British. The latter were largely RAF personnel. Most of the Army quarters and the Staff College, where my father was employed at the end of his career, were undamaged. Those like us who had connections out there, were anxious. The English community was a small world, and we hoped it had become no smaller.

It was my first summer at Sedbergh. The cold winds from off the fells had died away. There was no rugger, and endeavour had to find other avenues, perhaps not quite so significant. But instead of mud and bruising there was the sun and the hills became very inviting. Winder, which towered over the town was a quick steep journey. Beyond was Higher Winder which we usually bypassed to reach The Calf standing a little over two thousand feet from which you could view a panorama of rough and distant places. Further to the north east were Cautley Crags where buzzards nested and Cautley Spout, a sudden and spectacular drop of water. Black Force was a long run to the north west towards the gap in the hills by Tebay where three routes, which now includes the M6, pierced their way. Many hills but very few people. On a half holiday you could make them your own. From time to time an extra half holiday was decreed and the hills were ours for many hours. At three o'clock everyone had to be at least two miles out. Those without ambition or will sat on the second mile stone; others went into distant places and after much exertion arrived at farmhouses which dispensed ham and egg teas; life at its most simply satisfying.

I remember one magic afternoon climbing into the high places and singing a song that seemed to catch the day, *I feel like a feather on the breeze.* And another in winter when darkness was falling as I made my way with others from Cautley Crags. There was deep snow and at one place we could only just squeeze through a gap in the drifts. We arrived back glad to have returned before we froze. And there were the rivers. Three rivers, Clough, Dee and Rawthay, flowed by Sedbergh, and a little further away the Lune. It was to the latter that we could go in summer when time allowed and bathe under the arches of the viaduct that carried the railway from Low Gill to Sedbergh. This was cold water without compulsion, a refreshing freedom from the restrictions of a tightly disciplined community. Was this a tough school? Come with me to the Lune and take a dip.

And come on to the fells not just to run over them but to look more closely at what inhabits them. There were the birds: buzzards, peregrine falcons, plovers and many others. Strong young men were content to care for them and examine them and follow their movements, ringing the young and receiving news of them as they landed in far off places, noting down in meticulous detail all that they found.

This offered to my brother Bill an unusual escape. He was a brilliant cricketer, and his performance at Stratton Park had been so outstanding that it gained a paragraph in the Cricketer magazine. He looked set for a brilliant cricketing future at Sedbergh. But something went wrong and he became disenchanted with the game. His housemaster with splendid understanding said he need not play but instead he could pursue his other passion - birds; which he did and he found happiness. The school was mad on games, but the hills could not be gainsaid. What other school could offer an escape like this?

At home the caravan was moving on. We left Blackheath and its delightful garden and the woods through which we had bicycled and the friends we had made and found ourselves for some reason in New Milton, a small town on the edge of the New Forest. It lacked the class of the nearby Milford-on-Sea, and my mother, who had a keen sense of hierarchy, said, "The trouble with New Milton is that there are so many shoppies", by which she meant shop assistants, an inferior class. I don't know whether this gentle snobbery came from the life she had lived in India, or whether it reflected what was undoubtedly true, that in the thirties you knew your place. That is of course not your geographical location, which in our case was uncertain, but your place in the social scale.

We set about getting on terms with this new environment. A tennis tournament in Milford-on-Sea helped us to get to know the right people and a friend came and showed us how to trap moths by a night lamp and how to pin them to a board and the New Forest was near enough to sample; and if you really wanted to rub shoulders with the nobs there was always Lymington, a place defined by boats. It was a gentle and unremarkable time. But this was only marking time as my mother was preparing to return to India where her husband was waiting for her. I remember reflecting as the holiday drew to a close on the harsh necessities of our life and why my father had got no further than colonel. There was no bitterness but a strong regret.

Back at school I was suddenly more important. The seniority of a year at a boarding school means a lot. You can then greet the new boys and do …what? That is the point. You can assert your seniority crudely and roughly, or, to be more frank, bully. You can accept them coldly or you can help them on their way. In your hands lay the ethos of that small and unique community, the boarding house. It was a test that required a brave person to get right; it also depended crucially on the quality of your peers. Got wrong it could bring misery of the special kind that only boarding can bring, and it brought it to many people, and it brought on the system a shame that has taken many years to put right. I had the priceless advantage, as I have described, of a community of largely good people, several of them from Stratton Park, and we prospered. The going was hard but there was little evil. And the housemaster, watching and hoping, must have been pleased at what he saw, though he would remind himself, as I was to do, that the price of safety is eternal vigilance.

While I was attuning myself to my new world, the world outside was beginning to show alarming uncertainties. On the fourth of October Mussolini invaded Abyssinia. He had been eyeing it as the only independent African non-colonial power, and he wanted an empire badly. His chest-beating creed demanded it, and anyway they had met with a disastrous rebuff in 1896 and he wanted revenge. There had been border skirmishes towards the end of 1934 and in January 1935 the League of Nations was asked to arbitrate. It moved with a fearful deliberation. Sir Samuel Hoare told the League of Nations that the British government supported collective measures against Italy and the League decided by 50 votes to take action. This was the crunch. The pity is that in these years there were too many crunches and at each one there was failure. France was unwilling to move.

The term ended. I have in my hand my report from it. And I read with amusement the report on my Greek from a man of huge erudition, ruthless demands and strange ways. "He would be distinctly good if he were not so amazingly inaccurate." Next year I was able to turn the tables on him. Without his knowledge and with the complicity of my housemaster I entered Greek for School Certificate and passed. He contained his surprise well. But I had reached my frontier in the language.

On another frontier there were dark doings. On the 13th of December Hoare and Laval the British and French Foreign Secretaries published their proposed treaty with Italy. It was unbelievable. It was a carve up of Abyssinia giving Italy their share of the bargain. The western nations erupted and Baldwin, who had just been re-elected with a thumping majority, had to sack him. And we all asked: what was going on? Was the way open now for a real stiffening of the sinews?

And where was I? The reader may be wondering. Another aunt had stepped into the breach, Aunt Hilda. She was married to an officer in the Indian Navy with three daughters and a son and lived on the outskirts of Guildford, a semi-detached house bordering on the railway line but with access to a pleasant countryside. They were good to be with and were to hold the fort at critical times in the future. A double tragedy in the family lay many years ahead, but now all was well. Here I was content to see the year subside, attuned to the new pattern of my life; and looking forward to a year that was to contain more than I could have foretold.

1936

The year started on a sombre note. On the 20th of January Stuart Hibberd, the BBC's most majestic announcer, told the nation. "The King's life is drawing peacefully to a close." And then, "Death came peacefully to the King at 11.55 pm" The truth was not quite like that. We now know that the King's death was expedited by the doctors in order that the announcement could appear in the next morning's Times, by giving him a massive dose of cocaine and morphine in his jugular vein. Death was clearly near at hand, but there are various ways of doing things. It had been bronchial catarrh with signs of cardiac weakness.

The next day Edward VIII was proclaimed King from the balcony of St James's Palace. Mrs Simpson was watching from within. In Sedbergh market place I was part of a guard of honour that fired a *feu de joie* to celebrate the great event. It was a tricky operation. The firing had to go along the ranks and you had to get your shot in at the right moment. We had a rehearsal in the school gymnasium and the noise was shattering. In the marketplace the shots resounded, I believe correctly, and the watching crowd of country folk and schoolboys cheered. We had a new King. Who was he? My parents had met him briefly on one of his imperial tours. It was in Burma in 1922 and they were among those invited to have a meal with him. They saw a man who without regard to the trouble he caused toyed irresponsibly with the arrangements. Tedious formalities were not his line; and formality was the pattern of the Raj. All this must have sent some warning signals, though the fact that he had been pushed on to this tour against his will can hardly have helped.

Mr Baldwin said in a broadcast, as he was bound to, "The young King knows the confidence we repose in him." We liked the look of him, and when in his first broadcast on the first of March he declared, "My constant effort will be to continue to promote the well-being of my fellow men", we believed him. But there was one comment which said all sorts of things, and reflected the views of many who knew him "He was of too lively an intelligence for his job." It was now a matter of setting in train the many arrangements necessary for his coronation, which was fixed for the 12th of May 1937.

But at Sedbergh other and more sombre events were to unfold. Illness fell on the school on a scale that can best be illustrated by the report of the school medical officer which I have by me. 75 admissions to the sanatorium, of which 61 were measles. "The measles epidemic was a very severe one, many cases being complicated by some broncho-pneumonia to which one boy unfortunately succumbed. In addition to this 2 cases of cerebro-spinal meningitis developed in boys convalescent from measles and after many weeks of severe illness, though at one time apparently recovering, both died, the final cause in each case being cerebral pressure." It was in the words of our doctor a triple tragedy.

And for a small community devastating. Three boys dead. In my house there were two Batt brothers, Peter and Michael, from Stratton Park. Michael died, and I heard from my bed – I had succumbed to measles – the agonised cries of Peter mourning his brother. There was news of a miracle drug M and B, and a master drove furiously to get a supply. But it did not cure. And there were funerals. When the young are buried there can be little comfort. The hills did not offer much solace, only a wintry backcloth. And few had the will or in some cases the strength to climb them. The school was unable to function, and those in charge took the only action they could: they brought the term to a very premature end. How often do schools close like this?

For the headmaster GB Smith, a quiet thoughtful man who had patiently strengthened learning in the school, it was too much and he resigned that year. His successor JH Bruce Lockhart gave us a polymath – musician, international rugger player, artist and virtuoso language teacher. He set himself to bend Sedbergh to his will and we were aware of someone firmly in charge, and telling us to do things differently. The staff, who were his instruments, I gather bent unwillingly. But that, I also discovered, is what happens when teachers are told to change their ways. They command pupils, but are unwilling themselves to be commanded too forcefully.

We were dispersed to our homes. There was to be distance learning. We were to take with us our school books, post our work to our teachers and await their comments. There was a snag: where were our homes? If you tear up the script you have to improvise. Many people had to make plans before they were ready. Where should I go? My housemaster had to act as a proxy parent, which I suppose he was anyway, and offer plans. I'm not sure how much my parents were consulted. He said that, there are two alternatives: to stay at the bursar's house or with my grandmother. The first suggestion was novel and alarming. We must get away from this place of sorrow and not stay with a total stranger. Bursars manage figures, but can they manage guests? I was quite certain. It was Granny, and so loaded with books I went to 21 Camden Hill Mansions welcomed as only grandmothers can and prepared to do some swotting, as School Certificate was looming. I bought Trevelyan's great trilogy on Garibaldi and I was seduced by Philip Guedalla who painted the past with sharper colours than it had any right to have. And in that lovely drawing room I was surrounded by many memories of Burma. I read and read. The past was beginning to claim me. Bill and Iris went elsewhere. Granny thought I needed a holiday, which I certainly did and I found my way to Blounts Hotel, Clifton Gardens, The Leas, Folkestone, as my letters to my parents, proclaimed. They were now in Rawalpindi, a town near what is now the capital of Pakistan, Islamabad.

"Folkestone, I have made up my mind, is a very nice place." It was a quiet interlude; tea with Burma friends, some of whom recalled embarrassing reminisces of my mother when young, "She needed a great deal of chaperoning", a recognisable comment, and coffee at the Leas Cliff Hall with a band to listen to and a visit to the super-cinema to see Fred Astaire and Ginger Rogers dance remarkably and sing *Isn't it a lovely day, Dancing Cheek to cheek, Top hat, White Tie and Tails*. Staying at Folkestone was to be refreshed unambitiously.

Refreshment comes in many sizes. From a Folkestone hotel to the Norfolk Broads. My housemaster and his assistant took Bill and me and some others in the house on a cruise designed to blow away any lingering sorrows. They were teachers who cared, and they wanted to refresh us. It certainly did that. Norfolk was at its coldest and the wind was fitful. But the Broads offer opportunities of harmless mishaps, of which there were plenty, and our boat was filled with more laughter than wind. On one occasion I found myself trapped in the lavatory which must be the smallest room yet devised; I was rescued and greeted with mock relief. It was an interlude made for convalescents.

Having lost most of a term, we returned to one of mammoth length. But we had recovered; most of the shadows had receded and the fells were shining. What was not so certain was the situation in the world. Reading the portents the government issued on the 4th of March a White Paper on rearmament; and three days later Germany reoccupied the Rhineland. It caused a sensation. The thirties are always a looking back. This was the moment when we could have stopped Hitler in his tracks. They were craven days. France, who we were to see as a country unable to locate its heart, took no decisive action. And Hitler, to the astonishment of his generals who said he was mad, walked in. The government appointed a Minister for the co-ordination of Defence, an ineffective figure.

Perhaps the study of Garibaldi took my eyes off the world, but more was to happen that we could not ignore. Abyssinia. The sanctions countries talked about were derisory and were abandoned. Italy rained gas and routed their enemy and on the 6th of May Mussolini announced the annexation of Ethiopia, as it was now called. He had gained his empire. Haile Selassie fled to Britain and took residence in Bath; where he maintained his dignity. I was to meet one of his sons at a Christian holiday camp. On the 4th of July he addressed the League of Nations in a speech which must have brought a sense of shame to many people. "I am here today to claim that justice which is due to my people. And the assistance promised to it eight months ago when fifty nations asserted that an aggression had been committed…God and history will remember your judgement."

And in another part of the world we saw the beginnings of a terrible shedding of blood. Spain, where in July the forces of General Franco started their operation against a government that was falling apart. At last the term ended. I had taken School Certificate and was reasonably satisfied and prepared for my next port of call. It was Aunt Hilda's turn to take care of us. They were down in Cornwall. But before I could travel there I had to become a soldier. The Officers Training Corps is one of the world's stranger armies. It is meant to provide a reserve of officers for a possible conflict, and maybe we were beginning to think along those lines. It offered some rudimentary discipline not available in the classroom or the playing field; and it offered to the officers, who were members of the teaching staff, a chance to augment their income. For some of us it was fun and a chance to command that might not otherwise come our way, creating in its path some petty tyrants; to others it was a crashing bore, to be endured. So it was off to Tidworth Park to a week of parades and polish and battles, those splendid engagements in which there is excitement without danger and camaraderie of a different kind from what we had known at school. And it was a week from our holidays.

That week passed, and lugging my kitbag, an awkward piece of luggage, I boarded the Atlantic Coast Express. After a smoky journey along a line that no longer exists I arrived at Padstow, ready to become part of another family – it was Aunt Hilda - and to enjoy what north Cornwall so supremely offers: waves that carry you excitedly to the shore and leave you breathless and longing for the next one. In the years ahead it was to be a special haven.

That summer our gaze was not entirely on the sea. In Berlin Hitler was presenting the Olympic Games, hoping to use them as a stage on which to show to the world the supremacy of the true Nordic race that is, Germany. They certainly showed the full panoply of the new Nazi Germany and gave the world startling glimpses of what was to come, but in one respect the script went disastrously wrong. An American negro, Jesse Owens, won both sprints and the long jump, in which he broke the world record. He left the other runners standing: the film of the 100 metres remains firmly in the mind. At the presentation of the medals Hitler turned firmly away, unable to look on a lower order; and he was further shamed when the German Women's relay team dropped the baton. I saw a woman distraught as only a German under Hitler's eye could be. I also saw grace. Jack Lovelock won the 1500 metres in a world record time of 3 minutes 47.8 seconds. His trainer said, "He was the fittest man I have ever seen" and probably the most graceful. Unable to shine on the games field I discovered that I could run and looking at this elegant runner I took another look at my stride.

Memory fades. I have since discovered much else about those Games. It seems that Britain and the USA almost pulled out because of the disgraceful treatment of the Jewish athletes by Germany, but the authorities got the blessing of Baron de Coubertin the founder of the Olympic movement by offering him a huge bribe. And there was a final irony. Jesse Owens, though loathed by Hitler, was received with acclaim by the German crowds, who could reasonably wonder how he was received in the society of his home country.

The Christmas term started as it always did, new boys arriving and older boys taking the next step up the ladder. Tanned faces and new expectations. But this term something happened which made everything else seem strangely secondary, and it was to impinge on the school in an unexpected way. It was the King. His coronation was fixed for the 12th of May 1937; but things were happening. In July the King and Mrs Simpson toured the Mediterranean together in the yacht Nahlin, and there were photographs. But the British press was asked to respect the King's privacy. For many months American newspapers 'of a certain type' mentioned the King and Mrs Simpson. Ten years before she had divorced from her first husband; in October she obtained a decree nisi against her second husband. In the middle of October the

Prime Minister drew the King's attention to the gossip and warned him. The King said he was prepared to abdicate.

The British press, with a self-control which must astonish us today, agreed not to publish anything on the matter, though the presses of other countries had no such inhibitions, and on 26th of October The New York Daily Mirror announced with banner headlines, 'King to marry Wally. Wedding next June.' The news broke in Britain in a most extraordinary way. On the 1st of December The Bishop of Bradford, perhaps appropriately named Dr Blunt, gave an address at his diocesan Conference in which he used the following words, "The benefit of the King's coronation depends, under God, upon two elements: first faith, prayer and self-discipline and the self-dedication of the King himself. We hope he is aware of his need. Some of us wish he gave more positive evidence of his awareness of the need of Divine guidance."

Having no knowledge of the crisis facing the King he was merely reminding him of his spiritual duties. But the effect of his swords was explosive. In the words of that master wordsmith Malcolm Muggeridge, "He was like an elderly visitor at a Swiss mountain resort, who, wandering amiably along in knickerbockers, carefully kicks a stone and releases an avalanche."

The British press thought this was a heavily coded message to say that the ban they had been obeying had now been rescinded and they came out. On the 2nd of December The Times reacted moderately "The Bishop and the King – a pointed address." On the 3rd the floodgates opened. I remember going past my housemaster's study and seeing on a chair the blazing headlines, The Daily Mail, "The King wants to marry

Mrs Simpson. The Cabinet says No." The Daily Express had headings over seven columns.

What was going to happen? It affected Sedbergh in a way that took us by surprise. The Bishop of Bradford arrived to take a confirmation service at the school chapel. On leaving the chapel building he was amazed and alarmed to find himself face to face with the world's press. Poor innocent man. Inaccurately but understandably I wrote, "This evening was the annual Confirmation Service by the Bishop of Bradford, who gave his usual fine address. You perhaps have heard that he has startled everyone by attacking the King furiously for his proposed marriage."

What was to happen now? Breathless days followed. Earlier the King had suggested a way out: a morganatic marriage. This is a marriage in which the wife does not take her husband's rank, and their children, though legitimate, are without right to the dignity of their father and their claims on his estate are limited to his personal property. The Cabinet said No, and on the 4th of December told the House, "There is no such thing as a morganatic marriage known to our law", though it is in France.

On the 8th Mrs Simpson said she was willing to part from the King. What did we think? Prince Charming had his followers, the man who cared for the unemployed. His tour of the Welsh mining valley and his plea, "something ought to be done to find these people employment" had touched us and made us want to like him; and the Archbishop of Canterbury, Dr Cosmo Gordon Lang, who had declared his opposition to the King, was booed in public. Churchill was strongly for the King;

but most did not like the taste of it; and the commonwealth countries were firmly against. At school we took sides, perplexed.

On the 5th December the King told Baldwin that he was going to abdicate. On the 10th Baldwin addressed the House. As a Prime Minister his grip was loosening, but this was a masterly performance and he went through the stages of this sad business, using his words with a precision that was received with acclaim. That evening the King made his farewell speech from Fort Beldevere. "You must believe me when I tell you that I have found it impossible to carry the heavy burden and responsibility and to discharge my duties as King as I would wish to do without the help and support of the woman I love."

On the 11th the Abdication Bill received the Royal Assent. The Evening News commented, "All those brilliant hopes are brought to nothing." We have had many years to judge those words.

The year was not without its compensations. India enjoyed "a political repose such as the country had not known since the Great War" and awaited great constitutional changes.

And Penguin Books were born. They were launched uncertainly; the book trade doubted if books at this price, sixpence, were possible. But Woolworths came to the rescue with a big order and they were in business. Andre Maurois's *Ariel*, Hemmingway's *Farewell to Arms*, EM Forster's *A passage to India*, which stood for all that my mother was against. Edmund Blunden's *Undertones* of *war*, a poet's graceful tribute to horror. And then the Pelicans, where you could afford to learn. Shaw *The intelligent woman's guide to socialism"*, Leonard Woolley's *Digging up the past*, James Jean's *The mysterious universe*, and Freud's *Psychopathology of everyday life*, which for young learners was an entrance to a world that intrigued and excited. And with the words came a design so perfect that today reissued they make us marvel at their brilliant simplicity and they adorn T Shirts.

These books arrived at the moment when I was ready, ready to explore what men who could turn their thoughts into great words were writing, at a price that I could afford. I read and I learnt and I felt enlarged, and while the hills still beckoned they were having to compete with the study. I was drawn to the countryside: Adrian Bell's haunting Suffolk trilogy and AG Street's farming saga *The endless furrow*; the reality of simple things, men striving with the land. One that I remember particularly was a glimpse into a startling future in Olaf Stapledon's *Last and first men*.

And to bring an understanding of what was happening there were the Penguin Specials, books rushed out to reflect present discontents and controversies. There was no shortage of thought about what was going on; which was quite a lot. There were many more problems than answers. There was an increasing awareness that the world was going astray.

1937

"The pleasures of that gorgeous holiday still lingers" I wrote to my parents in Rawalpindi. It was a good start to the year, a trip to the Swiss Alps at Leukerbad where in the company of other schoolboys I attempted to ski and was further surprised by joy, a spiritual awakening by an ice rink. Granny, who was rapidly assuming the status of a patron saint, had financed the holiday, the fortnight costing just over thirteen pounds. A cousin came with me. He did not share the joy and was to go spectacularly off the rails. What makes us the people we are?

I was now old enough to attune myself to the world and a Europe that was becoming less and less certain of the direction it was going; and the politicians lost no time in agonising.

On the 19th of January Eden made a statement on the international situation. He said that non-intervention in Spain was justified. It was the civil war, a fearful confrontation between a left wing government and a coalition of generals under Franco and the Catholic Church. The conflict had torn people's hearts apart. Young men queued up to go there and if necessary die to help destroy the forces of evil, that is, Franco's armies. Occasionally the motives were less worthy. In the Second World War one of my sergeants told me that he had gone to that other war because he could not stand the boredom of his former life, which was as a member of a greyhound racing betting syndicate. In the bigger war he proved to be an unwilling soldier, persuading himself into collapse when the going got too tough. But the huge majority echoed the outburst of idealism that injected into bland years something worth fighting for. On the 26th of April German planes, flexing their muscles for a greater contest, destroyed Guernica, a devastation that epitomised total war and which Picasso transformed into a masterpiece. The Penguin Special *Searchlight on Spain* outlined the bitter issues. Couldn't we do something? No, said Mr Eden. He may have been right, but for many it was the hallmark of those years. We were not lions led by donkeys, as the Germans described us in the First World War, but idealists led by men in grey suits.

Attlee attacked these men bitterly, accusing them of bowing to every whim of the dictators; but his party was in turmoil with a left wing 'implacably' opposed to rearmament. For the young it was perplexing.

At Sedbergh we had a sixth form lecture every Friday evening with a speaker from the world outside. One was a tub-thumper and we treated him roughly, so roughly that the headmaster wrote the speaker an apology and delivered to us a fierce rebuke for our ill manners. We had views and we were unwilling to hide them. The Spanish Civil War had lit a flame.

But we had a King to crown, Albert Frederick Arthur George, on the date originally fixed for Edward, the 12th of May. On the 11th of May the King replied to a loyal address, "For my part I shall do my utmost to carry on my father's work for the welfare of our great Empire." We were allowed four days off from school, and coming so soon after the beginning of the term it was a splendid extra. And my mother was home with Robert. Her choice of a new home was unusual. In India she had met a Miss Fevez, who said that she was going to open a guest house near Guildford and perhaps we might like to patronise it. So we did. It was not a success. It was on the main road, had cramped accommodation and it showed us the wisdom of the saying that you should not do business with friends. But it did us for a bit; our life was a succession of bits.

We all went to Granny's flat and awaited the great day. We had seats on a balcony on the top floor of the John Lewis building in Oxford Street that was destroyed in the War. To get to our seats we had to climb from one balcony to another, which was unnerving.

Shortly after 10 am the royal procession left Buckingham Palace, the Mall, Trafalgar and Whitehall. "Sirs", said the Primate, "I here present unto you King George, your undoubted king." At 2.40 pm the King and Queen appeared at the door of Westminster Abbey annexe and then the Embankment, Northumberland Avenue, Trafalgar Square, Cockspur Street, Pall Mall, Piccadilly Circus, Regent Street, Oxford Street, Marble Arch, Hyde Park Corner, Constitution Hill. From our lofty station our view was limited to the tops of carriages and the heads of the marching men, but it was a noble sight, particularly the serried ranks of the Empire, men of every hue and many races and reflecting so much of my family's service. Bill was not with us. He was with a squad of senior cadets from Sedbergh lining the road by the Victoria Memorial. Many helped to make that day go well. The new King spoke that evening to the nation, "If in the coming years I can show you my gratitude in service to you, that is the way above all I should choose." Facing a position that he neither expected nor was equipped for, and scarcely able to get his words out, he attracted both our loyalty and our sympathy. We hoped that he would succeed. And we were pleased with our new Queen. We made our way back to Granny's flat, weary but happy to be together, the day's rejoicings for the time being pushing to the side growing uncertainties. And I took the train back to the north.

Mr Baldwin retired on the 28th of May and on the following day received the Garter. We felt he had done us well. We had to wait until we could pass judgement on his successor, Mr Neville Chamberlain.

And then the holidays. Family holidays are milestones to maturity. The family photograph albums show us gathered by beaches and we try to remember where it was and how old we all were and what sort of time we had. There is laughter and sometimes the tears that nostalgia can bring. 1937 was important for us. It was the first seaside holiday we had unencumbered by cousins; it was just us and we had time to make up. And it was Cornwall. We had taken a bungalow for six weeks at St Agnes and to that we aimed our motor car. Getting there was a day's journey.

There were of course no motorways and dual carriageways barely existed. There were just bits. In 1934 the North Circular, the Colchester by-pass and the Dorking by-pass had been completed and in 1935 George V opened the Great West Road, and in 1937 there were just 27.5 miles of dual carriageway. It was an extended game of patience and you were doing well if could average over 35 miles an hour. Cars were unheated and overheated. The luggage was tied on to a rack at the back of the car, and most cars had running boards, which as far as I can see, served no useful purpose. Changing to a lower gear was not entirely straightforward; it entailed double de-clutching.

So we set off very early on the 29th of July leaving suburban Surrey well before dawn. My mother did almost all the driving; my father, when he was around, directed the car rather absent-mindedly and there were sometimes scenes. Our first target was the A303, the spine of our journey. The Hog's Back, Farnham, Basingstoke, then eschewing the A30, Andover, Stonehenge, peering at the great pile at dawn, Salisbury Plain, where the army had shredded the country, the map reader's desert. And then we stopped the car and got out our wireless set to listen to a great sporting occasion. Sydney Wooderson, our outstanding middle distance runner was attempting the world record for the mile at Motspur Park. It came through loud and clear on our rather cumbersome portable. And he did it: 4 minutes 6.4 seconds, beating the existing record holder the American Cunningham by 0.2 seconds. We rejoiced, put away the wireless set and continued our journey in good spirits, joining the A30 and on to Honiton notorious for its bottleneck (I remember reading a comic piece in Punch, 'See Honiton and die'), Exeter, skirting Dartmoor where the hound roved, Launceston, Bodmin Moor and off the A30 south of Newquay, St Agnes. We had arrived. Tired, hot, hungry and not in the best of temper. But we were there. All together. There was no one else. We could get to know each other.

Which we did. Today the world's surfers come to these beaches and stand bronzed on their long tapered boards and standing roar to the shore, turning to where the waves will carry them best. Then no one stood on anything. Families took their pieces of wood and lying on them coasted excitedly to the shore, shouting with glee when they caught the wave right and when they just sank tried again. No one had wet suits; we just went on until we were too cold to continue. And then it was time to have a picnic and as the day drew to its close prepare a meal and talk or just sit and wish it could always be like this. Dad would not be with us for another year, but it was a splendid dress rehearsal.

And what tunes were going through our heads and echoing from our wireless set? *The love bug will bite you if you don't look out, They can't take that away from me, Shall we dance? There's a small hotel, It looks like rain in cherry blossom lane.* Gracie Fields was at the height of her powers, her virtuoso shrieks and her genius for capturing her audiences moved and amused us; the mill girl from Oldham sharing her joys and sorrows with us. And the crooners purred, gentle words softly spoken and taking us far away. Love was the order of the day.

But the show must go on. There was a significant parting of the ranks. A family, never easy to identify as a unit, was splitting up. Bill had left Sedbergh and was going to Sandhurst to prepare himself for a career in the Indian Army. He did not choose it; his parents did. He proved an excellent soldier serving in Burma with distinction and being wounded twice and twice mentioned in despatches. But it was a directed life, a return to the east that he had not chosen. With Iris also being directed – or misdirected – options were not becoming easy.

The world outside was moving uneasily. On the 5th of November the text of an Air Raid Precautions Bill was issued outlining in detail what to do in case of an emergency that we were beginning to think might happen. And at the War Ministry was Hore Belisha. Having launched a high profile assault on road casualties, with some effect, he was now turning his considerable energy to the Army. He was an authentic new broom, seeking to raise the standard of officers, which included cutting out dead wood, and to improve administration. One report described its effects as follows. "The general effect of the minister's activities was to revive the enthusiasm of the junior officers and to effect a change in the spirit of the Army administration comparable in the opinion of many to that wrought by Haldane in 1906."

The senior officers were not all so enthusiastic. The interface between a flamboyant Jew and army generals was not an easy one. One general, who distinguished himself in the war, said, "Most of the top soldiers in the War Office were afraid of him." But things were happening. Faint ripples reached the Sedbergh School Officers Training Corps when nearer the conflict the Bren Gun arrived and we gazed at this remarkable weapon, the best the infantry ever had, and we said a tearless

The Road From Mandalay

goodbye to the Lewis Gun, a weapon known for the frequency with which it stopped. We were struggling from one war to the next...

Germany was finding many ways to flex its muscles. Its command of Grand Prix racing was now complete and on the 2nd of October at the International Grand Prix at Donnington, German cars, Mercedes and Auto Union, took the first five places. They were in fact the only ones to complete the course. This was raw power and we had to reckon with the same names on every podium: Carraciola, Von Brauschitch, Rosemeyer. It appeared that not even Nuvolari could keep them in check. But England now had an unexpected foothold in this world of speed. The Germans had seen a winner in a young man called Richard Seaman and he joined the Mercedes team. He was to meet his end on the track, crashing when leading in the Belgian Grand Prix, but for a time his skill delighted us.

And we could continue to break records. Malcolm Campbell was still at it. He turned his attention to the water and on Lake Maggiore broke the world record with a speed of 126.325 mph, capping it shortly afterwards with 129.50 mph. He was incorrigible. We admired these from afar, but there were excitements nearer home. There was Brooklands, that saucer of rather bumpy concrete where cars of all sizes strove for mastery and where I went if I could, because Weybridge was not too far away and there were special deals with the Southern Railway. It was a world of fast rich young men: Earl Howe, Sir Henry Birkin, the Hon Brian Lewis, the Siamese prince B.Bira, Whitney Straight and others who got there just by their skill: Raymond Mays, Pat Fairfield, Freddie Dixon and the jockey George Duller. And most remarkable, the beautiful Mrs Kay Petre who handled the massive Railton Special.

There were handicaps; the smallest, a very hotted up Austin Seven could compete against the ERA's which were Britain's best and the massive machines that John Cobb brought into the field, roaring round and round. The shattering noise and the pungent smell of racing fuel and the air of excitement remains with me still.

Meanwhile our caravan moved on. Our stay with Miss Fevez had taken from my mother the chores of housework but it had also taken from us a real family home, and anyway it was an expensive way of doing things. Where next? We asked no questions but awaited results. And the next result was rather good, a house in the north west corner of Guildford, Pit Farm Cottage. It was agreeably *haut bourgeois* with a tennis club just down the road and a golf course not too far away at Merrow. And it was a comfortable house. It was 1930s ease, a hoping that it would continue like this, but wondering if it would. My mother moved there in the summer and we joined her for the Christmas holidays.

But my own studies had taken a dramatic turn. I had reached the classical sixth, but it was quite clear that I was not a classic; my Latin stumbled and my Greek barely moved. The extent of my ignorance was fully revealed when I went that summer to Bradfield College to see in a unique setting the Greek play they put on each year. It was Oedipus Tyrannus. It was beautifully done, but following what they were saying was a pretence and I knew that I had reached my frontier. I was presented with what was a remarkable scenario. They said, "We hope to turn you into a historian. Take some books home, read as much as you can, and at the beginning of next term we will test you to see if you are a historian. If you are you will sit for a history scholarship for Oxford next November." It was by any reckoning a tall order.

Seldom can the sixteenth and seventeenth centuries have been so roughly handled. I force-fed myself with the work of a generation of scholars, Trevelyan staying most clearly in my mind. How could I distinguish the commanding personalities of those years from the people that they governed? Why did one thing lead to another and not to something else? Why did peace-loving Englishmen start killing each other in 1642? And through it all, through Henry, Mary, Elizabeth, Cromwell, the stern hand of religion. And was Cromwell a saint or a monster? What did the people of England think amidst this buffeting of their faith? Many years went by in four weeks. The present mattered less than the past. My main respite, from my studies, after the interlude that was Christmas, was going out with the West Surrey and Horsell beagles, running through damp undergrowth and across muddy fields to a bloody conclusion, finding the cold air a wonderful antidote to midnight oil.

So the year ended with expectations; for me a new land of books and for the world uncertainty not yet turning to crisis. And a rite of passage. On the 5th of December I was confirmed by the Bishop of Borneo, an unexpected echo of the East. He was standing in for the Bishop of Bradford, the man who had stumbled unknowingly on the truth about Edward VIII. I stumbled too to reach my place in the service as I had sprained my leg badly on the rugger field. Flesh and spirit met, which is a fair description of the public school.

1938

My labours succeeded. I was asked to write and hurriedly I did so, wondering whether it would all make sense. It did. They said that I seemed to be a historian, and I hoped they were right. So I made my way to a rather elite collection of students. They called themselves Clio, after the muse of history, and they met not in a form room but in the school library. Surrounded by books in a place apart we thought quite a lot of ourselves; but we thought a good deal more of our teacher. Mr Sumner might not have passed his teacher training; there was never a class plan and his lessons had no recognisable shape. But he gave them a shape of his own. He sat on the edge of the table round which we sat and turning over the pages of a book he talked. His words took us through the years wisely and colourfully. We could nod and we could laugh. We found that it was good to work.

And it was necessary. I was to take a history scholarship to Oxford in November. The target was the Hastings Scholarship to The Queen's College. In the 18th century Lady Elizabeth Hastings had founded a scholarship which had funds at its disposal that few foundations can have matched. And it was confined to a small number of schools in the north. The desire to nurture learning in the north that had founded and revived Sedbergh now offered a chance to reach the university. It was my best hope. There was work to do.

But you do not only go to Sedbergh for learning (though with WH Fowler once on the staff learning was certainly there). You go for the hills. As the climax of the school song so brashly declares, "It is Cautley, Calf and Winder that make the Sedbergh man". And there is one trial of strength that the hills offer that is unique to the school. It is the

Wilson Run. This was started in 1881 as the Ten Mile but gained its present name in 1913 from a member of the staff, one of those legendary figures who give their life to one institution. The first mile is along a track and the last two miles along a road, but in between across the side of a fell are fiercesome challenges: plunging heather, relentless gradients, running streams and one place where you have to scramble. There is no race like it, and from time to time national newspapers declare that it is a cruel and excessive test for boys.

We never considered the cruelty but were well aware of the test. It certainly created huge interest in Sedbergh and the neighbouring areas. Locals opened books, though I never saw the odds nor did I know from where they got their information. A classics master composed rhymes based on Latin verse metres describing those favoured. My own name finished a hexameter as Rhodio Jam Jam. They said I had a chance.

The race took place in March. During training there had been an unusually dry spell but rain started five days before the race and on the day of the race there was a squally wind and thick mist which blew in our face in the last part of the course. The course itself was very heavy. In other words the conditions were bad, adding to the challenge of the rough country over which we had to run. The race proved remarkable. Stuart Alexander, who was to die at El Alamein, was the favourite. (Eleven winners died in the two great conflicts.) He was a friend with whom Bill spent many of his holidays. He had won in the previous year and was in good form. He set a cracking pace, so cracking that many who tried to follow shot their bolts fairly soon. I wondered why I seemed to be so far behind. If I was fancied, why wasn't I doing better? I had been overrated. It was a struggle. Some were clearly dropping

Richard Rhodes James

back, having misjudged the fierce pace, but there must be many still ahead. I had no idea where I stood. Plod on. Meanwhile strange things were happening at the front. Whitfield was running second and hoped he could force Alexander to too fast a pace. He did not seem to be succeeding but then suddenly just less than half a mile from the finish Alexander broke into a walk; he was done. Whitfield went on to win by almost three minutes from Alexander who was still almost a minute ahead of the next man - which was me. I had long given up trying to guess where I was in the race and was agreeably surprised to hear that I had come third. To come round that final corner and be acclaimed by the crowds was a welcome boost to one who was still trying to find himself. And at the special concert that always took place that same evening the runners mounted the stage in their finishing order. That was the importance we attached to this unusual trial of strength, Sedbergh is certainly a different place.

It was good that my mother was there, with Robert aged almost five, who trailed around and tried to be part of the picture. She came up from time to time, heroic drives up the A1 grandiloquently billed as the Great North Road, and then across England by a road which shows a beautiful land but takes some time to do so: Otley, Ilkley, Settle, Skipton, Kirby Lonsdale. On one occasion her car came to a grinding halt en route. I believe it was the little matter of oil. She called into a garage and pleaded helpless in her special way. It was big ends, and a major job was required. The man worked through the night and the car was ready the following morning. I got the impression in those days that because work was not easy to find that work when found should be properly executed. This was especially true of the north. And one can compare rather ponderously the attitudes of today's workers. But those were desperate days.

While I was struggling through rough places things were happening in a rather wider world that started the shock waves rippling. Week by week uncertainty crept on us until by the end of the year hope had almost ebbed away. The first shock was in March when on the 13th Hitler invaded Austria, the Anschluss. Germany had devoured Austria. The sight of cheering crowds and the dark tales of what Hitler had done to the chancellor Dolfuss, and the news that terrible things were now being done to Austrian Jews; this was crisis on a new plain. It is difficult at this distance to recollect what was the measure of our concern. Certainly our minds were beginning to concentrate and writers were telling us, what should now be evident to all, that disaster loomed. In Clio we had to lift our minds from the past and see what the present held. Penguin Specials poured out their messages. *Blackmail or war, Europe and the Czechs, Mussolini's Roman Empire, Germany puts the clock back, The Jewish problem, What Hitler wants.* And a rather limp sentence in the National Register, "The League played only a minor part." What must surely have disturbed us was the resignation of Eden, the Foreign Secretary in February. He was at loggerheads with Chamberlain, particularly over Italy and Spain. Where were we being led?

Fortunately, the world was not all politics. On the 2nd of April Oxford won the Boat Race a result that gave fresh impetus to a contest that was threatening to lose its interest. And in May we were moving again. I was sorry to leave Pitfarm Cottage, a place of comfort and endeavour. Was the rental period up, or was it too expensive? As usual we asked no questions and looked forward to the next stop, ready to adjust the address we put on our letters home from school. It proved a short move to a house in Wonersh, a village a few miles south of Guildford, a place of no distinction but reasonable comfort. And Dad was coming home. So when the summer term ended and as the family foregathered the holidays took on a new dimension.

We got into our car and set off for that long drive to Cornwall, more squashed than before. No seatbelts but a close cramming. Robert was sick at about Stonehenge, but otherwise all was well, and we were complete. I wonder if we thought that this might be the last holiday gathering for some time. Perhaps it was best not to look too far ahead. So we swam and lazed and ate easily prepared meals and did not listen to the wireless much except perhaps to hear the tunes that the world was singing. It was good that it was still a singing world, much aided by Bing Crosby. *I've got a pocketful of dreams, You must have been a beautiful baby, Two sleepy people and too much in love to say goodnight, The Lambeth Walk* and that special piece of writing *Those foolish things.*

What was Dad thinking? We never really plumbed that gentle mind but listened to his quiet encouragements and pulled his leg good-humouredly about his passion for healthy food. Those weeks were important ones.

It was good that the Australians were in England. There were the usual massive scores. In the First Test England scored 658 for 8 and both Australian inningses were over 400 runs. In the second both sides had inningses of over 400. Both were drawn. There was no play in the Third Test, which perhaps not unsurprisingly was at Old Trafford. Australia won the Fourth Test with a century from Bradman and some powerful bowling from O'Reilly.

And so we came to the Oval and once again Dad joined me, and together we watched. It was by any standards an extraordinary match. England batted first and made 903 for 7 wickets. In an innings lasting 13 hours 20 minutes Hutton aged 22 scored 364; there were centuries from Leyland and Hardstaff. Fleetwood Smith had the remarkable figures of one wicket for 298 runs. Australia was a bit of a disaster. Bradman and Fingleton were injured and could not bat, and Australia was bowled out for 201 and 123, defeated by an innings and 579 runs, a figure that will surely never be surpassed. To have seen this with my father made it a kind of bonus. And for a Sussex fan it was good to see that they drew with the Australians and their first innings total of 453 was the highest of the match.

In another field of sporting endeavour on the 24th of August Sydney Wooderson broke the world half mile record with a time of 1 minute 49.2 seconds. And on the land we were getting ever faster. Campbell had at last to put Bluebird to rest and two others took up the challenge and moved to Bonneville Flats, Utah: John Cobb and George Eyston, both devoting their lives to breaking records. George Eyston's Thunderbird was a particularly monstrous vehicle with eight wheels and 6000 horse power. They chased each other, I think most of us backing the rather less monstrous vehicle of John Cobb. On September the 16th Eyston hit 357.5 mph and they packed up for the season.

And so while Rome burned….

And it was beginning to. One thing was leading frighteningly to another. Hitler's claim that he had no more territorial ambitions already looked absurd. First it was Austria, now it was Czechoslovakia. The Germans in the Sudetenland area of Czechoslovakia were crying for help; they said they were being shamefully treated. Their complaints were discernible; their cries, becoming increasingly loud, held a fearful menace. Hitler the bully was going to act. It was the time for panic stations.

On the 3rd of August our envoy Runciman flew to Prague to talk. Sir John Simon made a speech in which he said that Britain stood by Czechoslovakia, and on the 30th the Czech government was urged to make further concessions. The journeys started. On the 15th of September Chamberlain, Sir Horace Wilson, and Mr Strang flew to Berchtesgaden, Hitler's mountain lair. There was a volte-face on Czechoslovakia; territory was to be conceded. We heard this and wondered. On the 22nd Chamberlain flew to Godesberg, and on the 28th he addressed the House; they must accept the principle of self-determination. Now we can see the slippery slide to surrender. Then we were desperate to do anything to avert war. But war seemed very near. On the 17th Chamberlain wired to Hitler, "In view of increasingly critical situation, I propose to come over at once to see you with a view to finding a peaceful solution. I propose to come by air and am ready to start tomorrow". On the 27th the fleet was mobilised and all RAF recalled from leave. The London City Council formed a plan to evacuate 500,000. Trenches were dug in Hyde Park and ARP shelters hurriedly prepared. My mother considered moving north, perhaps to Sedbergh. It was good to be in a safe school.

Drama was in ample supply. On the 28th Chamberlain interrupted a speech he was making in the Commons to say that Hitler had accepted one more talk. There was wild enthusiasm and a throwing of papers. Anything but war; a feeling that Hitler must have relished. There was such a holding of breath that the air must have been rather empty. And then his return on the 30th. Getting out of the aircraft at Heston, waving the piece of paper and proclaiming "Peace with honour". Munich. The honour was not easy to locate; we had left Czechoslovakia to its fate. Duff Cooper resigned from the government; Attlee said that they had witnessed a victory not for reason and humanity but for brutal force. Churchill raged. Someone cruelly remarked that Chamberlain was the first man to crawl at 230 miles an hour

I can recollect only a feeling of enormous relief. The Sunday Pictorial mirrored this feeling in its leader. "Let us praise ourselves, the people of Britain. For the last few weeks we have walked into the valley of the shadow. And we have been unafraid. We have looked squarely in the face of evil. And we have seen it recede." This was stretching it a bit. We were scared stiff. But we were not at war. Bombers were not about to appear. Gas masks – 35 million were said to be in store – were not now needed. The trenches we had dug could remain unoccupied. And my mother would not have to go north.

She was in fact in London. There had been another move and our new address was 229A Earls Court Road, the road that had welcomed us from the east in 1927. It was a commodious flat – or I think you would call it a maisonette - over Buckle and Cross the grocers. My only recollection is that it contained the coldest bedroom I have ever slept in. From there my mother could view the political scene with less immediate trepidation while realising that the stakes had risen considerably. Munich gave us a breathing space, but breathing spaces are temporary affairs. The future would have to be reconsidered.

Meanwhile I had other things on my mind. What was going on did not provide the ideal conditions in which to prepare to persuade Oxford University that I was just the material that they were looking for. To hedge my bets I also applied to Magdalen College, but they were awkward about my lack of a birth certificate seeming to doubt my existence. Their entry exam was in January, and Queen's in November, so I could let that rest and hope either that I would succeed at Queen's or that Magdalen would change their mind and see that I was.

I travelled to Oxford and for a few days wrote furiously. The past seem to be manageable, but three hours on 'Indifference' extended my word-spinning to its limit; my neighbour seemed to have a good deal more to say. And with a curious snobbery I observed a neighbour whose jacket pocket sprouted fountain pens. At the interview I said little. The almost pathological shyness, which afflicted my growing years, stemmed my tongue, but I was to learn that academia judges you by what you know. My mother had come up to see me, and I was moved by her care. We took a meal together and then she returned to Earls Court Road and me to Sedbergh. And waited.

There was good news. An Old Sedbergian at Queen's very kindly sent me a telegram; I had been awarded a Hastings Scholarship. Lady Elizabeth had been very generous. Eight scholarships had been awarded: three in classics, three in mathematics and two in history. The other historian was the boy who did not seem to be able to stop writing. I was told that my essay was my least successful effort, which I had anticipated and that my Latin and Greek gave me an advantage over those who had not really studied these languages. Oxford still believed in a classical spine.

What followed showed me that although my own family was an imperfect community I should not feel too sorry for myself. On the 20th of November I wrote, "I seem to have been writing letters continually for the last three days. I have had eight telegrams, four from Oxford and one from the grannies, the Mashiters and the Turbetts, and six letters, from Aunt M (+2/6), Aunt Evelyn, Sheelagh Turbett, yourself and of all people, Mr Inglis! I have already used up one packet of envelopes and I have one more letter to write. It is all very exciting and great fun."

It was indeed. So the year ended for me in deep satisfaction. For the world it ended in a deep uneasiness about the future.

1939

What a year. I had qualified for university and could have left school. It was decreed that I should stay. The Queen's College had rewarded my promise but that was a flimsy structure which must be built on. So I had the luxury of being a scholar without portfolio, studying without compulsion and reading what delighted me; it was a kind of dream scenario. And from that mountain fastness I was able at my leisure to see a world plunging into darkness and a family that was reaching crisis point.

Munich had given to every day a wake-up call. War had been avoided but not finally dispersed and it must be prepared for. Preparations came without delay. In January they came in a flood. 16th: Orders for material for making 400,000 shelters. 23rd: Campaign for volunteers for National Service. 24th: Albert Hall rally. 26th: ARP circular to intensify training. In February, on the 8th lists prepared of households eligible to receive free steel shelters. 13th: the government contemplated the erection at an early date of 50 holiday camps each capable of accommodating 350. On the 15th increased borrowing powers for defence expenditure.

While this was happening my mother was making the biggest decision of her life. She saw that war was imminent and that if it came she and her husband would be separated for an indefinite period. She wanted to join him, but whom should she take with her? The reader is invited to consider what he or she would do. A son was due for the university, and he would stay; another was in the army. That was fine; but what about a daughter of 16 and a son of 6?

The decision my mother took I have long pondered over. She took Iris, 16, and left behind Robert 6. Iris she had already misdirected and deprived of a university education, for reasons that are not entirely clear, but I presume it was her view of women's education in general. Iris was to go out to India and find a husband; there was no shortage of males. Iris, who bore the wounds of misdirection, has written, "My mother was planning my trousseau from the moment we stepped onto the *Strathnaver.*" This is to telescope the years, but the intention was clear. There must be a wait, but at the end of the wait there would be a husband.

Robert was a different case. Why was he left behind? I have thought that it might have been the memory of Monty and the fear of another tragedy, and the usual unwillingness of the British to submit their children to education in India; in other words the reasons we were all brought back to England. But during a war… The decision was made quickly; so quickly that there was some doubt as to whether my mother had paid the rent for 229A Earls Court Road. She would leave in March. And she would take out a cousin who was slightly older.

This cousin would find a husband; but for her there were to be no happy endings. With the cousin she took two dalmatians. Her energy was always looking for new outlets, and dogs filled the few gaps in her inactivity. Over the years in India she bred and showed her dogs with some success adding bull terriers to her pack.

I made my farewells in circumstances that I could not have foretold. During the Easter term my insides had been causing continuous problems and the school doctor thought that it might be the appendix. So he took action, of an unusual kind. He put me on a train to Nelson, a Lancashire town at the quality end of the cotton industry and told me to report to the Reedyford Memorial Hospital. There I would be examined by a doctor and if the conditions demanded it they would take out my appendix. They examined me. I received an amusing letter from my friends at school, "Did you pass the exam, or were you ploughed?" anatomically a little distasteful, but a good laugh. I was ploughed. The doctor looked ancient and it was said to be his last operation. His handiwork, it seems to me, could have been a little neater, and I don't think he found anything troublesome, but it was done. I relaxed and listened to the great radio comedy ITMA, "*It's that man again*", with Tommy Handley; he was convulsing England. It had me, as they say, in stitches, holding both my sides.

My mother came to see me; she said she had had to change five times and there, to the best of my recollection, we said goodbye. This time there was no anguish, no regrets, no feeling that things should have been otherwise, no feeling sorry for myself. I was now an independent unit and could operate as I thought fit. The war, if it came, would pose problems, but we would see. There was Robert of course. And that was that. It was not clear when we would meet again.

So, after a few days in bed in Nelson, being outrageously spoilt by the surgeon's wife with games of backgammon fuelled by lavish helpings of pâté du foie gras, whose care suggested that they had no children of their own, I returned to Sedbergh. I could not run in the Ten Mile, but I was not unduly disappointed. I was aware of other runners who had shown during training that they were rather faster than me, and I preferred to remain in the record books as the boy who finished third.

So I could read and I could watch; watch the gathering clouds and wonder with increasing uneasiness where it would all end. On the 26th of March the government decided to introduce a bill to call up all men between 20 and 21 for three month's training and then serve for 3½ years in TA or special reserve. On May the first the Military Training Bill. 300,000 to be registered in the first year, of which 200,000 would be called up, 'militiamen'. All would receive a shilling a day for six months training.

I wonder if in these uncertain times anyone focussed on the government's White Paper on Palestine published on the 17th of June. The objective was the setting up within ten years of an independent state. Arabs and Jews were to share in the government; the Jewish population should not be allowed to exceed one third of the total. There are few limits on the things that a war can change.

For me there was a bad start. On April the first Cambridge won the Boat Race by four lengths and normal service was resumed. But there were more serious matters afoot. On March the fourth Sir Kingsley Wood, the Air Minister who looked more like a bank manager, told us

The Road From Mandalay

how many aircraft we had: 1750 and by the end of the financial year there would be 2370, and the RAF strength 100,000. Barrage balloons were being actively organised. And on the 15th of March Germany marched into Czechoslovakia. Everything fell apart. Munich was exposed for what it was: a fool's charter. One comment makes one wonder how many fools there were around. "To the government this new act of aggression, so completely at variance with their predictions, was disconcerting in the extreme." But there was some sanity. "To the opposition this latest stroke of Herr Hitler caused little surprise. They saw it as only the natural consequence of the Munich settlement." Bar miracles, which Hitler would be unlikely to be a party to, it must be war. But the hesitation continued. On the 25th of April the Labour party reaffirmed its opposition to conscription, but two days later the government's decision to introduce conscription was approved. Public opinion was now forcing the government to hasten the pace. The British Ambassador to Germany was recalled. And, in a development at which we can now agonise consultations with Russia opened.

On the 31st of April Chamberlain said that in the event of action threatening Polish independence the government would be bound to lend all support to the Polish government. I believe that Hitler was surprised that we kept our promise, but in view of the kind of politicians he had to deal with this was perhaps understandable. It was a time when we were trying to locate the steel inside the distinctly velvet glove.

The year unwound remorselessly. On the 7th of April Italy had invaded Albania and occupied Tirana. I found it hard to equate these jackals with the easy-going braggarts of Bordighera. But Mussolini could not be gainsaid. Chamberlain said that in the event of threats to the independence of Greece or Rumania the government would lend all support. Our promises were expanding.

There was a pause when the newspapers turned our attention from the world to a major tragedy at home. On the first of June at 1.40 am the submarine Thetis left the yard of Cammell Laird for acceptance trials. It submerged in Liverpool Bay and was reported overdue. A marker buoy which the submarine had released was sighted at 9.20 am. At 7.54 am on the 2nd the submarine was located 130 feet below the surface. It moved until the stern was 18 feet out of the water and there it was for all to see. Four men escaped by the Davis escape apparatus and were picked up. Every possible apparatus for salvage was deployed, but it proved impossible to lift the boat and 103 men perished. The tragedy was caused by the flooding of a forward compartment when they thought that a torpedo tube had been left open. For a time it held us appalled.

The term ended and I left Sedbergh and its hills and the struggle to overcome books and mountainside with thanks that I had had a base on which to build a life, an anchor when much seemed to be shifting. It had been good to be there. And this certainty was now facing a new challenge. Previous separations had been finite; the possibility of war changed all that. Technically I was now independent, but in the days ahead there might be few independent people. We might be on His Majesty's service. There was a plan for some in the boarding house to take a boat on the Norfolk Broads, but the uncertainties of the times forced us to cancel this. And we waited to see what would happen.

Where was I to live? It was with Aunt Hilda again, who was my anchor; I was now the only adult member of the family in England.

The Road From Mandalay

This family provided me with great kindness and with a home until such time as the Army caught up with me; I did not volunteer but hoped that I would be allowed time to take a degree.

And we waited to see what would happen. It was quite a lot. On the 9th of August the King inspected whole of the reserve fleet in Weymouth Bay. A complete Black Out was carried out over nearly half the country and bombing raids were staged over the eastern counties to test defences. "Highly encouraging" was the report. I wonder; anything less would have done little good to morale.

International crises did not deter those trying to go faster than anyone else. These were achievements that provided a refreshing antidote to the fumbling failures of our statesmen. On the 23rd of August John Cobb achieved 368.85 mph. But in the air German now won the crown with 469.11 mph in a fighter aircraft, an event which must have given much unease to those who were preparing our own air defences.

Also on the 23rd came perhaps the most shattering blow of all. Russia and Germany signed a non-aggression pact. Our own wooing of Russia had been a lame affair. And now…here was *real politik* at its starkest. It was the season for cynics. We now knew what kind of world leaders we had and that surely Germany wanted war. The days unwound relentlessly. 24th: Emergency Powers Act passed in all its stages. 26th: Germany annexed Danzig, the corridor they had craved for so long. She then turned her venom on Poland, history's Aunt Sally. Britain reaffirmed her support for that beleaguered country.

And what was I doing during these terrible days? Rushing to the colours? No. I was playing golf in the morning and tennis in the afternoon. It was the thirties' middle classes playing out for the last time the too easy rhythm of those years. It was the end of a world and we could not guess what lay beyond. Those days have taken on almost the appearance of a dream. We were not to see their likeness.

On the first of September at 5.30 am Germany invaded Poland. The news reached me when I was playing golf with my cousin on Merrow golf course. In an absurd parody of Sir Francis Drake and the Armada I turned to my cousin and said, "Shall we finish the round?" We did. On the same day there was complete mobilisation. On the 3rd we declared war. And the King in a special broadcast said, "For the second time in the lives of most of us we are at war. Over and over again we have tried to find a way out of the differences between ourselves and those who are now our enemies. But it has been in vain…We can only do the right as we see the right, and reverently commit our cause to God… ask my people to stand calm, firm and united in this time of trial." He stammered out his words, and it was almost as painful for us to listen as for him to speak.

The thirties were almost over; a dramatic goodbye to years that were never quite sure where they were going.

6.
Into war

It was war. What, when we were not enjoying ourselves, should we do? I took an early part in the defence of my country. I was instructed to go to a neighbouring house and wait at the end of a telephone, for what? Apparently for a message saying that we were being invaded. I was not sure what I was supposed to do in the event of such a message, but I took up my lonely vigil. I spent several nights without sleep and, growing increasingly worn I harboured the treasonous thought that I wished the invasion would happen and my vigil would be at an end. But of course it was the 'phoney war' and on land nothing warlike was happening. I returned to Aunt Hilda's house where we barricaded the windows with sandbags and laid plans for a shelter in the garden. And we made sure that the black out was in good order. We would guide no enemy to our house. We were in for many, many dark nights.

And so to Oxford. In October 1939 it was as lovely a city as ever: the High, The Broad, the Cornmarket, the Giler, the Parks, the Radcliffe Camera, the Bodleian and the colleges to show that we had a past that could not easily be shaken. But as war came it was a strange place. There were many empty places. Some had cut short their studies and decided to join up. Some, due to come up, had decided not to. Some knew that their studies would not be completed; and wondered how long they would be allowed to remain at university. A few, because of the nature of their studies, would be allowed to go the full course. It was a patchwork that became apparent in post-war reunions when we compared our pasts – and saw that some empty places at the table were tragic ones. There was Sidney Keyes, who came up in 1940, the exquisite poet of the war years whom I remember as a handler of words who held court in Queen's with another poet John Heath-Stubbs. Sidney perished in Tunisia and we lost a great voice. John, almost blind, I remember for his gently rasping words and pungent phrases and groping his way down the High. Words flew and we listened. Oxford deals well with words. There were some whose academic horizons seemed limited. Geoffrey Evans burst into my room and shouted in triumph, "I've done twenty minutes work today". Alas, he did not survive. There were men of sport. In the room opposite mine in the front quadrangle was Peter Fanning. He was probably the most distinguished oar of his generation; he stroked Radley College when they won the Ladies Plate at Henley, a competition that was open to colleges as well as schools. This was a rare achievement. But he was among the sixty Queensmen who did not come back from the war, and by a sombre coincidence I saw the announcement of his death in a facsimile copy of the Times for 5 May 1945 brought out to commemorate sixty years of peace – for some. We were that generation.

The Road From Mandalay

There was a wide political spectrum. The two leaders of the Fascist Association, remarkably allowed to operate, were closely monitored. And there were Marxists. The chief of these was Edmund Dell. He went away to the war and the conflict must have mellowed him. He returned briefly to lecture at the college before a distinguished career in industry and fifteen years in Parliament where as a Labour minister he moderated Bennite extremes with well measured common-sense.

Some of the tutors had gone to war; others would follow.

My own history tutor was John Prestwich, who by chance was an Old Sedberghian. He was so deep in books that the mountains must have been a profound distraction. He was, I believe, a particular expert on the thirteenth century. He had published nothing but was content to pass on what he knew to a very timid student who made up for his silence in speech with brightly coloured words on paper; and he had to keep recalling me to the facts which were to me a tiresome discipline. His dryness was a necessary antidote to my exuberance and it seemed to work as he said he thought I might get a First. Oxford needed people like him.

Before long the war took him off, to Bletchley Park, where he assisted in the mammoth task of breaking enemy codes; his exactness was admirably suited to such a job. In his place came Menna, his wife whom he had tutored for her Finals. The scene really changed. She was a charming Celt for whom the past sparkled; for a halting Anglo-Saxon it was an enriching experience; they were enjoyable times. And to Rhodes House and Lord Elton who had tutored Ramsay Macdonald's son. His scholarship did not satisfy those who knew more. Indeed I commented at the time with the scorn of youth, "Unfortunately I have been having Lord Elton again as one of my tutors. He is quite the most superficial historian in Oxford; but he has the knack of getting people through exams". He certainly had, and he had a considerable gift for words and he gave wartime encouragement talks on the wireless wholly unscripted. I remember tutorials with him chiefly because he spent the entire session trying to light his pipe and never quite succeeding. Those studying history at Oxford, certainly in my day, could lead an easy life going to as many or as few lectures as they liked. We could be choosy and I chose AL Rowse. An acquaintance of mine, a distinguished historian, said of him, "he was a good man, but never found the peace he sought." What attracted me was the savagery of his thought, ideas shooting out of a mind never really at rest, and forcing one to focus; a cut above other lecturers whose ideas could be culled more conveniently from books, and what interested me was that while he spoke caustically he wrote gracefully.

My studies also took me to Magdalen and to Bruce Macfarlane and the narrower confines of academia. He was said to know more about the fifteenth century than anyone else. When a book came out on this period he took it carefully to bits and explained what was wrong. Scholars feared his pen and there was a general hope that he might publish himself and give the others a chance to have their own back. But he never did. There was just one very short book *England in the age of Wycliffe* and nothing else. His research was prodigious but he could not face the challenge of publication. Oxford today would, I think, be unwilling to employ men like him and John Prestwich. They taught with much care, and they had a big influence on those who studied those far off centuries. But today who wants teachers now when university jobs come up? Publish or ... you lose your funding.

As I write the history faculty at Oxford is deeply uneasy. The priority it has given to teaching has left too little time for the creation of the books that the fund-providers require and the faculty has slipped a bit down the league tables. There has been a whip-round to fund – the leisure to write. Temporary lecturers are being employed while the scholars write. An Oxford historian writes, "And why did I write? Partly of course to meet the demands of the Research Assessment Exercise on which our Faculty will be judged (and financially rewarded) at the end of next year, and for which we famously scored only a 5 last time round, (while Oxford Brookes gained a coveted 5* - there are issues here of prestige as well as money)". It is the eternal conflict between extending knowledge and distributing it. There is no financial reward for good teaching. There was one tutor who could have answered any criteria, Norman Sykes, one of our great church historians, a man from the north. He wore his scholarship kindly and encouraged me to believe that there was something there.

And there were Collections, a progress report part written exam, part interview; we were paraded in front of the fellows and they told us what they thought of us. At one interview I was told not to work too hard, advice which must surely not be common. Was I too earnest? I was certainly very withdrawn. I read a paper to the College Historical Society entitled Historians of the Nineteenth Century. It went on for an hour and a quarter and at the end drew a drowsy commendation. They said they liked it, but I was not convinced.

Unable to either hit or kick balls successfully, sport was out. So I ran, a pursuit that Sedbergh had fostered, and with fewer people to contend with I found myself running against Cambridge in cross country and three mile. The cross country was at Cambridge and on land that is now hemmed in by the M11 we struggled across very muddy fields, which was a kind of agony, ending up in Granchester Meadows. My third place was not enough to give us the victory; we had the first, but the rest were nowhere. The illustrated press report said, "Cambridge had the advantage of being better accustomed to the heavy ploughed land." But it was good to see that other place, where my future would ultimately lie, and to go along that railway line that wandered through scattered places sometimes uncertain where it was heading; and where Bletchley was its Clapham Junction. Now unlikely bridges and pointless station roads plot its course and plans are hatched to start it up again. In the spring of 2006 an energetic young entrepreneur started an airline to bridge the tedious gap between Oxford and Cambridge. It would take just twenty minutes rather than something over two hours. He hoped for a steady flow of businessmen feeding on the learning of the universities, a world of software and business schools. Alas, he got his sums wrong and the service folded after a few weeks. And the tedious journey continues. Ox-Bridge remains defiantly discrete.

Running had its uncertain moments. On one occasion I was due to run in an inter-college competition. I thought it had been postponed and was sitting in the Queen's College Hostel in Iffley Road studying *The history of the laws of England*. I glanced across at the track and was horrified to see that not only was the meeting in progress, but that the relay in which I was the last leg had already started. Throwing my book aside I dashed upstairs, changed and ran across the road in time to take over the baton; fortunately it was a four by one mile relay. I did not win but was glad just to have taken part.

There was, as we had to remind ourselves, a war on. Those of us who had no strong objections were told to join the Senior Training Corps, with the promise that if we passed Certificate B we would go straight to officer cadet training units missing out the lower echelons of the army. We paraded once a week and were instructed partly by students. There was one painstaking undergraduate instructor whom I remember vividly. He had gold rimmed spectacles and black hair brushed firmly across his forehead. He looked rather like a Wellsian draper's clerk, a kind of intellectual Mr Polly, but he had a profound knowledge of the Vickers Medium Machine gun. He told us how to dismantle it. The first item to be dismantled, he said, was the Pin Split Keeper Outer Casing Muzzle Attachment, and we had to believe him. And this, he said, is the Muzzle Cup. The bits came off, named with precision, until we were looking at the gun's oily entrails. There was also a fine lecture by a sergeant on how to assemble a double apron barbed wire fence, a little masterpiece of precision. Distinguished people visited us from time to time, the most memorable General Carton de Wiart a famous warrior. He had won the VC and had clearly lost some limbs. He had a black patch over one eye and a useless arm; indeed he seemed to be tied together with string. We stared goggle-eyed and wondered at the nature of gallantry. To say that he was a role model was to push our horizons a bit. And there was General Swinton who told us how he had invented the tank and how they tried to disguise its development. (What is a *tank?*).

We simulated manoeuvres, pretending to assault Oxford from Boars Hill. Oxford itself was safe enough. Apparently Hitler decided to save it from harm, hoping to use it as his capital. But we plotted its destruction on a fine summer's day and hoped that our tactics would pass muster. I was told to attack a farm. My answer did not agree with my examiner's, but I was declared satisfactory.

War in Oxford proved to some people more than a game. The strain told. One student rushed up the High smashing all the shop windows. And there was deep tragedy. On the 17th of May 1940 I glanced out from my college and saw opposite by the entrance of University College an ambulance and a police car. Inside terrible things were going on. As the undergraduates were coming out of lunch John Herbert Fulljames after a furious argument mounted a nearby staircase, opened a window and aimed a rifle at the students. He killed Charles Frederick Lorraine Moffat; and he also wounded Dennis Graham Melrose in the chest and Pierre de Kock in the heel. He was taken away.

While this was going on, something of a family crisis was afoot. My mother must have had pangs about leaving Robert behind. She wrote to me with a demanding request. Could I go to the school in Great Missenden where Robert was boarding and gauge how he was and if I felt that he was feeling the strain recommend that he came out to join them in India. It was quite a responsibility. I went to the school and thought Robert was unsettled. I wrote, "Regarding the war, I'm afraid Robert knows far too much, and I think it is worrying him. For this reason, I think he should come out to India before the bombing starts." Robert sailed from Tilbury on the 29th of June 1940. It was the last convoy to go down the channel and it was bombed continuously, several ships being lost. Many years later in an article in The Times he described his experiences. "We were just the bunch of frightened, lonely children, wondering what the heck was going on, what was going to happen tomorrow, what was going to happen when we got to the other end."

The party was in the charge of a woman who could most reasonably be called a beast, punishing savagely. In one fit of rage she threw out of the porthole Robert's treasured teddy bear. The ship finally docked in Madras on the 29th of September. Robert has written, "Eventually we got to Madras and I was reunited with my parents, whom I hardly knew…and it was there that I learnt to sail, to climb and to be happy and so the nightmare came to an end". After the war Robert said that he had not been feeling unsettled and said he was sorry that I had subjected him to such an ordeal, but I have never doubted my decision. He was to escape the separation that was the lot of the rest of the family. Indeed with a war on a greater separation was avoided. He should never have been left.

In the summer of 1940 this war was in crisis and past and present had become significantly entangled. I was taking my first year exams as the British were being rescued from the beaches of Dunkirk. The fifteenth century can seldom have seemed less relevant. On two absurdly different levels, our soldiers reached safety and I satisfied the examiners. One was a miracle, the other a reasonable return for a rather earnest student. By the end of that furious blazing summer with the air above a battleground I knew there was a good chance that I would be able to pursue the other centuries. But it was not certain. I wrote in June

1940, "There is quite a likelihood that the university will not open next term."

We were told that it would, as civilised a judgement and hope for the future as you could wish with the skies crowded with battling planes. Ashamed to be seen idling when my country was struggling to survive I signed up for the Oxford University Forestry camp. We were to help cut down and cut up trees in the Wye Valley. Pits needed propping to sustain the maximum output of coal and men to cut up the props were in short supply. We pitched our tents near Tintern, but had little time to share Wordsworth's thoughts on the lovely abbey ruins. Arms fresh from wielding pens struggled to lift logs and to pull saws and we were discouraged to see in neighbouring openings on the forest the work that we were doing undertaken by horses. One slope was so steep that we had to step aside sharply when finishing the cut to avoid being struck by our handiwork. Officials came to inspect our work and told us that it was very unsatisfactory. Perspiring we gave the official some silent thoughts and continued. Distant noises in the night told us that the cities of South Wales were being pounded. It was a not so quiet reminder of the two Britains.

Our relations with the local were not wholly satisfactory. Most of them thought we were 'conchies', people who were considering this their war effort. This was understandable because some conscientious objectors were working in the area. And it was not helped by some considerable wassail one night; the local cider was potent. The wassailers were arrested and were hauled up by the vicar who was in charge of the Local Defence Volunteers, later named the Home Guard – Dad's Army.

There was, I wrote, altercation. I don't think we were a great success, but we must have added something to the sinews of war,

A week and we folded our tents and returned to our homes hoping that we had done good. I cycled to Guildford, a journey made less sure by the total absence of road signs but helped by a kind lorry driver who gave me a lift up Birdlip Hill, the steep rise that takes you up the sharp escarpment of the Cotswolds. Indeed he took me to Swindon, and I finally arrived at my dear aunt's at 10.46 pm.

Oxford opened and gave me another year. As I approached my final exams in the summer of 1941 I contracted mumps, with complications, and there was a possibility that my future might be jeopardised in delicate ways. "You will be alright", said the doctor, and the future proved that he was correct. And it did not prevent me taking my exams.

I was grateful for that other year, but could not postpone my enlistment any longer as my country said it needed me. On the 10th of October 1941 I reported for duty to Sandhurst. It was a strange intake that paraded on that famous asphalt. We were civilians straight from university and with no credentials but the passing of a fairly meaningless military test and the feeling, which contemporary society fostered, that men like us were of officer material. Our instructors, officers and NCOs all from the Guards, were presented with an interesting challenge. The possibility of reversion to the ranks, to a life we had never experienced but dreaded, kept us anxious to succeed. But our brand of intelligence might respond to the mindless shouts of the NCOs in ways that they had not come across before. It would be overstating the case to say that we bullied them; we certainly caused some of them to be ill at ease. Was this disgraceful snobbery or the skill that the army taught you of acting to your own best advantage? Only the sergeant majors, men endowed by nature with the gift to deafen and terrorise, could cause us to quake and our own Company Sergeant Major knew with an intuition that I remember with admiration just how to cope with these superior people: let them know that you have got them taped. The officers had the most powerful weapon of all; the power to decide our future. We could not displease them.

Overarching all was the stentorian figure of Regimental Sergeant Major Brand. He was said to have the longest cautionary word of command in the British Army, winding up for the final bellow which would tell us what we were supposed to do; he was never difficult to locate. We regarded him with a mixture of terror and laughter, wondering what the persona was behind the decibels and to what regimen he subjected his family. Was there life after the "Fall out"?

There was another noise that took us by surprise. It was a trumpet echoing through the dining hall in the evening when we had returned from soldiering. It was the trumpet of Humphrey Lyttelton. He was training for the Grenadier Guards but that did not let this prevent him from spelling out his skill in triumphant sounds. Those sounds had a marvellous future; the war took him but it brought him back. For us they brought some entertainment when we needed it.

We were not always playing soldiers, but we were always active. Sport. Here the Army encouraged us to be physically flexible and believed that sportsmen made good soldiers – which is largely correct. Running was my forte and Oxford had prepared me well. I found myself leading the cross-country team and rejoicing in activity without uniform. Our own course started up a long hill and while we attuned ourselves to it our opponents were soon breathless and we had little difficulty in overcoming them. On one occasion we ran against the RAF at Halton, where the apprentices learnt their trade. I found myself in front but was uncertain of the way. I battled on, weaving through Wellington bombers on dispersal and the others obligingly followed. I kept in front and was surprised to see the joy of the opposition. I had beaten their star, the catering officer, whom they did not like at all. They were glad to see him worsted. Did their food get even worse?

So in our various ways we became soldiers, and then officers – in that order; being first ground down and then built up. It was a life of ceaseless action, running from one assignment to another, changing our clothing several times a day and trying to show that we could command, and then at the end of the day supping in the grand dining hall. Some of the exercises were carried out on bicycles and on these occasions the commands were those used for the cavalry; good clean fun. Hearing terrible tales of other Officer Cadet Training Units where survival seemed scarcely possible, we cherished our luck. We were tested, but not too harshly. On one exercise we were dumped by night several miles out and told to return without using roads. If we used roads we would be taken back to the starting point. We marched down the railway line and were deemed to have succeeded. Indeed our company commander, an interesting mixture of enthusiasm and pomposity, commended us for our spirit. Instructors were of many kinds. One was a civilian, Mr Knight who taught us elementary field engineering. He held barbed wire in his hand and said, "Grip it tightly and it won't hurt you." His hands were a mass of cuts. He became known to us as Knight of the Bloody Hand. There were some interesting relationships. In one platoon was a member of the Wills family, the tobacco manufacturers, and the platoon instructor was a tobacco farmer. It was said that this cadet received very favourable treatment. My own platoon instructor, a Coldstreamer Doccy MacGregor, we regarded with awe and some affection and we rewarded his encouragements by winning the Drill Cup. We were also mesmerised by the polish and glitter of his uniform. Reflecting, I have hoped that he was able to take these qualities into battle.

I celebrated my twenty first birthday not with wassail but doing extra drill. Our platoon had been heard talking in our classroom and like a lot of naughty schoolboys, a stage we thought we had passed, we were reprimanded and had to march furiously up and down: on a cold January day, doing a movement which for obvious reasons was not usually carried out: presenting arms at the double. And through it all eyes were on us. Were we good enough? The price of failure was too awful to contemplate. Three terrible letters loomed over us – RTU, Returned To Unit – we had failed. There was one cadet so feeble that one wondered how he ever got there and he just had to bear the days until he was told he had failed. His name was Rideal. If he is still around he can encourage himself with the thought that we regarded him not with scorn but with a gentle pity and a quiet thankfulness that we were not as bad as that. Some were clearly on the edge and you could tell them from their anxious faces. All looked forward to be approved. The border-line cases were put into a special squad, commanded by Major Harcourt-Vernon. To be there was to cast a serious doubt on your future. Not to be there was a huge relief.

The Road From Mandalay

So in March 1942 having survived every scrutiny they could give us, we passed out on that vast parade ground, responding to the unique command, "In review order, advance", remembering to count thirteen and march up the steps to the grand entrance followed by the adjutant on his horse. And we were now declared fit to command. On that parade ground my father passed out in 1905, my brother Bill in 1938 and my younger daughter was to pass out in 1995. It is a place of memories. And I remembered it many years later when my daughter was there. There was a dinner night for the girls' dads, and after a splendid evening we paraded on the following day on the exact place where I had done all my drill. We were drilled and inspected and as we carried out our uncertain movements I thought back many years. On this following morning we climbed into the uniform we had been so anxiously awaiting and which we had been measured for in the Camberley tailors, those commissioned into the Guards looking so resplendent that the mud of war seemed to be an affront.

So what next? For me there could only be one answer – a return to the East. Only thus could I see my parents again in a war whose length it was not possible to forecast. I sought the Gurkhas and I had connections. If you have strings, pull them. My brother was in the 6th and an uncle of mine had commanded a battalion of the 3rd Gurkhas before the war, and leaning on the uncle I was accepted for the 3rd Gurkhas. On the 23rd of March I sailed from Liverpool. It was not a troop ship but a very small civilian vessel *The City of Hongkong*, which carried a mixed load of passengers. There was a clergyman who sat almost continuously at the bridge table smoking cigarettes elegantly from a holder, a strong young man going to help govern the Sudan, that country which because of its recruiting policies was known as a country of blacks ruled by blues, a group going to the Friends Ambulance Unit in China and purveying a courage of a special kind, a man who had been sunk and machine gunned in the water and who trembled; and a woman whose status and lifestyle we never really discovered; and a few officers.

We started in a large convoy, but when dawn broke on the third day we were surprised and a bit alarmed to see that we were by ourselves; the rest of the convoy had turned left into the Mediterranean and our ship with a top speed of thirteen knots was alone for three and a half weeks, our only glimpse of land being Ascension Island. It was a boredom of a kind that I had never before experienced, the sea having little to offer; but I learnt that boredom comes naturally with soldiering and is to be preferred to what punctuates it: moments of extreme fear. We ate prodigiously; I remember five course breakfasts. Once away from England – those few hundred yards from the quay made the difference - we were no longer rationed. Food was available wherever we went and we collected it. I do not think I have ever eaten so much.

Thus bloated we sailed into Cape Town harbour to what must be one of the finest landfalls in the world. The harbour was full of ships, including the *Queen Mary* and the *Queen Elizabeth*, both troop ships and carrying soldiers, about 13,000, in conditions not dissimilar to the old slave ships. They were preparing to invade Madagascar, a necessary but not very important operation. The inhabitants of Cape Town were splendidly hospitable, though their greeting had lost some of its cutting edge because they had recently received the Australians whose indiscipline could be taxing. I walked along the seashore until I was confronted by a Zulu guard armed with a large spear. He suggested that I go no further. I saw his point, as you might say, and retraced my steps.

As we docked at Durban we were greeted by a lady singing at the quayside. She did this to every ship as it arrived, and her patriotism was rewarded after the war with a decoration; a splendid lady. We changed ships and boarded a genuine troopship the *Windsor Castle*, which was sunk a year later though without casualties. Its captain was so devout a Christian that he refused to practise convoy manoeuvres on a Sunday and he held a Bible Study in his cabin each day. I shared his faith and I admired it.

So mid April we landed at Bombay. I had returned to my early childhood days. It had been a long pause. A road back.

My parents' wedding, Maymyo, Burma, 10 July 1918

The Raj family, Mhow, India, 1926.
I am on the donkey on the left

Stratton Park, which nourished me

Sedbergh, the school in the Cumbrian hills.
Photograph: Lathwell and Associates

Reunited. Agra, Christmas 1942

Temporary warrior. 1944

Haileybury. The buildings in which young men trained to govern India

Two families. 1976.

2005

My last visit to the East to remember the fallen.

And to see where I began

7.
Battle

Bombay. The Gateway of India, the huge imperial arch. The place where journeys began and ended, looked on with either expectation or deep relief and a pondering about the future. I thought that for me it would be an ending. Now it was another beginning. The war had separated us; now I was using it to bring us together. As I left the *Windsor Castle* and awaited instructions, did I recognise it? Some echoes remained: the shouts, the smells, the strange tongues, the squalor, the apparent confusion, the feeling that the land we governed was so foreign to us, but which we did our best to govern. And right at the back of my mind: how long would we remain here?

I was instructed to proceed to Bangalore, where I was to attend an induction course, to attune me to the country and its ways and the army I was to enter. I must start again. I boarded the Deccan Mail and on a journey that took me through Poona, where Monty lay, and over the Western Ghats. I was reminded that the British in India travelled in style – if you were an officer or belonged to a reasonably high place in the official hierarchy: four bunks with bathroom attached and ample space for your luggage. 'Other ranks' had to make other arrangements, being allotted inferior accommodation. Bit by bit the past was starting to come back.

War can do many things to people. The officer in charge of our induction course seemed a rather sad figure, a bit of a Granny, reputedly the oldest major in the Indian Army and waiting for retirement, a move from obscurity to obscurity. I was therefore surprised when much later I found that he ended the war by commanding a brigade and being awarded the DSO. Leadership is a strange business.

I enjoyed Bangalore, then not a computer city but a pleasant town lifted above the heat of the neighbouring countryside and I became a little more at home in the east. When soldiers arrived from England, they were sometimes met with a taunt from those already out there, "Get your knees brown". I was beginning the tanning process. But my mind was elsewhere. My parents were awaiting me, and given leave I set off to meet them and to bring about the reunion that the war had engineered. They were in Naini Tal, a hill station in the foothills of the Himalayas where the British went to cool off in the hot weather. I took the train to Khatgodam and then boarded a bus for a somewhat hazardous journey up the mountain road, parts of which had been washed away by the monsoon. Mum and Dad greeted me; we were together again. And there was Robert, the boy I had despatched to the east and also Iris. She had found her man, and a splendid man he was. They had been married on the first of March 1941 at St Stephens Church, Bareilly in the United Provinces, "and afterwards at 4 Cantonments," a full Raj wedding. She was eighteen. Now she had with her her son, who is today a distinguished academic, an anthropologist whose work has often taken him back to the east.

There are some ironies. Iris's husband was a tea planter, and after the war worked in Assam. With three children they were faced with the same agonising about separation as Iris herself had been, though this was somewhat abated by the arrival of air travel. And Iris, herself an academic, had to pit her powerful mind against the mind-closing *longeurs* of the tea planters club. Had Central Casting stumbled? I attended Alan's christening at the church by the lake, a splendid gash in the hills, and then after a few day of being a family again I set off to join my regiment, hoping to lead Gurkhas into battle.

That was not quite how it turned out. The 3rd Gurkha Regimental Centre was in Dehra Dun, a town in the foothills of the Himalayas. The mountains were a splendid surround; across a valley the hill station of Mussoorie, where I was to convalesce from one of several bouts of malaria, and beyond them range after range of very high places. And here I met the magnificent soldiers who hired their services to the British with laughter, endless willingness and gallantry. Those who command them would command no other. I was due to join the 2nd battalion who were serving in Italy, but the colonel in charge, having taken a close look at me, decided otherwise. I was not a warrior. I was too diffident to lead men into battle. What do commanding officers do when faced with men like this? They send them on courses. So I learnt some engineering and how to maintain and mend cars and fight fires. I was even for a time the second in command of an Indian convalescent depot.

A month in hospital with dysentery further occupied me. And Christmas with my family at the Cecil Hotel, Agra. It was *all* the family; India had brought us together. When would we meet again? Sadly the Taj Mahal, surely the world's greatest building, was in scaffolding, but it was too great to be more than slightly marred, and nearby were the remarkable ruins of Fatepur Sikri, a magnificent town that had to be abandoned because, some say, it had run out of water, or perhaps because it was in too isolated a position.

Meanwhile there was a language to learn, or rather to relearn. The words that I had spoken spontaneously all those years ago had left me, and I had to do it all over again with my *munshi*, the language teacher. Having surmounted this I raised my sights and started in on Higher Urdu. This involved the Persian script, very akin to Arabic, a most graceful thicket to unravel. The munshi who took me through it said that his grandfather had been converted to Christianity by Lord Roberts. I was just getting to grips with the set text when the army called me away and things started to move. I also started to learn Gurkhali, the language of Nepal and hoped that I was understood. And I continued to wonder what would happen to me.

While I was wondering India was stirring. Growing up in England I had watched from afar the surges of Indian politics and the attempts of Britain to contain them. Now they were in my midst in as sharp a form as they have ever had been. On 8 August 1942 the All India Congress Committee issued the startling call *Quit India*.

The British authorities discovered a plan to sabotage British rule by strikes and attacks on government installations. They gave their traditional response by locking up all the Hindu political leaders. The wreckers struck, torching public buildings and tearing up railway tracks. The disturbances were concentrated in Bihar, the United Provinces, Bengal, Delhi and Rajputana, but here for six weeks they were close to revolution. More than 60,000 people were arrested 1,028 were killed and 3,125 seriously injured, though the total number shot dead may have been 2,500. More than 300 railway stations were destroyed or severely damaged. Within a month several hundred people had been killed. The Viceroy told Churchill that it was the biggest rising since the Mutiny of 1857.

The news reached us at the 3rd Gurkha Centre. No one was allowed out and the safety of the women, always the panic centre of the Raj, was given top priority. We felt suddenly insecure, preparing for battle, but with another kind on our hands and for a short time we were besieged. The pressure eased and by the end of the year by force of various kinds and mass imprisonments the Quit India movement had been suppressed, but we had been frightened. We could now concentrate on the Japanese.

And I had to find my way to the battlefield. It happened in rather an unorthodox way.

There was another course, but this time with a special twist to it. It was a cipher course and it was in Mhow. I found myself again in the place where I had last lived in India in 1925. I described this return to the past in a letter to my parents "The evening I arrived I rode round the cantonment. First up to One Tree Hill and then down to our old bungalow. There it stood, just as it was all those years ago – the dhobi's pond into which Billy once pushed the dhobi's son, the steps at the back on which the bearer used to leave his cricket bat after it had been oiled and under which we once caught a snake, the space behind on which we used to sleep in the hot weather (once in a high wind the beds were blown over), the pond in the front garden into which I remember falling at least once, the servants' quarters where I used to squat down and eat chapattis. Then I went down past the club, this too exactly the same, with the chairs laid out on the lawn and down to the bazaar past the cinema where we used to go and see Jackie Coogan." It was a moving return.

I finished the course and was declared a fully trained cipher officer. It was time to take stock. The 3rd Gurkhas clearly did not want me and it was time for radical action. On the way back to the centre I called in at General Headquarters in Delhi and as a trained cipher officer asked for an exciting job. The man from the Military Secretary's department looked up his files and said, "Ah, Yes. I think you will find this exciting. Report to 111 Indian Infantry Brigade at Ghatera". The colonel at the regimental centre was much relieved when I told him, and I set off. The man in Delhi was correct in his description of the job. It was July 1943.

I was to serve the strangest man I have ever met: Orde Wingate, and join the force which called themselves the Chindits. He had left his mark in Palestine and Abyssinia, in each showing himself to be brave, ceaselessly inventive and almost impossible to deal with. Earlier in the year he had taken a brigade where no brigade had ever been – deep into Japanese territory, being supplied entirely from the air. He had startled the Japanese, inflicted minor damage, lost a third of his force and gave to a theatre of war that was the despair of Churchill something quite exciting. He also unknowingly gave to the Japanese the thought that land previously believed to be impossible to operate over might be the area from which they could launch their attack on India, thus leading them up the (very rough) garden path.

Some said he was a genius, others that he was mad. No one thought he was ordinary. I believe that more has been written about him than any other war general: three full length biographies and a host of other works, including one of my own. He has been worshipped and hated, though it can be said on his behalf that those who worshipped him were generally the warriors. One bit of hatred appeared in the Official History , in which the writer, once publicly discomfited by Wingate, (he discomfited many), took his revenge by penning a passage that broke the rules of official histories by launching a personal attack, using every means including a deliberate misquoting to destroy his reputation. His friends have used the years since then to attempt to right this wrong and to salvage his reputation. The argument continues.

This was the man whose force I was joining. Another and far bigger incursion into enemy territory was being planned, one eventually involving six brigades; and it was being assembled in a way that only Wingate could have achieved. His earlier escapades in Palestine and Abyssinia had attracted the attention of many people, but especially one man thirsty for new ideas with which to grapple with the enemy: Winston Churchill. Churchill saw the Far East as a theatre of war bogged down by a hostile terrain and incompetent generals. In Wingate he saw a man who could break through the crust of tried and too often failing ideas of war; and in a remarkable leap of faith he had taken Wingate to the Quebec Conference in August 1943, which met to plan allied strategy, and invited him to spread his ideas before the Americans.

This was a formidable undertaking for a brigadier, but Wingate was different and he mesmerised the Americans as he outlined his vision. In return they offered him support of a kind that they had never offered before: a private air force of gliders, light planes, fighters, bombers and transport aircraft.

This was the force that was to enter Burma in 1944. Much of this was still to be put into place. The brigade I was joining in July 1943 was to be the spearhead of the new operation along with 77 Brigade which had been in the path-breaking operation earlier in the year. Yes, we were to be called Chindits, a mispronunciation of the word Chinthe, the mythical animal that sits at the entrance to Buddhist temples to guard off evil spirits. Our more ordinary name was Special Force - and - the name designed to obscure our identity - Third Indian Division, though we came to be far larger than a division.

I got off the train at a wayside station in Central India. The jungle barely allowed it space and the rains were in full swing. I was dressed for the office and was unfit. I was joining a band of men who were barely dressed at all and who had been engaged for some time in achieving the level of supreme fitness that Wingate demanded. I met the people who were to be my companions at Brigade Headquarters for many months in danger and exhaustion. Joe Lentaigne was the brigadier. He had proved in the retreat from Burma to be a soldier of skill and courage as a Gurkha battalion commander and had been decorated. He was a very likeable man and being an Irishman a very talkative man who took good care of his men and was good to work for. The brigade major, his chief staff officer, was a man quite out of the ordinary. Jack Masters had a razor sharp brain, a wide understanding of the world, and an encyclopaedic knowledge of the USA. In the Indian Army he was generally regarded as rather too big for his boots, but of his capacity there was never any doubt and I found him a fascinating companion and his thrusting mind a constant challenge. He later became John Masters, a successful writer, telling tales of India with the purposeful narrative strength of a very intelligent soldier, tales laced with the love of flesh which was never far from his mind. A too human person. The intelligence officer was John Hedley. I have met few people less anonymous: a large Old Etonian with a booming voice, an inexhaustible appetite for work and a very warm heart. He had worked in the Far East in business and knew the ways of those who lived east of Suez and he amused us with some of his findings. With him you knew that you were with a human being. Frank Turner was the animal transport officer, caring for our only means of transport, the mules who without murmur or ill will carried all our heavy equipment. He was the definitive west country man, his friendly brogue giving commands and dispensing care to men and animals alike. The Gurkha muleteers although they could not always understand him held him in some affection.

Briggs ran the Signals. He was a Yorkshireman who had worked in Customs and Excise and viewed life with some of the sharpness of the North. The oddest figure was Frank Baines. Coming from a distinguished west country family he had run away to sea and became eventually and improbably the Conservative agent for Wimbledon. He was trained in camouflage. "I have come from the Camouflage Pool", he told us, "where the sedge is withered and no birds sing." He commanded the brigade defence platoon and his own brand of zest and a splendid flow of words gave a difference to our days together.

The brigade comprised four battalions: two Gurkha and two British, the Cameronians from Glasgow and The Kings Own Royal Regiment from Lancashire. The Gurkhas moved easily in wild country; the British had to learn the ways of a new world.

There followed the process of preparing for a special kind of war, operating in enemy territory and receiving all our supplies from the air. It required unusual fitness and the ability to carry large loads in far away and rough places. For me, straight from easy places, it was a struggle that I could hardly manage. The first march left me hobbling and wondering what made me ask for adventure. The country we trained in, Central India, was the area that Kipling chose for his Jungle Books: gentle undulations punctuated by scattered jungle. It was good to look at only if you had not just walked many miles under damp loads that tore at your shoulders and rubbed your thighs. On one exercise we lost our way. Where were we? We had a thought to ask our base where we were, but they were none the wiser. We found our way but felt very foolish. We were getting better slowly.

The rain stopped, but in its place was a much larger problem. We had settled unwisely by a river and malaria struck. Hundreds succumbed and brigade training had to come to a grinding halt. I caught it myself and was taken to a hospital at Jhansi, the place where the family had suffered many years before. The powers that be were alarmed - we were in no fit state to confront the enemy – and large quantities of sharks liver oil arrived, to be taken by every man every day. Slowly we regained strength. Christmas came and we celebrated as soldiers do. The future might afford little wassail and we made merry.

The time had come to go to war and we travelled slowly to the front. *Slowly* is a reasonable description. It took us six days by train and steamer to reach Sylhet in Assam. We were in charge of our train and could determine its pace. It took another eight days to march over the hills to the Manipur plain south of Imphal the main base of operations; to the east lay the front line. The original plan was that we should march into enemy territory as the previous expedition had. It was a prospect that held no delight for us. But we heard as we marched over the mountains of the extraordinary plan that Wingate had hatched for us. He had been to Quebec, he had seduced the Americans and we were to fly into Burma, advance parties in American gliders to prepare air strips and the rest by Dakota transport aircraft. Fighter aircraft would support us and light planes carry out our wounded. We were rightly amazed. Whatever people thought of Wingate, no one could doubt that he was unusual. No one else could have put all this together.

So that is what we did. On the ninth of March 1944 I climbed into a Dakota at an airstrip north of Imphal along with twelve Gurkhas, two mules and one pony, just under the maximum weight of 6,000 lb. Far into enemy territory two strips had been prepared by the glider-borne advance parties to receive us. The engines roared, the animals shifted uneasily and we were off. At 11.15 p.m. we arrived at our destination, an open space east of the Irrawaddy River. In that open space was a flare path lighting twelve hundred yards of runway, a sight that I have never extinguished from my memory; for this was enemy territory. We circled for half an hour – in retrospect a dangerous delay – and, a little bumpily, landed. We had arrived. We had now to carry out our task. This was to harass the enemy.

First we had to cross the Irrawaddy. Things went badly wrong. Gliders landed on the sandbank with outboard motors, but there were problems getting the motors to function and many of the mules refused to swim. What should we do? We threw some of our heavy weapons into the river because they would need mules, and we left behind to operate east of the river a larger force than we had planned. It was a bad start.

News reached us that Wingate had been killed in an air crash. Our inspiration had gone. Our brigadier, Joe Lentaigne, took his place, an appointment that was difficult to understand and unhappy in its outcome. It was a serious piece of miscasting and how it came about remains a mystery. Joe did not really go along with Wingate's ideas and he had not the strength to stand up to the man who now held our destiny, the American General Stilwell. Our future was uncertain. It did save us from embarrassment. Joe had shown during his brief command in Burma that he was too old to be there and his nerve had gone. Where he should have been we often pondered.

There followed weeks in which we attempted to inconvenience the enemy by ambushing his convoys, blowing some bridges and destroying supplies. It certainly inconvenienced them, but whether it really required a brigade is something people have continued to wonder. I remember those days as days of toil: marching many miles under huge loads and then settling down to encipher and decipher messages, to ask for food and to report our activities. The rhythm of our days centred round the air drops. Every four or five days the Dakotas arrived and dropped the things we needed; above all our food. Along with five days' rations was a 'luxury' drop, tinned fruit and bread and tea, a welcome relief from the splendidly packaged but very bland American rations on which we depended, rations which had originally been designed for twenty four hour operations. I grew very weary, but there was little fear. Almost our only apprehension was whether the Dakotas would arrive.

In April our role changed and we were given a job that almost saw the end of us. We set up a block on high ground a few miles west of the railway line leading to the northern town of Mogaung to attempt to prevent the railway being used and to draw off some of the enemy forces. We called it Blackpool, a grave misnomer. It was wholly misconceived. It was too far from the railway to carry out its main job, was an easy target for artillery and as a defensive position broke most of the rules of war. Before long the enemy got our range and started to pound us. John Hedley had the lugubrious task of counting the shells. In one bombardment he reached two hundred and each of these bombardments killed about twenty people. We seemed to have little future. To hear the shell leave the gun at the other end and wonder where it would fall was to feel a special kind of fear.

And then the weather closed in and the supply aircraft found it difficult to reach us. The enemy attacked and with little food or ammunition and faced with annihilation Jack Masters gave the order to retreat, which miraculously the enemy allowed us to do. On the 25th of May we staggered out and struggled over the mountains to the haven of a large lake, a two day hell that not all who started it survived. The block had cost 70 killed, 50 wounded and 100 missing. The horror was that we had to despatch some of our desperately wounded as there was no hope of succour and the Japanese would show them little kindness.

It had been a bloody fiasco. We collected ourselves and tried to gird our loins. Many fell sick and not a few died.

I had one NCO left, the splendid Corporal Yuille, who said, when men were complaining of the miles we walked, "I walked further looking for a job in Glasgow." We were now a spent force and should have been relieved. But our commander Joe Stilwell, who loathed the British and at times questioned their courage, determined to run us into the ground; which he did. Eventually after weeks of increasingly futile wanderings there was one sharp action which gathered a VC. Jim Blaker of the 3\9th Gurkhas charged the enemy position, was mortally wounded by a machine gun and in his dying breath urged his men on. His bravery was a splendid counterpoint to the weariness of us all. One British battalion, tried beyond the edge of its endurance, went on strike, an awkward predicament behind the enemy lines. And in another a company refused to attack. They had had enough. A medical check revealed that there were 125 fit men in the brigade and Joe saw the point. We were flown out at the end of July. We had damaged the Japanese, but at a cost that I have never found easy to justify. What it did do was to give me an experience that I would not easily forget and give an extra dimension to whatever job the post-war world gave me. Wingate's flamboyant Order of the Day contained the words, if I can remember them correctly, "It will be good to say 'I was there'." Shades of Henry V perhaps, but stirring in its own right. The strange man gave colour to us all.

8.
Other lands

Malaria struck me again and I joined many others of us in hospital. In Burma we had taken suppressants, mepacrin and pemacrin, which turned us yellow but kept us whole. When we stopped taking them the germ, free at last, could go into action. A sergeant in the next bed first of all told me of his gallantry and the medals that he had won and those that he anticipated. And then he revealed to me the details of his private life, extending my knowledge of the flesh wider than I could ever have imagined. It was a world wholly new to me. Perhaps it was time I discovered how the other half loved.

There followed blissful convalescence at Mussoorie, a Himalayan hill station whose mountain air revived me and leave with my parents at Quetta in what is now Pakistan, where my father now worked. It was a journey that showed India's railways' communicative face. Change at Lahore on to the crack train, the Karachi Mail, change at Rohri Junction in the heart of the Baluchistan desert, one of the hottest spots in the whole sub-continent. Then up the spectacular ravine of the Bolan

Pass, pushed and pulled up what I believe is the steepest broad gauge line in the world with escape lines in case the train lost control. Onto the beautiful plain of Quetta where winter brought snow and summer a gentle heat in which the British could find relief from the searing heat below and where the Army set up its Staff College. My father, having finished his career but unable to return home to retire, was employed as Mess Secretary, an old warrior catering for the needs of the rising stars of the Army he had served those years ago; a last service. I could not say where I had been, though I am not sure quite why, as the Japanese must have been fully aware of our activities. So our conversation was rather more restricted than it could have been.

Special Force reassembled again in the Central Provinces and prepared for another operation. We trained but the spring had gone out of our step. On 1 February 1945 we were declared 'ready for war,' again, and on 2 February General Sir Oliver Lease, Commander of Allied Forces South East Asia came to see us and tell us that we were no longer needed. The mooted plan that we should be landed by glider north of Rangoon was dead. He said he was sorry; but we were not. Without Wingate we had lost our identity.

When a military force is broken up, you have to do something with its component parts and with the people who make it up. My own future was decided for me. Joe Lentaigne greeted me and said he would see what he could do for me; which he did. He acknowledged my contribution to the operation by giving me a mention in his despatches - I was not a warrior as the Gurkha colonel had guessed, but I had learned to endure - and he arranged for me to attend an intelligence course, apparently a sought after assignment, in Karachi. I went there by unusual means – by flying boat. There was a lake in the middle of India near to our main headquarters and here flying boats landed as part of a service operated by C Class flying boats chartered by the Royal Air Force. It was the type that had set up a pioneer service from Southampton to Durban, a five day flight with many landings in strange places. It was an unexpected way to say goodbye to people I had served and suffered with, lifting off the water; unpressurised and so unable to climb above the weather and seemingly unheated but as spacious as a drawing room. And then after a few hours we were lowered gently on to Karachi harbour, a controlled splash surrounded by many boats. After the war managers in the airline industry dreamed dreams of flying boat luxury, but the idea never really got off the water; it was totally impractical. And when now I say I went in a flying boat many have asked, "What *is* a flying boat."

Intelligence. We were to be instructed in what commanders wanted; information. What is happening "on the other side of the hill"? Are commanders, to use that phrase that surrounded them, 'in the picture'? What can we do to abate the fog of war? How can we make sure that the information we have remains in the right hands? Security. If we felt a little pompous, we would say that we were not fighters but thinkers, easing the load on the commander's brains and freeing him for action. And so in a secluded corner of Karachi we pored over maps and wrote reports and tried to understand the Japanese, a difficult but very necessary task. We went up in Tiger Moths piloted by civilians who were so used to these splendid little planes that they threw them around with an abandon that sometimes unsettled us; and from them we were told to read the countryside, as we were told to try to read the enemy's mind.

I do not think I impressed the instructors. At the end of the course we were given our postings. Many were sent to specific jobs such as Brigade Intelligence Officer or even for the very successful Brigade Major. I was told to report to a headquarters and await instructions. The question: was - which headquarters? There followed what was probably the longest train journey in the war. I was told to report to Calcutta, which involved crossing the entire width of India, across the Sindh Desert and down the Ganges Valley, the heart of British India. I reported there. No. There was a mistake. Report to Madras, and so down the east coast, an area which in peacetime the Army seldom frequented and was often to referred to as the 'sloth belt.' I reported to Madras. No. There was a mistake - another one. Report to Bombay. Along the line that had first taken me back to India I reported to Bombay, wondering if I might face another circuit of the subcontinent. But this was it. I was to be a very junior intelligence officer in 34 Corps which was preparing to invade Malaya and recapture it from the Japanese. This was Operation Zipper, which the wags said had been so named because nothing was buttoned up.

The wags had something. Brave men landed and pored over the beaches trying to choose the most suitable stretch of shore. The bit they found was so unsuitable that the Japanese, we later discovered, had practically no troops in that area; only a fool, they surmised, would try that bit. We did not know this but patiently put things together hoping that we had got it right. And my part? Playing around with names of places and trying to make sense of them for the benefit of those who had to use them. The tedium was relieved by a game of rugger in which I dislocated my shoulder; I left the field and a lady doctor watching yanked it back. And it was further relieved by seeing the same film four times in a week, the truly delightful family saga *Meet me in St Louis*, which, if I were to deploy self pity, would remind me of what a family life could be.

D Day drew near, but when it came it was a strange scene. I was sitting in my room when extraordinary news greeted us. It was a mammoth bomb, of a kind that no one had ever imagined. Bit by bit its enormity was fed through to us and we began to have optimistic thoughts. We did not have to wait long. The Emperor of Japan asked his subjects to think the unthinkable and to lay down their arms; and the war was over. 34 Corps could now proceed with its task, but without opposition. Zipper was a walk over.

We climbed into our ships and sailed unimpeded. During the voyage I started writing the account of my adventures in Burma that John Murray published thirty years later. We landed at Port Swettenham on the 21st of September. We discovered the quality of the beaches we had chosen – we would have been seriously bogged down – and were glad that we had no enemy. Instead we were greeted by our former adversaries bowing down to their conquerors and trying to be as helpful as they could. It was a weird scene. They presented every officer with a Japanese officer's sword. The certificate allowing me to bring my sword through customs is one of my more interesting documents. We spent the night at Port Swettenham and then took the train to Kuala Lumpur. The trains were beginning to function normally. One officer, who had previously lived there, arrived at Swettenham to find his bungalow intact, his car in the garage and his servants waiting for him.

Kuala Lumpur showed no signs of war and all services were functioning. I wrote, "Several officers have been so struck with the country that they are applying for jobs here. There is a general feeling that England will be an impossible place in which to earn one's living after the war." My own future I hoped to secure by writing to the Provost of Queen's College asking for an early release. But underneath the outward exterior of calm there were many wounds. The Intelligence Department set up their office in the buildings of the Yokohama Specie Bank, "sniffing out bad hats" as I wrote to my father, and here I listened to stories of men and women who had been grievously misused by the Japanese. And listening I gained a further insight into the nation we had been struggling against in the jungle. It was not easy to know what to do with this information; guilt was in so many places. We hoped we brought solace and some justice.

But it was time to move on. 34 Corps, having taken over Malaya, had fulfilled its main function and was broken up, a Corps that never fought. Once again many bits had to find new slots in the intricate network of war. With the war officially over expectation was less tense; danger did not seem to beckon. But it is unwise to predict too hastily. I was told to report to an area where conflict still raged and a war that few today know anything about. It was Indonesia. This had been a Dutch colony for many years and the Dutch naturally wanted it back. They had seriously miscalculated. Their former subjects, who most believed had been well governed and were content, exploded. They took up arms, many of them from the Japanese, and said they would kill their masters. These were an easy target. Many thousands of Dutch civilians had been interned by the Japanese and were awaiting liberation. Now they were facing death, and had to be rescued. And the British had to do the rescuing helped to some extent in a supreme irony by the Japanese. It was a tricky situation. The British force commander, General Christison, was told to occupy only the key areas and make no attempt to pacify the whole country. To the Dutch this was a betrayal of Britain's duty to a loyal ally. To the Indonesians it was a cloak behind which the British planned to reintroduce the Dutch army and destroy the republic. A brigade arrived and went into action. There was fierce fighting round Surabaya and the brigadier was murdered as he toured the city trying to secure a peace. One battalion of the 3rd Gurkhas lost 22 killed and 32 wounded. It was as bloody as that. Nehru said that Indian troops should not be used and the Americans said that American vessels should not be used to ferry Indian troops from Bangkok to Java. Tense operations followed. Are the British nature's dogs-bodies?

I made my way, taking the train down the spine of Malaya to Singapore. Here there was another scene of unreality. I stayed for a few days in Raffles Hotel and we dined in marble halls on tins of bully beef. I bought a typewriter for 120 Straits Dollars and by an open window I tried to learn to type 'The quick brown fox jumped over the lazy dog' with limited success. I saw the film *Rebecca*, which captured me. It was a strange recall. Thinking of Stratton Park I have always thought of Manderley, and as Rebecca came round the corner in that gripping climax and saw the burning house I saw in my mind the ruins of that school where I had once lived and learnt, and which now lay in ruins.

I waited for a ship for rather too many days and observed a country trying to get back to normal. There was a meeting of many races. "There was a big dance last night at which there were British, Australians, Dutch, Chinese, Malays, and Eurasians. The Dutch are vast and Teutonic, though I don't suppose they would favour the description…. The Dutch seem to be built on a vast and somewhat earthy scale, but at least they are full blooded. They appear to have survived the ordeal very well." A little knowledge is of course a dangerous thing. Once in Java I had to revise my stereotypes. Then I boarded an LST (Landing Ship Tank), a hulk of very hot metal, to Batavia, known to us now as Jakarta.

Was I going to finish my war facing death? No. I was appointed to a unit which could possibly be described as the sump of the British Army. It was 554 Lines of Communications Sub Area, a unit that held together a part of the supply chain; necessary but calling for little skill and no courage. I was to be GSO 3 (the lowest staff rank covering training and operations) and Intelligence Officer, at last able to wear three pips on my shoulder. I collected information and then told my commander, Colonel Mitchell, and others at the headquarters what I thought was going on. It was a life of bits and pieces. "I have a queue of strange people at my door every day. The Indonesian Minister of Health turned up the other day and a crowd of other officials. The Prime Minister wanted his car back and the local Mayor wanted to know if we had seized a certain building." It was a harmless if busy way of appearing to be important.

There was a bit of black comedy. Some fanatical Muslims had started a non-vulnerability course by which those who attuned themselves to the right vibes could not be killed. The course received what must have been a mortal blow in the death of the chief instructor. Otherwise I could only retail news of fighting and casualties and a feeling that it would be a hard struggle and a hope that the Dutch could be safely extracted. We were in fact besieged in Batavia; travel outside was only possible under armed escort.

Inside the city the unreality continued. There were thousands of Dutch anxious for their safety, and there was free alcohol. The Japanese had held huge stocks, and you just helped yourself; which we did. There were parties of some proportions. One could make up perhaps rather tasteless jokes about Dutch courage, but those interned needed every support they could get. They were a frightened people awaiting rescue. There was a strict curfew. So when the curfew hour approached there was some very dangerous driving as officers, well oiled, tried to reach the shelter of their quarters before being apprehended. Most extraordinary of all was the currency situation. There were two currencies, the Dutch guilder, which had been reintroduced and was very sound, and the Japanese guilder which had been printed without limit and was therefore technically worthless. But the local shopkeepers were terrorised by the rebel Indonesians. They were ordered on pain of death to deal only in Japanese money; so we traded in worthless money, and every week the British troops were given a free issue of Japanese guilders. It was the economics of a madhouse. I sat on a committee which tried to find a way of dealing with terrorism, but we found none. Peace would only come with the handover of power to the Indonesians, and this the Dutch, with a stubbornness which we did not know whether to applaud or decry, refused to do. So we guarded them and hoped that we would not have to stay too long.

My own stay was to be short. I received a letter dated 28 January 1946 from the Adjutant General's Branch, New Delhi, which read, "Approval is accorded to the Class 'B' release of Lt RJR Rhodes James. The above named officer, if willing will be released as an Arts student and should report to Oxford University, Oxford immediately on release". The Vice Chancellor of Oxford University had asked for my release and the Government of India had agreed. In other words I had jumped the queue. My mother had been busy and she must have known the right people. She told me that the person who handled my release was a Mr Gandhi. Much paper flowed to make sure that everyone who needed to know about me was informed; it surprised me how many people were interested. On the 2nd of February I said my farewells, my war ending rather feebly, and boarded a Dakota for Singapore. The weather was not good and we had to come down to a few hundred feet above the sea and I was glad to land. The strip at Singapore required care; there had been a nasty accident not long before.

There had also been a number of accidents to planes taking troops home, and many were now preferring to go by sea. On the 19th of February I left No 1 Transit Camp and boarded *The Monarch of Bermuda*, a ship that was burnt out a year later. We called in at Colombo and lunched well at the Galleface Hotel. Then up the Red Sea and the Suez Canal, the journey that my parents and my uncles and aunts and had made so often. The Mediterranean was uneven, so there were days of uncertainty, but at the end the sure knowledge that we would be free – for what? My parents were at home, their last journey done; no more journeys, no more separations, indeed as it was becoming clear, no more Raj.

We landed at Liverpool on the 23rd of March 1946, four years to the day since I had embarked for the east, a rather grey Sunday. Some people on board had made a bet that it would be raining; we landed on the first fine day for some weeks. We were met and there was a kind of reception, and the officer in charge of troops was thanked for what he had done. He had in fact been a bit of a disaster, so there was a dissenting murmur in the ranks. With my baggage and my Japanese sword I went over to Woodside Station, Birkenhead and awaited a train to take me to whatever the future had in store. It was one of those trains that wandered across the land seemingly uncertain of its destination. It gave me time to watch the land go by, a bleak and tired land; but still green. My immediate instructions were to take 21 days leave, study closely the enclosed memorandum giving information regarding clothing, food coupons etc and report to the Civilian Clothing Depot Grange Road, Guildford. And there I went, to an area where I had lived on several occasions and kitted myself out with what my country offered me, preferring a tweed jacket to the rather odd suit that the authorities mistakenly thought was the latest thing. And I received a letter from the Under Secretary of State for India saying that four months in the ranks and 49 months commissioned had earned me a gratuity of seventy three pounds ten shillings and a post-war credit (I think this was one of Keynes's ideas) of one pound twelve shilling and sixpence, being reckoned at six pence a day for 65 days from 1 January 1942. "In the absence of the necessary documents from India the above calculation must be regarded as provisional".

I had now to reconstruct my life.

9.
Re-entry

In 1946 Oxford was strange in new ways. Two cohorts clashed and tried to get to know each other. There were those who had come straight from school – there were no 'gap' years - and there were those who had served in the armed forces and in a few years had grown old. These had been in faraway places and seen things that they were not always willing to describe. Many had been decorated for gallantry; one I met in the Athletics Club had won three Military Crosses and done things that I later discovered were quite remarkable, and one in the Christian Union had three Air Force decorations. All of us ex-servicemen, whether brave or just enduring, had to start to think again.

But first of all – what should I read? The university had given me a degree in history in 1941 and had generously allowed me to continue my studies, beginning at the term I became available. They would give me another degree in four terms in any subject I cared to choose. This really was *a la carte* education and it must have involved some deft administration. I was looking for something not too narrowly academic and with some connection with the real world and chose PPE, Philosophy Politics and Economics. At this time multiple subject degrees were rare and PPE faced an ongoing criticism that it had too many bits. There is an interesting comparison with Cambridge. At Cambridge there is a single subject Economics, but in science it is Oxford that specialises, offering separate degrees in physics and chemistry and at Cambridge a combined degree in Natural Sciences. No matter. My mind was not attuned to depth, and I hoped to wander between these subjects and find something I could grasp.

Not only did the university give me freedom to study what I wanted. It gave me tutors of a remarkable quality. In economics I had WW Rostow and Charles Hitch. Rostow was then a young visiting professor from the USA, but he later became John Kennedy's economic adviser and the writer of a very influential book, *Stages of economic growth*. Hitch later became President of the University of California.

They listened carefully to the stumblings of an ex-serviceman. It was a gracious stoop. The Provost was Sir Oliver Franks, who had risen in a career that can have been matched by few from junior lecturer in philosophy for ten years (elected at the age of 22) to a chair in Moral Philosophy, and then to the Civil Service where he rose to the very top, Permanent Secretary at the Ministry of Supply. His mind was made of a special brand of steel (or, some would say, ice) which he put at the disposal of any who wished to use it. There were quite a few of these, and he was only in Queens for a short time before leaving to become Ambassador to the USA, then chairman of Lloyds Bank and Provost of Worcester and then to other areas of distinction; including the chairmanship of a committee enquiring into the Falklands War at the age of 77. He was also asked to examine the structures of Oxford University. He was a very safe pair of hands. As for Queens, it was good at an uncertain time to have a firm hold on the tiller, if only briefly.

There was also the question of lecturers. Could I understand what they were saying? There were some known for their lucidity. I remember Mr Mabbott, who described ideas so that we could understand them and here gathered the ex-officers in their British Warms overcoats hoping to understand. Of course there were some renowned simply for the power of their words and they attracted people from every subject. AJP Taylor held us; he knew just what he wanted to say and he said it with a conviction that bent our minds in his direction. He was a performer. He swept into a packed lecture hall and without further ado and without a single note he launched into the past, his words colouring the truth and fashioning it with his own brilliant ideas. He and Bruce MacFarlane came from the same college; they show how wide was the spectrum of Oxford teaching. And there was Isaiah Berlin whose words spun out of a mind that needed no script. They say he lacked the finer points of scholarship, but it was exciting to see a mind like this at work, breathing out in great gulps what he believed to be true. I could understand big ideas; the verbal gymnastics of the philosophers I could only grope after.

One tutor I was glad but surprised to meet. Dennis Nineham had come up with me in 1939. He soon showed to us a mind of exceptional quality, surprising examiners whenever he encountered them. And when I returned he was chaplain and tutor in theology. From there he gathered momentum: two chairs in theology at London University, Regius Professor of Divinity at Cambridge, Warden of Keble College and Professor of Theology at Bristol, his wisdom put to the service of many causes in the Church of England. And by a curious chance he was for twenty seven years a governor of the school where I spent most of my teaching life. His razor sharp mind submitted the scriptures to such ruthless scrutiny that sometimes in my more impish moments I rather had pity on them. He was now one of our tutors.

The war had taken its toll on my body and my spirit. I went down to the Iffley Road track and tried to rekindle the energy that had brought success in 1941. But something had gone, and anyway there were many more people to compete with and I struggled in the university second cross country team and finally gave it up. It was galling to admit defeat. I noticed a young medical student, Roger Bannister, who I believe ran the mile in 4 minutes 50 seconds.

And my faith had been severely damaged by the fleshpots of Batavia. It was restored by the support of friends and by CS Lewis who showed me with words that have seldom been equalled that Christianity is both intellectually respectable and logically and experientially inescapable. The university took a less favourable view of his writing and denied him the final academic rewards that his exquisitely imaginative scholarship deserved. *Odium academicum?* Yes. Of a kind. The huge success of his religious writings had generated a special kind of envy disguised not too successfully by the opinion that he had published nothing of real academic depth. This judgement was not shared by Cambridge, which came to his rescue and offered him the chair he so richly deserved; the shame was that he had little time to enjoy it.

Ivory towers are never totally immune to the realities of the world. As we entered 1947 Britain experienced one of the coldest winters it had known since those legendary days when oxen were roasted on the Thames. A contemporary at Queens recollects seeing a photograph of an old Morris Minor being driven across the iced up Thames between the college barges and Iffley. A blanket of ice and snow descended on the land and lasted for the whole of the Hilary Term, a name given by Oxford to what Cambridge calls the Lent Term and schools the Easter Term. Whole areas of the country were cut off. I listened to an epic radio broadcast about a village that was lost in the snow and how rescuers finally broke through. Even Oxford was barely navigable. I remember staggering into a lecture at Somerville College and being greeted with rather a frosty glare by the lady lecturer. I thought it was rather an achievement to have arrived at all.

My parents had come back in the previous year and were now living in Oxford at a house belonging to an aunt and uncle, a family that was to face disaster. It was in North Oxford, that area where few houses are small and where there is an air of quiet grandeur, where many hope they could afford to retire and where nowadays few can. It was no Latin Quarter. My father had spent forty winters in India. This, his second winter at home, he spent facing a kind of arctic. He pushed a pram to the station and there filled it up with coal, returning with its load through the snow to heat a house that was not built for warmth. His willingness to face whatever came his way was undimmed. He cannot have imagined that the country which he had yearned to return to for so many years would greet him thus. For me also it was a different scenario. My education had been a life apart. Now at a stage when most people left home for university I was living at home. It was a to-ing and fro-ing that was not wholly satisfactory, but it was a kind of catching up.

There was another dimension: a brother becoming a teenager. I had sent Robert out to India to escape the war and rejoin his mother and father and I think I did right. Now he was back and needed directing. He had a brief stay at a prep school, not one of the best, and then up to Sedbergh. The holidays posed a problem; he was a generation detached. I did what I could. I set out with him, in a punt. This simple statement needs enlarging. It was a camping punt, equipped with a canvas cover in whose shelter you slept. As we headed out of Oxford, Robert reclining in the back of the punt said to me, "By the way, I don't punt." So I punted for forty miles, towards Wallingford and back. I gained a close knowledge of the bed of the Thames, sometimes in the good places hard and shallow and in others deep and soft when despair would creep in. And every night we tied up and slept and my arms told me that they had been exploited. It took a week. I never really discovered what Robert thought about it all; he seemed to be satisfied. I also took him on the Norfolk Broads, hiring a yacht, Spearwort, hired because it was very cheap, and I soon discovered why. It was unimpressed by any breeze that came its way and we edged fitfully in no particular direction, hoping that we were not being mocked. A stormy day spent on a lee bank gave me too much time to reflect and wonder what we were doing there. Robert must have wondered too.

But brothers apart I had my own future to consider. What should a degree lead to? Had war changed perspectives? Those who had 'had a good war' hoped that their skills might be as marketable in peace as in war. Many, happy just to have survived, hastened to find a place in the new world. The landslide Labour victory in the 1945 General Election supposed that there were dreams to dream; no more repeat of the heartless thirties, the years when resolve might have saved us from the calamities of war. We needed new men and new ideas.

So we sat our exams and hoped that they would lead in the right direction. I satisfied my examiners, who continued their kindness by giving me a 2nd, which I was surprised to receive. Today it would almost certainly be a 2:2. They must have taken a particularly generous view of my philosophy papers in which I spun words and hoped that they had meaning. Absurdly, I took my exams in an MA Gown. I had qualified for this meaningless status by the passage of years since first starting at Oxford. In one exam a thunderstorm raged, and it echoed eerily the sounds of artillery in the monsoon. Memory sometimes does one no good.

And then? It was to teach. I wanted to tell people what I knew and, refuelled spiritually I felt I had something special to pass on. I did not embark on any teacher training. I thought I must enter the market before it filled up. So it had to be the private sector which required a meaningful CV and the ability to impress headmasters. The Oxford University Appointments Board, seeing my aims, handed me details of vacancies at public schools – this was a term that we were then not ashamed to use. Marlborough was not able to help and the Royal Naval College, Dartmouth turned down my application. So, after a pause brought about by horrendous floods following the freeze, I set off to an interview. Canon Bonhote was an austere figure who had had the task of seeing the school through the war and of uniting two schools, an operation that required determination and tact. He had just a year to go. He greeted me and said, "Before anything else, your expenses. How much were they?" "One pound", I said. On the 2nd of May 1947 he wrote to offer me a post for September. It was a school that was to take thirty four years of my life and to take my mind back to a past that I thought was over.

10.
Echoes of the east

Haileybury College, the school that was to take up almost all my teaching life, was imbedded in the east. The buildings it occupies once housed the East India College, which moved there in 1809 from Hertford Castle. They were designed by William Wilkins who later designed the National Gallery and Downing College, Cambridge; Humphrey Repton oversaw the landscaping. "For the education of young persons appointed to the Civil Service in India… Established by the East India Company. The object of this Establishment is to provide a supply of persons duly qualified to discharge the various and important duties required from the Civil servants of the Company in administering the government of India…to administer throughout their respective districts an extensive system of finance; and to fill the important offices of Magistrates, Ambassadors and Provincial Governors."

Up to then the servants of the Company, having gained nominations, were sent out at the age of sixteen to continue training at Fort William College in Calcutta. This was clearly much too young. The original plan for the College was to take boys at fifteen and send them out not earlier than nineteen. What were they to be taught? Here aspirations and reality tended to come apart. There were four sections: Oriental Literature, Mathematics and Natural Philosophy, Classical and General Literature, Law, History and Political Economy. The connections between this and the efficient government of India may not seem evident. To teach these subjects there was a collection of largely distinguished academics. The name best known to us today is Thomas Malthus, who spent twenty nine years at the college. He was the Professor of Political Economy and History. He was the man who frightened the world by asserting that population was bound to exceed the resources necessary to support it, an imbalance that could only be righted by abstention from reproduction or by death from disease or starvation; an assertion that we think we have proved wrong but which continues to disturb. When I took over the direction of economics in the 1960's I thought much about my predecessor, as I explained to my pupils how wrong he was. Memories of India might perhaps have made me pause just a little.

An old Haileybury student with twenty years service in India commented, "The education given at Haileybury was a bad preparation for an Indian civilian, and that, instead of learning Greek, Latin, Sanskrit and how to extract cube roots, a lad destined for India should be made to devote himself to the acquisition of the vernacular and should moreover give a good deal of attention to agriculture and land-surveying". What was obvious to all who attended the college was that erudite academics are ill equipped to control the young; ill discipline became at times quite scandalous.

But what brought the College to an end and made my school possible was the arrival of competitive examination instead of nomination, and the appearance of 'competition wallahs' the fruit of the dreams of Macaulay and others to bring in a meritocracy. This arrived in 1854 and the College was doomed.

On the sixteenth of July 1855 Parliament passed "An Act to relieve the East India Company from the obligation to maintain the College at Haileybury". No new students were to be admitted after the 25th of January 1856, and the last student left in 1858. The outbreak of the Indian Mutiny in 1857, in which forty one old students lost their lives, and the end of the East India Company came to expedite the whole process, and the records describe in vivid detail the gallantry of many of the old students in that terrible conflict. Charles Le Bas, the third principal of the College mused sadly that no longer would those who went out to serve India know each other. A kind of camaraderie had gone, and with it the strong Christian ethos instilled into the students, to whom knowledge itself was never quite enough.

I have in front of me a list of all the old students of the College from its beginning until it closed at the end of 1857. It is a catalogue of service that illustrates perhaps more graphically than anything else what these people, some of whom my forebears knew, did for a race whom they tried to understand and whose efficient and upright government was their first concern: Judge of Meerut; Commissioner of Jessor; Collector and Deputy Agent at Jaunpur; Assistant to Civil Auditor Lieutenant Governor, Punjab; Collector of Customs, Calcutta; Opium Agent, Benares; Inspector General of Police NWP. There were many who died too soon, in various parts of India and those who are marked as "Died at sea", on their way home. One was more specific, "Died off Ceylon".

So it was over. What now was to happen to the imposing buildings left behind? For a short time troops were billeted there; the Company's army quartered there before being disbanded. On 30th July 1861 the estate was sold by auction to the British Land Company for £15,000. One suggestion for future use was a lunatic asylum, another a workhouse and there was also a rumour that a Roman Catholic Seminary was going to be established. But finally in 1862 "It was determined to endeavour to establish at Haileybury a new Public School, that genuine, and at its best, noble English institution, as impossible to describe in a few word as is the character of 'a gentleman', which it helps to mould." The school opened in 1862.

There was one connection with the east that brought many echoes and took me back to square one. In 1874 Cornell Price, housemaster of Colvin House, took a few boys to help start the United Services College at Westward Ho! in Devon with a special emphasis on preparation for the Army. This was the school that Kipling attended, made famous by his novel *Stalky and Co.* By the turn of the century the school was starting to fail and arrangements were made for it to move to Windsor and help start up another school, which became known as The Imperial Service College. The Second World War hit both The Imperial Service College and Haileybury College hard, and it was decided to amalgamate them into one school at Haileybury in 1942, an operation that required the merging of two sets of traditions and a good deal of diplomacy. Thus Kipling's school had come back to where it had started, and one boarding house bears his name.

A private school seeks distinction by the quality of its old boys. It is good to have someone really famous who can reflect glory on his old school; and, when his obituary appears the world can see what helped to make him the man he became.

Haileybury, not flush with the very famous, has one trump card, Clement Attlee. Being a man with a touching loyalty to institutions he was very willing to be played. He addressed the sixth form on being a prime minister, an occasion jocularly referred to by some as a careers talk, in which he told us that his main task was to keep the cabinet ministers from talking too much; and when there was a new building to be opened he opened it.

For me there was an extra dimension. Here was the man under whose direction we had given up control of India. In the summer of 1945 the Labour Government came into power dedicated to the rapid withdrawal of British power in India. There were two main decisions Attlee had to make: who was to oversee the withdrawal and how quickly was it to be carried out. Wavell, the Viceroy, had brought to the Indian scene a totally new initiative, but he was out of phase with his masters – Attlee did not care for him - and in his laconic way he dismissed him. Wavell had been the focus of too many pressures and his efforts to find the right answers were never properly recognised. Attlee, in what he described as an inspiration, chose Mountbatten. "Dickie Mountbatten stood out a mile. Burma showed it." He had decided there to give the government of the country into the hands of Aung San, a choice that showed considerable insight. The country of my birth would not want any more British to manage them.

The other question was: when? Attlee wrote, "I decided that the only thing to do was to set a time limit and say – 'Whatever happens, our rule will end at that date.' " . And then, "You should aim at 1 June 1948 as the effective date for the transfer of power." The relationship between Attlee and Mountbatten was a critical one. Attlee was not afraid to delegate. Buffeted by complex questions at home and an increasingly volatile succession of events in India and with a cabinet that had little understanding of the east he was content to say, "Mountbatten should be given a large measure of discretion to amend the details of the plan, without prior consultation with His Majesty's Government." He certainly was. To general amazement and some alarm Mountbatten chose 15 August 1947 for the transfer of power. (Wavell had himself once suggested 1 Jan 1947 as a suitable date for the handover). Attlee minuted, "Accept Viceroy's proposal", a decision-maker at his most laconic. And so the transfer took place, and about half a million died. The Raj was no more. Attlee was not the kind of person to ponder what might have been, or what Old Haileybury might have made of it. India had to be freed and he had allowed it to happen. And to outline the details of the freedom, he sent out an Old Haileyburian, Sir Cyril Ratcliffe, known at school as Squit (a not uncommon appellation in boys' schools) with the fiercesome task of drawing the boundary between India and Pakistan, six weeks in which to divide 300 million people. This he did, and we still ponder the consequences of his political geography.

Attlee impinged on my past in another way. I had served in the Indian Army under General Slim and I shared with almost everyone in that force an immense admiration, indeed affection, for a great soldier.

In 1947 Montgomery was finishing his spell as Chief of the Imperial General Staff, and question of his successor arose. Attlee decided that it was to be Slim. Montgomery disagreed; you could not have an Indian Army officer in that position. There was a suspicion that he was afraid that he might be outshone. He was indignant when Attlee persisted. He said, "I have already told Crocker that he is going to succeed me." To which Attlee replied with a riposte that is not easily forgotten, "Well, untell him!"

This is the man I found myself meeting at Broxbourne station in 1954 and inviting him to get into my car for the drive to Haileybury. I was the president of the school Senior Literary and Debating Society. Each year we held a dinner to which we invited a guest who we hoped would be distinguished. We asked Attlee and he was delighted to accept. I drove to Broxbourne Station and awaited the great man. The station knew he was coming and there was a touching excitement among the staff; here was their man. The train wheezed to a standstill and out came one of the most ordinary great men of our time; akin in a way to Harry Truman. He climbed in, turned to me and said, "The minister of agriculture has just resigned." He had left the House of Commons during one of the great debates of the post war years; it was the debate on Critchell Down. This was an estate in Dorset owned by a Commander Martin. It had been taken by the government at the beginning of the war in the national interest, but for reasons that were wholly unsatisfactory it had not been returned. The debate revealed gross incompetence or perhaps worse in the lower reaches of the Ministry of Agriculture and the Conservative minister, Sir Thomas Dugdale, though cleared of any responsibility, felt bound to resign.

Attlee had chosen to leave the scene and visit his old school. As we were on our way, he turned to me and said, "My greatest problem as Prime Minister…" From the man who had confronted the atom bomb I was expecting something significant "…was in choosing bishops. Whenever I chose an old Haileyburian, people got suspicious." His loyalties were unquenchable.

We dined in the gallery of the school dining hall. We offered him wine, but he was unable to accept. He had just been inoculated before going on a trip to China. China was very much out of bounds to the west at that time, and his visit was frowned on in many quarters; but frowns never disturbed his simple certainties. Afterwards we repaired to my bachelor quarters and he talked, about the past and the school. He became again just a Haileyburian, and we listened and wondered at this heavily disguised greatness. His ordinariness came out in a tale about those years. In the old dining hall boys could read while they took their lunch. But he was so brow-beaten that the only book they let him bring in was the school address book. Many years later he was on a parliamentary delegation to Canada when he met an Old Haileyburian; shall we say Tomkins. "Ah yes", he said, "Tomkins. 22 Acacia Avenue, Brentford." Tomkins was surprised at this feat of memory, but did not ask what had brought it about.

I drove him back to Broxbourne Station and the stationmaster was there to greet him again. He climbed in; second class, and the train steamed slowly out of the station. The liberator of India had been through an evening of very small things and seemed to show delight in them. He was willing to be ordinary to those who shared his loyalties and to show that sense has no need of pretensions.

11.
Shaping the young

Fresh from name-dropping, I must retrace my steps. It was September 1947 and a world trying to find itself. Germany was a starving and shivering ruin after the coldest winter in living memory. France was beginning to repair the damage that its friends had inflicted on it and was starting the process of trying not to remember too much about what went on when the Germans were there. America was drawing breath and trying to consider where it stood. Its arms, its men and its money had contributed massively to the victory of the free world. Was its contract over? Having given so much did it owe more?

And Britain? It had won, but the trappings of victory were not easy to discern. The fierce winter had left it battered, with coal stocks barely enough to heat its homes and power its factories. Scarcity continued unabated and bred, as scarcity must, evasion and deceit and it generated wealth for sharp people and produced a new word for the English language, 'spivs'. The rationing that had made the war a marathon of self-denial was still with us; and that included bread and butter

– and much else. Sweets were not freed until 1952 and meat 1954. It would have been reasonable to suppose victory would have granted us earlier freedoms. But it did not. We loosened our belts, but by fewer notches than we had expected. Sir Stafford Cripps, the ultimately ascetic chancellor, told us that we must indeed tighten, though in one moment of quiet despair he said that perhaps it was better to retire to bed. Cars were almost unobtainable. They were so scarce that second hand they cost much more than when new. The latter were governed by supply, the cost of production, the former by demand which could not be met. Those who had privileged access to new cars had to promise not to sell them for three years to avoid large windfall profits. The street lights could now shine, but after the wild rejoicings of the victory days Britain was in sombre mood wondering about the future. It was also broke and was pondering how to balance its books. It was in hock to the USA, which was proving an unrelenting creditor; and it showed. Remembering the grim disappointments of the post-1918 years we just hoped that we could do better. With this hope we had voted in a Labour government with a massive majority. The scale of it came as a total surprise and the world was amazed that we had deserted our great war leader. But the voters had remembered the thirties and were unwilling to see them repeated. We needed a fresh start.

In this grey world I reported for duty at Haileybury. "Your starting salary", wrote the Master, "will be £280 per annum, resident, rising by £15 per annum to a maximum of £700". Resident meant full board and lodging in term time. The salary included an extra £30 a year because of my war service. I have my salary notice for the second term; it reads

£82. 4d. Here in 1862 fifty boys came to start a school. In September 1947 I found myself in a school that numbered 522 and a staff of 57.

In a ridiculously blank moment I thought: officers don't carry their own luggage; I am behaving improperly, and I asked someone if it was in order. My two worlds badly needed disentangling. And the luggage had a story to tell. One trunk had been sent by the Military Forwarding Officer. I had been told that this was a very unreliable form of transport, so I had put practically nothing in it. When it arrived it was clear that it had been dropped in the sea. Some time later I received a letter which read, "You may remember that you used my services as MFO in the war. I have started a travel company. Perhaps you would like to patronise it". Some letters answer themselves.

Round the huge quadrangle, almost as big, I believe, as the Great Court of Trinity College, Cambridge, the buildings of the East India College stared at me and reminded me of many things: my forebears and the families that formed the pattern of my life and the country that had taken their lives. Several of the boarding houses were named after Indian provincial governors: John Lawrence, Viceroy and Governor General; Sir Charles Trevelyan, Governor of Madras; James Thomason, Lieutenant Governor of the North West Province; John Russell Colvin, Lieutenant Governor of the North West Province. And there was Sir Henry Bartle Frere member of the Council of the Secretary of State for India. They stared at us from their portraits, sentinels of the buildings where they had learnt to prepare to run an empire. And by the chapel were memorials of forty who had died in the Mutiny.

My room looked out on to this quadrangle and from it I could observe all that went on. I was in the middle of my new world. It was a very small world but one that was to absorb me totally for many years in way that few jobs can. The school was emerging from the war as weary as the rest of the land. Many of the staff had gone away to serve in the war and had been replaced by others who were either too old or too unhealthy to serve their country. They had served the school well, but as role models they were imperfect and the boys did not always treat them well. They were willing second-bests. The school was grateful for what they had done but longed for young blood.

We, the new ones, were that young blood. We were expected to give fresh strength to a tired world. But we had first to find our feet. The boarding schools of those years were gaunt places and Haileybury was as gaunt as any. The buildings of the East India College were imposing but could never be described as friendly and the sleeping arrangements, unique to this school, were about as far from hearth and home as can be imagined. The boys in each boarding house slept in one huge dormitory, about fifty beds placed in two long rows. Apparently the first Master, the Reverend AG Butler suggested that the study bedrooms of the East India College should be converted into long dormitories 'for the better supervision of the pupils.' It was perhaps a high price to pay for supervision and as the years went by it became increasingly difficult to sell to parents. But in those days, when life had hard edges, we did not complain. It generated a camaraderie of a special kind, and it also amazed those from foreign lands who had always wondered about the British and their ways. A Dutch boy, who was invited to have one term with the school, described it to me as a hard system run by good people. Today it is study bedrooms again, and luxurious ones. At present fees hardness is just not on.

Boarding schools require good people. To say that it is a full-time job is to give scant meaning to that phrase. It is a place where the pupils do not go home. Buses do not take them off the premises; parents do not, except sometimes at weekends, wait with their estate cars. They are with you round the clock. Their cares are your cares. Having shut them off from the real world for much of their time you have to create for them another world and believe that it is a good one. If today you do not like this kind of life and may be tempted to complain to your union that you are being exploited you should go somewhere else and limit yourself to the classroom which, you may say, was where you were paid to operate. Having operated in tasks that had had few limits we were not too fussy. It was good to be at work in a place where excellence was the aim and to do whatever came our way.

Having achieved two (rather flimsy) degrees at Oxford I might have expected to be allowed to instruct sixth form scholars. But the job description said otherwise.

"Ex-serviceman to take general form subjects". I was required to teach Scripture, English, Current Events, Economics and Maths and in my second term Latin, mostly to thirteen and fourteen year olds. I also found myself doing a little Greek once. I was allowed to dip my toes into Economics and Current Affairs for a few periods with sixth formers.

Heady stuff. I had no teacher training, wishing to find a job when there were still some around, and my pupils had to bear the full weight of my inexperience.

Entering the classroom for the first time is a moment of truth. There had been no dummy run; this was it. I hoped that my words would capture them, that I would open minds and capture imagination. I was mistaken. I had too willing a tongue and talked too much and discipline started to crumble. And I had little glimpses of that special hell that only teachers can know: the failure to keep order. To be destroyed by the young is to look into the abyss. I sometimes did and left at the end of the lesson diminished and distraught. But to experience the rapt attention of the young and to find yourself capturing them and doing something to them is to reach the sky. In teaching heaven and hell are both fully represented. I experienced both.

The school could reasonably be described as a bachelor's heaven; which perhaps explains why there were so many around; there were nineteen of us. We fed in grandeur in a dining room that might have been the Mess of a very superior regiment, with a huge table once used by the East India Company and surrounded by the pictures of past empire builders. On guest nights we brought out the silver and passed round the port and tried to pretend that we were something more than just teachers. In the ante-room each evening the drinks tray was brought in and joined by other members of the staff we dined and drank and hoped to put back – some rather lavishly – what the day's struggle with boys had taken out, spicing our sips with that peculiar wit that teachers are wont to use, barbed fun that could be both amusing and cruel, and which we hope we did not try out on our pupils. Humour, I discovered, was a valuable but dangerous instrument, to lighten but not to wound. There was a grumbling, which teachers seem to regard as one of the rights of their profession, but there was little of the bitterness that can corrode staff rooms. Neither Mr Perin nor Mr Trail seem to have been in evidence. Has memory softened hard outlines? I don't think so. There was a quiet confidence that the private sector generated and we could laugh, prodding gently our boss or each other. Then having eased each other's day the married staff withdrew and the bachelors repaired to the splendid meals waiting for them.

Our only real contact with the outside world was the newspapers that were placed by one's place on the breakfast table; you read but you did not speak except to ask your silent neighbour to pass something. Women seemed distant, which indeed they were. We were a closed community within a closed world.

We each had a man servant, who brought us our weekly rations, butter and sugar and bread, the strange fruit of victory, and made our beds. Mine was a Welshman. Like most Welshmen he cared for rugby football. He had once played centre three quarter for Abertillery, but had been unwise enough to have a game with a rugby league club, which by the rules then applying expelled him from rugby union; his attempt to evade discovery apparently failed. He wanted to join the Army; but he said he could not pass the education test, because – and these were his words - he did not know how many z's there were in 'scissors'. He was very willing and cheerful but was clearly a sick man. He died too soon, a sad, bent man who did his best to care for me.

My room was splendidly central but it was fiercesomely cold. With all four sides open to the elements it gave the weather a commanding freedom, which it exploited to the full. When winter closed in – and then there were real winters untouched by the greenhouse gases now said to be threatening us – I sat in the fireplace with my overcoat on ready to shovel more coal on the flames, in moments of extreme cold switching on an electric fire. To reach the bathroom I had to go through a cloister and up a flight of stairs and as I was exercising every day the bathroom was a place I had frequently to visit. It reminded me very much of Oxford, that other place where the centuries had not quite caught up with the needs of civilised man. The school paid for the electricity and it should have been in their interests to provide warmer accommodation but the East India College did not make many options available.

Others were at my beck and call. If things went wrong there was an army of skilled operators to put them right: carpenter; plumber; electrician; clerk of works and behind them the source of all help. The bursar. You went to him with special requests and also complaints. Bursars at boarding schools are a special breed, who have to balance the books and know when to say 'No' as politely as they can. They have to be both accountant and welfare officer. If you are a bachelor in a school where bachelor accommodation is provided you are particularly dependent on their goodwill, as they do much to control your standard of living. You hope that they will give you what you want or if not have really convincing reasons for saying 'No'. We had to learn the right level of persistence. With no wife to give that touch of sweet harassment that ladies sometimes use to discomfort bursars this was not always easy.

We were well served, but we also had to serve without stint. We all had to take games. There were no bouncy young men in tracksuits from Loughborough organising fitness and manning multi-gym equipment. Clad in shorts we ran on draughty days across the games fields and tried to tell boys of varying ages how to play. Some listened eagerly to what we had to say; others showed either lack of interest or a positive dislike of what was going on. Some were fearful of physical contact, those who would later talk darkly of what they had been made to do and wish they were elsewhere. We blew whistles and hoped that we had got it right and that the players would understand why. And when the teams for which we were responsible were engaged in matches we stood on the touchline and in varying degrees shouted advice and scorn. The players had somehow to unravel from the conflicting shouts what was meant for them. What games did do was to change our relationships with our pupils. It was a free interplay of endeavour; bodies rather than minds. No one had to keep order. You could not be destroyed. And after the traumas of the classroom it was a kind of resurrection; at one with your enemies.

There was another area of activity spectacularly distanced from learning, which I had experienced myself as a boy. This was playing soldiers; or to be more precise playing soldiers, sailors and airmen in the Combined Cadet Force. Every Wednesday afternoon we deserted the playing fields and went on parade. When I was demobilised in 1946 I did not expect so soon to climb back into uniform, but that was the way it was and I hoped that a few medals would do something to raise my esteem in the eyes of the boys who wondered at the effectiveness of some of my other activities. Some boys, given the brief authority that went with non commissioned rank, shouted commands with zest. Many found it a crashing bore, Wednesdays usually were. Stamping feet and listening to imperfect lectures on the Bren Gun and the reading of maps did not stir much blood.

But of course on occasions something more exciting happened as I had experienced at Sedbergh in a rougher terrain. We engaged in battle and called it Field Day. It was a battle fought away from the school and it took on the air of a holiday with (blank) bullets. Some attacked; the rest defended. The latter was the less demanding role and suited the less adventurous, although on the occasion when we fought in the snow on the Ashridge Estate it was a chilly business. The staff, thinly disguised as officers, decided who were dead and told them that their day was over, a judgement greeted by some with disappointment and others with relief. After the fight was over we tried to decide who had won and what lessons we had learned. There was one distinguished classic who said to his men as he attempted to retail the lessons of the day, "Now, gather round me in an amphitheatre". Did Caesar thus address his men? This was the Army. The sailors and airmen had other problems. The sea was not easy to come by, nor were aeroplanes. But we returned to school satisfied that different things had happened and that tedium had been successfully breached.

Once a year a battle became a campaign. We went off to Corps Camp and were soldiers for a whole week, as I had done those many years before. Sometimes it was Salisbury Plain, that area that the Army had successfully wiped off the map; empty spaces where men could fire real bullets and civilians were hard to come by. More frequently it was Norfolk and the Stanford battle area, another blank spot on the map where a village had been surrendered to war and where wartime runways were never far away. The first post-war camp in 1948 was there. There was no petrol – the war had seen to that - and all went by rail. It was a scorching summer. We changed at Ely and cooled ourselves by trudging through the Cathedral, our boots giving to that majestic building unfamiliar echoes and then chugging slowly to East Harling, an epitome of Breckland Norfolk, sand, bracken and a lovely church.

Here just three years after the real war we learnt to fight. Perspiring fun without danger.

We fought by day and sometimes by night. I remember one night attack in which a section commander was giving his orders. He turned to his men. "What shall we have as a recognition signal?" A voice from the darkness, "I can make a noise like an owlet". Alas, when the moment arrived nothing came out but a noise like an organ in its death throes. The attack was unlikely to have succeeded. It was all clean fun and there was a camaraderie of a special kind with the school nowhere in sight and teachers recognisable as human beings. It was also profitable; the officers received Army pay, which helped to fund the holidays that beckoned.

One of my tasks was to arrange the homeward journeys of the cadets, which meant working out a large number of railway journeys and obtaining the tickets, which fortunately the Defence Department paid for. There were some nasty moments. One boy, destined for Wadebridge in Cornwall was about to board the train when he saw that the ticket said Weybridge, many miles short. And there was one I seriously mismanaged. He hoped to go to Llanybyther, a rather obscure place in South Wales. The routing went badly wrong; after a long journey he arrived as the sun was setting at a terminus in North Wales. The journey turned into an uncovenanted initiative exercise.

Hoping to achieve, I volunteered for almost everything. Besides the Corps, in a moment of rashness I said I would assist in the boxing; which we then thought of as a noble art, designed to instil courage, grit, persistence and all the other qualities necessary to turn boys into men. Twice a year houses competed against each other to win cups and give honour to their community. And there was an annual fixture in which we competed with Dulwich, Bedford and Eton to win glory for the school. In one of these contests our man retired to his corner after a round in which he had been fearfully buffeted. His second, there to give advice, gave it and I heard him saying, "That's fine. Carry on like that." My own part was to repair to the gym and, quite simply, teach boys how to box. My only experience at Sedbergh had been one victory and one defeat, and an unwillingness to do more. With the smaller boys there were few hazards, but sometimes large sixth formers would come up and say, "Have a round, sir?" There are some forms of willingness that have their price. But to be willing was what mattered.

There was one rather curious job that I made for myself. I became for a time the master in charge of beagling. Which meant that on certain Saturdays I filled my car - in 1951 I had at last found one which dated from 1935 - and drove to a meeting of the West Lodge Hare Hounds, a suburban pack that hunted with a cross of beagles and basset hounds. The basset hounds sniffed and the beagles ran. It sounded a perfect combination, but we caught few hares. Anyway, it was a good day out and a togetherness of a kind that teachers find encouraging.

Being young we could take a position somewhere between elder brother and uncle, treading a fine line between camaraderie and authority, encouraging but remaining distinct and decoding the unspoken words of those with whom you connected, "Sir is alright." And all the time fighting the temptation to be popular; respect had to come first. It was a togetherness apart. This was particularly true in one job that came every young master's way: to assist housemasters. They bore the burdens and responsibilities of this remarkable job; we were to provide the enthusiasm and to take some of the minor duties, giving the housemaster a brief respite from his ceaseless care. We helped coach their teams in the fierce civil war that houses fought against each other, engagements that generated loyalties as intense as any against other schools because your enemy was in your midst. We willed those fifty boys to win in whatever contest they found themselves, achieving an identity that brought satisfaction and giving to the housemaster's reach an extra dimension. In houses where all was not well - and there were some – the house tutors, for that was our name, found themselves delicately poised; between a housemaster whose touch was imperfect and boys who tempted you to take their side. What we could do was to wish our best for them and cheer them on and to learn lessons against the time when we ourselves would be running what one old housemaster described as temperance hotels. And we discovered what is a hard fact: choosing the right house was almost as important as choosing the right school. Within a larger area of good there could be pockets of evil.

With battles behind us there were still battles ahead. Fortunately on this battlefield I had splendid co-warriors. Jobs at independent schools are prized, and these schools can pick. How they pick shows how independent they are. One Master was keen to add to the sporting prowess of the school. He rang round to Oxford and Cambridge. Any blues? Yes, a rugger blue. Good. Subject? It doesn't really matter.

Teaching was a doing as well as a talking; a touch of *mens sana in sano corpore*. This has become a kind of a caricature, Kipling's 'flannelled fools and muddied oafs', but before the days of frenzied league tables it had a certain humanity.

What it did give was a splendid assortment of recognisably human people with the ability to laugh which the present strained generation seems partly to have forgotten. There was a refusal to be too earnest. One, whose academic credentials seemed limited, would come into the Common Room of a evening and cry, "Anyone for Scrabble?" Pomposity could be punctured by practical jokes. One, who took himself too seriously, put up a notice about a car he wished to sell. The riposte was another notice which read, "My Neapolitan uncle has a fleet of clapped out ice cream vans for sale." A young member of the staff was anxious to visit a girl friend on Speech Day. He received a note, purporting to come from the Master, ordering him to do three hours car parking duty. Another was invited to take sherry with the Master. He arrived and long pauses ensued until both parties realised that something was wrong. One of my duties was to put together the school calendar. I received some strange entries: School visit to the Chelsea Flower Show; Shooting match against Glenalmond (Away). One found his small car hauled up the steps at the entrance to the Science Block. And there was a dangerous game seeing who could drive round a lap of the school roads in the shortest time. I believe it was won by a master's wife. Good clean fun.

Sometimes unusual jokers came our way. This was when temporary emergency appointments led to hasty selections and strange people turned up. One such was hauled out of retirement. He had held senior posts, but he was well into his anecdotage and his aim was to tell tales more preposterous than anyone else. One remarkable story started, "The only time I ate human flesh was in a French cruiser off Sydney". We goggled and waited for more.

Yes it was good to have such colleagues, of whatever kind. And it was good to be young and amid all this camaraderie it was good to be willing to expend oneself. To teach in the morning and the evening, to run round the games field in the afternoon and to mark one's pupils' work and prepare for the following day until late at night; what more could one ask? The world outside was distant and uncertain; and in the fifties rather harsh, but this world was very worthwhile. And without a wife it could take all that one could offer.

I waited for that final prize: to run a boarding house.

12.
Other people's children

In 1956 I became a housemaster. In other words for seven days a week for eight months in the year and for twenty one years I looked after fifty boys, a father figure who for eleven and a half of these years was himself unmarried. It is a job fuller than any other in the educational world. It is a whole life.

As I write, the lists of those of boys, all 281 of them, lie before me; and indeed the photographs taken each year. They stare at me and light up many memories, not only of themselves but of their parents, the people who entrusted them to my care and whose confidence I had to deserve. I learnt that some of these thought I was great, and some hinted that they wished they had chosen another house, but the great majority appreciated that I was doing my best to make the most of their offspring, sharing a burden.

They came in a refreshing variety. There was a patrician figure, a baronet, who at that time was deputy head of the Army Legal Service. As the elder of his two boys arrived I explained to him the system of exeats. "Exeats?" he roared, "I didn't send my boys to a boarding school to visit them." One came to me at the end of a term and said he was removing the younger of his two boys, the elder having already left. He made this statement and then burst into tears. They were the tears of a man who was trying very uncertainly to fashion his future. He had planted tea in Ceylon but then left because of that country's uncertain state. He settled in Essex and started growing cricket bats; that is the special willow from which bats were made. But he wanted a wider world and decided he would move his family to New Zealand. The family set off from Liverpool Street for the first stage of their journey. But there were terrible second thoughts and the family retraced their steps. Happily courage returned and the family settled very happily in that distant country to grow fruit.

There was an admiral whose relationship with his sons became so charged that I found myself a rather bewildered go-between. One father, whom I had known as a boy, came to see me to discuss his son on the day a terrible tragedy hit the school. It was a pleasant spring Sunday afternoon. He sat down and without further ado said, "I thought I ought to tell you that the Master has just collapsed and died. Now I would like to discuss my son". I cannot remember into what cul-de-sac I directed that young life. I just remember groping for words and wishing I were somewhere else and wondering what manner of people there were.

There was one who lifted a lid on an unusual family situation. He was in fact a guardian. The boy in my care was the elder of two twins and was due to inherit a considerable fortune. The guardian regretted that he was the elder, if only by half an hour, as he thought he was not a suitable recipient of riches. The younger boy was much more suitable. What could I do about it? The conversation could clearly go no further, and died out in a cloud of regrets. The boy concerned found as part of his inheritance that he was patron of a church in Norfolk, and one half term he went off to preside over the induction of a new vicar. The Church of England has strange byways.

And there was one boy who had perhaps an even more unusual family. His father had been killed in Malaya, one of the first casualties in the communist troubles just after the war. His mother was in prison. Clearly an intelligent lady she was in apparently for what might be called a white collar crime, though I never found out exactly what it was. We corresponded, an unusual exchange of letters. I kept her in touch with her son's progress; she wrote back at length explaining the iniquity of her sentence and saying that she was taking active steps to make sure that justice was done. It seemed that her letters wearied the authorities and it appears that her sentence was lengthened. The holidays posed a problem for the young man. Kent County Council, who were his official carers, took considerable trouble to see that he had a billet and his friends at school were very kind in offering invitations to stay. The boarding house is a kind of family. He applied for Oxford University and I had to put in an unusual sentence, "His mother was committed by the courts". He entered Oxford but sadly did not last the course. He is today a prominent environmentalist, splendidly surmounting much.

I was interrupted in writing the above by the arrival of the post. In it was a letter from one of my former charges remembering old times and enclosing the copy of a letter I had sent to his father reporting on his first ten days at school in 1966. "You may be interested to have a progress report on Michael after his first ten days. My impression is that he is settling down well... He promises well and should have a good deal to offer to the school." Parents had to believe what I told them, but they must have realised that what I said had to be a reassurance and might not say all. Those surrendering their sons to a stranger needed their nerves settling. This applied particularly to mothers to whom the surrender was more meaningful but who, when the handover took place, generally hovered in the background, as this was a man's world.

These handovers were always a bit tense, an uneasy shuffling of feet and words, a searching for the right thing to say, a wondering by the parents how long they should stay and by the boys how long this was all going to go on. And then the goodbyes. In those days almost all had been to prep school, that area of our education system that really floors foreigners, and were used to partings; for a very few it was a new separation that they had been wondering about for some time and which had shadowed the closing days of the holidays. For all it was a step up into a world bigger than they had ever experienced. Those who had been big became suddenly small. Did they know what they were coming into?

And now they were mine. What would I make of them? I had read their reports from their previous schools, documents written with varying degrees of honesty, giving hope and expectation. Their entrance exam was meant to show how bright they were. It usually did, but there was one unusual case with a boy who had come from a comprehensive school and was not attuned to the Common Entrance Exam. He had made rather a hash of it, but he turned out to be outstanding and had no difficulty in gaining entrance to Oxford University. Others, over-coached, had apparently reached their zenith. Some made up for limited minds with a superb physique, the sportsmen that schools like this were always glad to have.

What sort of boys did I hope to receive? That is an interesting question. I wanted first boys with minds that could really achieve, scholars or at least those who could pass without difficulty the various tests that the examination system provided. And if they could reach Oxford or Cambridge, that would be a bonus. And I would like sportsmen. The morale of a boarding house relied and probably still does absurdly on its success on the field of play. Triumphs here were acted out on a stage for all to witness. To beat another house was to make a powerful statement; to fail to win anything was to cast a shadow and elicit demeaning comments from other houses. And I would like boys who whatever their resources had high ambitions and a willingness to do everything to achieve them. These I admired and would encourage and hoped to provide an environment in which they could have a go.

What sort did I get, and how did I get them? The former depended on the latter. It was a matter of the supply chain. Establish a good connection with a prep school and it might be possible to pick and choose. Being unwilling to blow my trumpet as loudly as I should I had only limited success here. But there was another source of supply. Some parents put their sons down for the school without specifying the house preferred. The Master had a list of boys he could allocate. This was an interesting situation. Some housemasters found it hard to fill their places and were allotted these 'wild cards'. To be filled up like this could be a humbling process. The Master might say to the parents, "I think we can fit you in", and to the housemaster," I think I can fill you up";

but there might be some gems. Looking down my lists I am grateful for the great majority of the boys who were entrusted to my care.

And how did I exercise my care? I hoped successfully, but you could never be quite sure. Certainty was a luxury that it was dangerous to entertain. There is a perhaps rather tedious saying: the price of safety is eternal vigilance. To be sure that all was well I had to know what was going on and this required many pairs of eyes. Having only one pair I had to look elsewhere for help; the whole system depended on these other eyes: the prefects.

I sometimes blush to think how much depended on these people. Had I appointed petty tyrants too eager to command or feeble young men unwilling to direct? And if I made a mistake about the head prefect the house could soon become unmanageable or at the least go in the wrong direction. I recollect one head of house who exercised his authority savagely, and when a boy ran away I had a dreadful feeling that this person drove him to it. I used to agonise about selecting the right boss. It was my good fortune to be very seldom let down. There was one occasion when having selected the head for the next term I had terrible second thoughts during the holidays and told the parents of the boy that I had changed my mind. He was justifiably incensed.

And what did I want these young satraps to watch? Simply, that wrong things were not happening, and that right things were. And there was one wrong that surpassed all others in my scale of values and that kept me awake at night: bullying. Taking other people's children into your care, charging them large sums and then have them treated cruelly is dreadful. The 1950's were rough days and Haileybury was a rough place. There was a lot of bullying. By whom? By young boys against younger boys. New boys were easy meat. Those who had suffered for being new were eager to take their turns as persecutors, with initiation ceremonies designed to humiliate; perhaps not the degradations described by John Betjeman in *Summoned by bells*, but still unpleasant.

Somehow I had to try to break the vicious circle, a circle that depended simply on those who had been there one term. There was no problem in the vast dormitory; it was too public for anything untoward to happen. But in the small living room where the most junior lived too much could happen. How could I stop it? Complaints from the persecuted were a non-starter for obvious reasons. I could enter on some friendly pretext and hope to gauge what was going on, but in the end it rested with the prefects. I had to train them as man managers and by my care show them how much caring mattered. It was in effect to turn a system of discipline frequently derided and criticised into a channel of care that could transform both the prefects themselves and the society they were supervising.

Sometimes I despaired and wondered what was happening to my charges, but I discovered, as teachers do, that one's endeavours are usually more successful than one thinks. A few years ago I had a pleasant surprise. I was involved in a correspondence in The Times about the huge number of churches one clergyman had just been appointed to look after. The parent of one of my former charges wrote to say how the clergyman I was referring to was coping. "Luckily Mr Lloyd (like your correspondent) is a former schoolmaster and had a great fund of energy and good humour. No doubt his new benefice will be as happy and well run as was Mr Rhodes James's house at Haileybury." This could not put back those sleepless nights, but it could add a glow to my retirement.

There was another surprise that I could not have guessed: I appeared in fiction. I was looking through Frederick Forsyth's thriller *The fist of God* and came on the following remarkable statement. "Terry loved Haileybury, then under the headmastership of Mr William Stewart; both boys were in Melvill House whose housemaster was Richard Rhodes James. Scorning having a go for a place in university Mike announced early that he wanted to make a career in the Army. It was a decision with which Mr Rhodes James was happy to agree." The author who had two sons at the school, seeking verisimilitude, had placed his hero in my charge. It was interesting to be imagined.

There were sadnesses. Three boys I had to ask to leave. One was thought to be involved in drugs, though I have often wondered whether we had got it right; one refused to work, an embarrassing dismissal as his father had just let us have some furniture from his firm at a heavily discounted price; and one who had obtained money by forging signatures.

There were tragedies. I had to tell two boys that their fathers had died and I did my best to comfort them. But to me the greatest tragedy happened in the spring term of 1962. On Thursday Alan went down with virus pneumonia; on the following Tuesday he died. Early in the morning the school doctor rang up and said, "I'm afraid he's gone". I could not face my colleagues at breakfast. I summoned the House and told them and there was the empty bed in the dormitory. There was a terrible moment when a master, not appraised about what had happened, asked his class, "Where is Whale?" There was a short memorial service in chapel. I was asked to read the Lesson but could not. After a few days the tragedy hit me and I collapsed and retired to the Sanatorium not having a wife to weep with me. That is how close a boarding house is.

Some days later I drove with the Master and the Head of School to Dorset for the funeral. Alan's parents had recently separated but were there to grieve together. Afterwards his stricken mother arranged for a memorial by the grave so striking that those who regulate cemeteries were a little uneasy. It was a bleak cold spring day and we returned to our work with some spring gone out of our step. A small plaque went up in the dormitory.

Happily there was nothing else as bleak as this; just the usual worries about the few boys who took up most of my time and who in my lighter moments I wondered should be charged higher fees. And some awkward times. I was woken late one night by the school doctor. A boy needed his appendix out. The doctor could not reach his parents; could I give permission for the operation. I dressed and walked to the San. The parents were followers of homeopathic medicine, which caused a slight catch of the breath, but I had no option but to give the go-ahead. Fortunately they caused no fuss when they were told that the operation had been carried out.

One boy faced me with a shock. He was a mature young man who had travelled and had an uncertain parental situation. He came to me one day, troubled. "I have done something dreadful". In the language of the day that could mean only one thing. "You mean you've put a girl in a family way." "Yes." I cannot recollect what I said. I only remember that I felt peculiarly helpless.

There was one problem that I found particularly difficult. That was complaints against the prefects. I had to back them up or lose the confidence of those on whom I relied so critically. But substantial grievances I could not disregard. It was a tight rope that I did not always feel I negotiated well, leaving either prefects who felt they had been undermined or boys who thought that the system was weighted cruelly against them. And I was always anxious when more than one boy came in at the same time. I smelt conspiracy and waited uncertainly for what they wanted to say. "Sir, we..." a fearful opening gambit. With singletons I had a simple method: just listen and say nothing, and it was amazing how often at the end of the monologue the boy would say "Thank you very much. That was most helpful." To be listened to, I discovered, is to be restored.

I beat, and until the climate changed and we said goodbye to a past that we remember with regret and perhaps shame, I allowed my prefects to beat. Today this is appalling. Then it was the framework of a discipline that was designed to be sharp and effective. In the right hands it was acceptable; in the wrong hands it was a tyranny that should never have been allowed to operate and it has cast a shadow over too many memories. John McCarthy, the Beirut hostage whom I remember as a boy in my time, said that his time at boarding school did something to prepare for the rigours of imprisonment. It is remarks like this that made me wonder from time to time what kind of world I was presiding over. It reminded me that the exercise in care, that I regarded as the running of a house, operated within quite harsh parameters.

Old boys returned and I discovered how they had fared, being prepared for surprises good and bad. "What do you do?" I asked one of my less gifted alumni. "I run a boozer", he said, and I wondered all sorts of things. Some arrived unusually. "How did you get here?" "By fire engine." He delivered them and one stood outside my flat. At a Corps Camp the Army laid on a parachute drop. An old boy dropped nearby. As he collected up his parachute I asked, "What are you going to do when you have finished your National Service?" "I'm thinking of becoming a monk." Some achieved a measure of distinction: the head of the Serious Fraud Office; the presiding judge in the trial of Milosovic. But as I glance down the house lists I see lives slotting quietly into the professions and the middle ranks of trade and industry. Two brothers achieved a distinction of an unusual kind: between them they fathered fifteen children.

What had I done to shape these lives? There was machinery for helping boys to decide their future. Then it was called the Public Schools Appointments Bureau. But 'Public Schools' is a phrase no longer used; it echoes an image that we are trying to change. It was later called the Independent Schools Careers Organisation. Its officials descend on schools and help boys to choose. On one occasion a boy in my house, a classic of some quality, sought an interview. I said, "What advice he did he give?" He replied, "He thought I was just the man for the Gas Board." In fact he gained a classics scholarship to Oxford and I believe is a solicitor. A distraught mother, whose son was in fact in another house (poaching like this was not really done), said "He's been offered a good job by Heinz, but there is a chance of Oxford. What do you advise?" Some questions are answered more easily than others.

Getting boys into university: that was one of the tasks of housemasters. Now with a huge increase in the number of universities and the entrance to some, anxious to fill their quota, embarrassingly easy to enter it is less of a problem. Then the openings were much fewer, and showing some condescension we were only really interested in Oxford and Cambridge and maybe the medical schools. For some time there was no UCCA or UCAS and we simply wrote round and tried to find open doors. And we assessed our charges. I learnt before long that attempts to turn geese into swans were unwise. One goose admitted, and future swans might be in jeopardy. A bit of frankness, a phrase or two that was strikingly not a cliché, were likely to catch the eye of jaded Admissions Tutors. There was one Admissions Tutor at Cambridge I wrote to and received no reply. After a long interval I rang him up. He was contrite. "I'm terribly sorry. There is no place for a historian, but if he will read theology I can take him". He did and the boy concerned has found a fruitful ministry in the Arab world, at present in the Yemen. Another boy one Easter holidays went round the Oxford colleges knocking on their doors and asking for admission. One of them obliged. It was delightfully informal and today totally impractical.

Once a year we were on show, as we continue to be. Speech Day. A distinguished person was invited to give away the prizes and to deliver weighty words. On one memorable occasion it was my former commander, Field Marshall Viscount Slim. One remark of his sticks always in my mind. "I have made it a principle to trust everyone I meet and I have very seldom been let down". The funniest speech of all was strangely enough delivered by another Field Marshall. I persuaded three distinguished men to come and speak: Lord Blake, the head of my old college, Sir Arthur Norrington, my wife's uncle, who had steered the Oxford University Press and became Master of Trinity College, Oxford,

The Road From Mandalay

and Lord Ballantrae who as Bernard Ferguson had taken part in both Chindit expeditions. He acted with typical graciousness. The original speaker had fallen out and I telephoned and asked him to stand in at about ten days' notice. He took a deep breath and said "Yes". And though suffering from throat cancer he travelled down from Scotland and gave us splendid words. But before these famous men spoke the Master addressed the assembly, usually at length, to tell them what a splendid school they were spending their money on. Housemasters entertained and parents who had never met before exchanged greetings and perhaps noticed for the first time that they might have only one thing in common: the money necessary for such an education. The boys hovered in the background, content to eat and drink what was on offer and to limit their conversation to each other.

I have a very bad memory, a failing which became a joke in my house, and away from their sons I found it very difficult to remember who was who. This was particularly important when parents started to discuss their sons, as they did on these occasions and I had to think fast if I was not to give advice in entirely the wrong direction. I hope they understood.

The afternoon drew on. Parents wandered round to see the full range of what the school offered and watch the cricket match in which it was hoped that the school team was being successful. And then they climbed into their cars and departed. I returned to my house, sank wearily into a chair and reflected on what a remarkable job I had.

As the years have gone by, I have seen how dramatically the scene and the job have changed. It is still remarkable but it is different and by all accounts a good deal more stressful, as the young seem less willing to be cocooned and their parents are seeking more value for their money. And are watching the league tables. And there is another big change.

Fast forward. Not long ago I went to a place that bore the name of the house that I had managed for twenty one years. It bore little else. Instead of a huge gaunt dormitory was a building that could have been mistaken for a five star hotel and which had won an award. And in it were not boys but girls. Girls had first come to Haileybury in 1972, about a dozen intrepid young ladies in the sixth form. As we were able to pick and choose they were highly intelligent. Rachel and I (this was *my* big change) had part of the oversight of them, and we had the task of interviewing them on non-academic grounds; would they fit in? It was a situation in which many lines could get crossed, and the criteria were not always clear, but over the years very few seemed out of place. And we were glad to have them.

Why? The reasons were mixed. Siblings could now go to the same school; boys' schools had much better facilities and maybe better staff than girls' schools; arguably it was good for girls and boys to learn to live together; and controversially the girls would have a civilising influence. But behind it all there was a hidden agenda that independent schools were unwilling to articulate: they helped to keep up the numbers. State schools may 'fail', independent schools may close down. The heads of the former fear the inspectors, of the latter the entry numbers. Independent heads are competitors in a market place that is quite demanding. But they seldom say so. They must preach success, and they must find the means to achieve it. And as I wandered round the new house full of girls, I was bound to reflect: where had all the boys gone?

The Road From Mandalay

Did the girls civilise? The first of them had quite a hard time. Boys do not willingly surrender their masculinity - or their immaturity; and the girls were frequently ahead of them in class. But as more girls arrived the boys found they could learn to be both male and civil. Something did happen. I certainly enjoyed teaching the girls; they were in general more eager and willing to learn and they were willing to be seen to try.

But they were sixth formers.

The girls I met at my recent visit were of all ages; Haileybury had gone co-ed. I was uneasy. I believe that younger girls need space. To add to the hard learning process the extra pressure of boys is to ask too much. The issue can become a little confused. One of the first intake of eleven year olds was a girl whose grandfather I had taught. I gather he had no grandsons but wanted to keep the connection with his old school. This is the kind of loyalty that schools generate. This was the quality of the school that had taken my years.

In the nicest possible way, girls have followed me. In May 2006 I returned to Sedbergh and refreshed myself with a school setting without compare. The archivist, who had been following my words said, "Come and lunch in your old house". Which I did, and I found myself dishing out food - to girls. The board in the room where we lunched proclaimed the past and my name reminded me of those distant years. Was the school, as the motto proclaimed, the 'hard nurse of men'? Was the Sedbergh girl an oxymoron? I just hope that the hills will do to them what they did to me those many years ago.

13.
Words

Single people have time to travel and teachers deal in words. Putting these two together I found that I had a ready market for my pen. Come with me.

In 1962 I went with a friend to Romania. It was the first year that the country opened itself to the west; it was desperate for foreign currency and offered us a cheap trip. What it was not so sure about was how much freedom to give us, and when it relieved us of our passports as we arrived we knew that our journey was unusual.

The travelling itself had its moments. We changed planes in Brussels and prepared to board the Tarom plane that was to take us to Constanza, an Iluyshin 18. Unfortunately the pilot had run out of flying hours, so while he slept we waited, and our escort said in a marvellous flight of English, "We will shove you into the restaurant." Which they did. As we approached Constanza we were informed that a lot of people were suffering from sunstroke and stomach upsets, which was discouraging; my friend did in fact get sunstroke which put him out of action for a few days.

The Times had a column 'From a correspondent' and it took three of my pieces from this holiday: one reminding the reader that Constanza was where the Roman poet Ovid spent his exile and moaned about it comprehensively in his *Tristia*, the second an account of a magical day in the Danube Delta where a myriad waterways mingled and huge and elegant birds gathered and the third a very different and rather hilarious gathering in the Carpathian resort of Sinaia where we spent our second week after a scorching seven days by the Black Sea. Parties from Czechoslovakia and Russia joined us in our accommodation and for an evening's entertainment we arranged a song contest. The Russians offered a vigorous piece called the Spaceman, the Czechs something gently Bohemian and the British – all they could do after hurried consultations was 'Ten green bottles' and 'The hokey cokey.' Unsurprisingly we won the booby prize of a bottle of mineral water; the Russians took the first prize, a bottle of vodka. It was good clean fun and a rather sharp look at our culture.

I wrote for Country Life a piece centred on the Dobrudja, a vast and desolate plain that lies between the Black Sea and the Danube with spectacular Greek Roman and Byzantine ruins and peopled by many races: Romanian, Macedonian, Lipovene, Ukrainian, Turk, Tatar, Greek, Jew, Italian. I wrote, "Take a country bus out of Constanza, watch the peasants get aboard and you will see enacted a vivid racial pantomime of the Dobrudja's stormy past." It was a land that had taken many years to discover who it was.

Richard Rhodes James

In 1963 I went to the USA on what I can only call a shambolic operation. An organisation was set up which called itself the Independent Travel Education Foundation. Its purpose was to take a party of Dutch and British teachers on a tour of American schools. Early on it was clear that something was wrong. We arrived in Washington to find that the hotel accommodation was totally inadequate. Sleeping arrangements breached most of the existing codes of decency and on the next morning after a night of deep embarrassment furious couples stormed the organisers. Normalcy then reigned. Buses went to different areas of the States and we could make our choice. I chose a trip which took in North Carolina where I stayed with a dentist in Hendersonville and then over the Smoky Mountains to Knoxville, Tennessee where we visited the State University and on to Louisville, Kentucky where I stayed with a small businessman and shared a bed with a French teacher; we went to the Blue Grass country, the land where America's most expensive race horses are bred and then to Canton, Ohio where I stayed with an unmarried head of a secondary school; she was a lonely figure and she implored me to return and tour the States with her. The next stop was Trenton and Princeton University, whose buildings looked remarkably like some at Oxford.

By this time the party had found American hospitality so exhausting that they pleaded to be allowed to stay in a hotel. We arrived back at New York to meet up with the other coach loads and to hear organisational tales of woe and news that the ITEF had run out of cash and that those who had paid for the next operation in the summer would lose their money. For me it had been a colourful and trip and I wrote two articles, one for The Times giving a general outline and one for Country Life on the Blue Grass country including a photograph I had taken of the greatest race horse ever, Man of War.

In 1964 it was the Holy Land. It was not then a troubled land; the only constraint was that the Israel visa had to be detached from our passport and having crossed from Israel to Jordan we could not cross back and took the only way out, which was via Lebanon where we drove up the lovely Bekaa Valley to the gigantic ruins of Baalbek. Before that we had driven by night across the desert to Petra, a place that cannot be compared with any other.

The Times took two pieces, one a look at Israel, the other the account of a walk I did with a friend. We left our coach at Safed, a town perched on the hills overlooking the Sea of Galilee, said by some to be the city referred to by Christ as the city set on the hill which could not be hid, and walked down from the hills to the Sea of Galilee. It was dark when we arrived at the road and we were about eight miles from our hotel. There was a bus in the lay-by. My friend approached the driver. "Are you going to Tiberias?" "Yes". Could you give us a lift?" The reply was sharp, "Don't you know it is the Sabbath?" and he drove off. I could not help thinking: a few miles away Christ had preached and said some sharp things about the Sabbath. "If an ox falls into a pit"… if two travellers are stranded …. Eventually a taxi drew up and a genial Jehu, unhampered by religious scruples, drove us to Tiberias.

My writing took me elsewhere. It is reasonable for a teacher to write about education. I offered some pieces on the independent sector to *The Teacher*, the official organ of the National Union of Teachers and they were willing to take them, to discover as I titled my first article, what happened *On the other side of the fence*. They wanted more and I did six articles for them before I ran out of steam. There was much talk at the time of the independent schools losing their losing their independence, and I wrote a piece for *The Spectator* which I called *Waiting to be integrated*. That was fine, but flushed with success I was unwise enough to follow it up with another, *Amber light for public schools?* I had failed to do my homework, got my facts wrong and was rightly slanged. I learned to take care. I did three pieces for *Crusade* magazine, entitled rather racily, *Crisis in the classroom,* a title that is never really out of date.

Did my faith reach my pen? Yes, it did in quite a striking way. I found myself by a chance encounter writing the leaders for *The Church of England Newspaper.* I wrote them every week for four and a half years, only missing out when I was abroad. There were two each week. On Saturday evening I got out two sheets of A4, gathered my thoughts and wrote to fill the pages. There was no fair copy and I sent them straight off, the whole procedure taking about an hour and a half. There was just one occasion when the editor did not accept them. Some time later I heard him tell a friend, "Richard did some free-lancing for me." I had hoped for a more comprehensive description of my work. In private he was generous.

I have with me all the words of those years 1961 to 1965 as I commented not only on the church but on the world and to recall them is to bring back a decade to which we look back and on which we blame so much: a general ugliness of artefact and behaviour as we tried to shake off the grim fifties. It was a dash for freedom that never quite succeeded.

There were years of hope. I wrote on 27 December 1963. "Nineteen sixty three will probably be remembered as the year when men tried to overcome the barriers of faith, race and ideology that separate them from each other." The Test Ban Treaty; USA trading again with the USSR. And the world reactions to the assassination of John Kennedy seemed to show a desire to grow closer together. But for the most part we watched the Russian leaders wondering what they had in mind; the gyrations of Krushchev were not always easy to follow.

It is interesting to see how often Africa appeared in my articles; perhaps it was an imperialist following the disappearance of his world. On 30 March 1963, "After seven years of bitter fighting peace has come to Algeria at last. It is a peace marred by explosions and soiled by blood. The Algerian tragedy has damaged France in almost every sphere. It has hamstrung politics, causing the downfall of the Fourth Republic and also of the Fifth as well. It has caused a heavy drain on French resources, both in money and in men. It has prevented France from giving an adequate contribution for the defence of Europe. It has been a standing embarrassment in her relations with Britain and the USA. It has branded her as a colonialist in an age when colonies everywhere are being given their freedom. Above all, it has divided the French nation against itself in bitterness and misunderstanding. Only de Gaulle could have brought a settlement."

In central Africa there was a frenzied grouping. Kenya, Tanganyika, Uganda, and Zanzibar tried to get together and failed. The Rhodesias and Nyasaland had a brief courtship and the burly figure of Roy Welensky tried to hammer something together. But the joins did not hold. And one by one new countries emerged. December 16 1961 "On December 9 Tanganyika gained its independence. Thus it joins

Ghana, Sierra Leone and Nigeria as a liberated African colony and looks hopefully to the future. How bright is that future?"

Belgium liberated the Congo, but seldom can freedom been more tarnished as many hands stretched to grab its great wealth and a new state arose to claim supremacy. Katanga is a name now known to few; then it split the Congo apart.

The UN fumbled. I wrote in 1961, "The weapon forged by the nations of the world to ensure its peace seems now sadly blunted, its present usefulness small, its future existence in jeopardy." The death of the UN Secretary General Dag Hammarskjold in unexplained circumstances "could not have come at a worse moment." Fund managers have to declare: 'Past performance is not a guarantee of future performance". There seems an inevitability about the Congo that casts doubts on this statement. Will it ever be a safe haven for our trust?

The sixties saw a deep thinking about Europe. September 1961. "The Prime Minister has made his long-awaited statement and committed this country to a participation in the Common Market...The controversy has been remarkably free of bitterness." And later, "Mr Sandys, Mr Hare and Mr Thorneycroft have been touring the dominions in an attempt to reconcile them to Britain's participation in the Common Market."

And to show what a roller-coaster politics is. 9 February 1962. "Britain is in search of an opposition. The Conservative Party continues to govern as if there was no opposition." But if the fortunes of political parties change, the problems facing the country and its rulers have a habit of repeating themselves.

Education. Health. Punishment. Transport. Are we ever satisfied with how we educate? In the sixties we articulated our concerns with two reports of commanding importance: in October 1963 Newsom, focusing on 13 to 16 year olds of average or below average ability and in that November Robbins on universities. Newsom recommended raising the school-leaving age from 15 to 16. I minuted two objections: a serious shortage of teachers and restless 15 year olds. Today does this seem all rather old hat? But at 16 what have we got to show for it? Newsom wanted the best for the less able and offered many ideas. As I only taught largely the more able the report was not for me. But I saw down the years that problems have continued to mount up.

Robbins was an altogether bigger affair. I was in London the day the report came out and saw huge queues forming at the Stationery Office. I went to the Economist Bookshop where copies were available and there were no queues. I described the conclusions as 'breathtaking'. Six new universities were to be established at once; by 1980 there should be 350,000 at universities (then there were 118,000). At an early stage doubts arose; and the appearance of the mantra, "More means worse". In September 1964 the Vice-Chancellor of Nottingham University announced that he was resigning a year early in protest against the lowering of quality that the Robbins Report envisaged. I wrote blandly, "All agree that many more should go to university, but there is little agreement about how many more." We are still mulling over this. There was an irony. In 1965 the Vice-chancellor of Essex University gave the Reith Lectures on the idea of a university. His own university was then in the midst of serious disturbances, reflecting the uncertainties of those times and the way in which in the sixties we seemed to have lost our way.

And theologically there was a great wandering. In 1963 The Bishop of Woolwich's *Honest to God* came out and cast doubts on what most Christians believed were the foundations of their faith and substitute for the firm word God what to some was the largely meaningless phrase the 'the ground of our being.' What should I say to my reader? I said that we must not "surrender the notion of grace or shrivel the Incarnation into something largely meaningless and put ourselves at the mercy of every wind of mood and mental stress." I hope that made sense.

Dr Beeching is a name from the sixties that never seems to go away entirely. It is interesting to remember what he did. I wrote on 5 April 1963, "2,363 out of 4,293 stations are to be closed and 5,000 route mile passenger services are to be withdrawn entirely. There have been strong protests. Scotland complains and an area most in need of economic assistance will be further crippled. Inhabitants of south Wales say there is now no link with central Wales. Hotel owners in the south-west claim that their trade will be ruined with almost the whole of the north Devon and Cornwall coast and much of the south coast cut off." I then said "Will rural life shrivel unless buttressed by rail transport? The answer is almost certainly no, provided of course – and it is an important proviso – that adequate bus services are available." Beeching today is still for many an unfriendly word. But what could he have done with crazy economics?

Our present problems were with us then. 17 January 1964. "Today the resources of the British Army are being stretched in a disquieting way. We are experiencing increasing difficulty in recruiting." And in the same year, "Last year there was more drunkenness in this country than for forty years." And on 22 March 1963, "An underlying feeling that something is wrong with our prisons is abroad…It is generally admitted that the state of some prisons is a scandal."

I laid down this pen at the end of 1965, when I also resigned from the Church Assembly, now the General Synod, where I had sat largely silent for fifteen years listening to too many words, seeing a church that wanted the best but was unable to engage the country's attention or its soul and seeing there the many different and competing ways in which we were trying to achieve this. Archbishop Fisher's passion was Canon Law and he was determined to bring it up to date, so we ploughed steadily through it. Few but the lawyers seemed to have the faintest idea what was going on. It was irrelevance on a massive scale.

My pen still moved in other directions but there was one window of opportunity which sadly I could not open. A man from the Oxford University Press came to my study and said, "Write something for us." I asked "About what?" "Anything you like", he said. I wonder how many writers are given such an open invitation. I thought furiously, started on a project on The Theory of the State, which received encouragement, and then realised that I was hopelessly ill-equipped for the task. So that was that. And back to the classroom and retailing other people's ideas.

Finally, there was one piece on which I have continued to delight. I had written a booklet called perhaps rather ambitiously *Teaching Christian Doctrine*. Not long after I received a letter from the publisher. "We have had a request from a man we know working at the Anglican Mission in the Diocese of the Arctic who would like to consider translating your booklet along with others in the Falcon series into Eskimo. We would like to give permission for him to do so". I have often wondered how such temperate concepts as The Lamb have been rendered. And I have also pondered what impact the ideas that I was trying describe have had on the drunken despair of so much of those frozen lands. I had in mind a good deal more than global warming.

14.
Return to the hills

The east was not easy to shake off.

My sister Iris had fulfilled my mother's hopes when she took her out to India in 1938 and she had married. He was a splendid man but his world was the east; he was a tea planter working for the Assam Tea Company, and this set up the very problems that Iris had herself faced. She had three children. Where should they grow up? To begin with Iris taught them herself with the aid of material supplied by that imaginative educational organisation the PNEU, the Parents National Educational Union. She was a natural teacher and they learnt well.

But the time came, so dreaded down the years, when they had to come "home". And the same question arose: who would look after them? The ironies continued. It fell to the lot of my parents to undertake the task that they had all those years before delegated to others, the caring for the family. Iris and Mac returned and prepared the ground. It was unusual. They bought a house in one of England's most lovely parts, the Lake District. It was near Hawkshead, the place where Wordsworth went to school and which today is almost trampled out of existence by the crowds that come to share it with too many others. In the fifties it was gently busy. Their house was just off the lane that skirts the hills to the north east and goes past a hostelry that draws many who know their Lakes, the Drunken Duck.

Just over the hill is a view matched by few in that lovely land, Tarn Hows, a lake cradled by the hills. Its beauty has been its downfall, but if you approach it in a snow storm you may find a place to park. A gentle walk and there it was, to strike the eye and never to sate it. The time came for Iris and Mac to return to India and to do the leaving, my parents to do the caring. They moved in 1954 from their latest rented house in a rather dreary village that overlooked Poole Harbour, where I found myself reading to Iris's children large chunks of Arthur Ransome, to this delectable spot, where Arthur Ransome had placed his carefree tales and there they stayed for ten years. I was unmarried and for the part of each holidays I went there and there I roamed at will.

Hills. I had known them in Burma as obstacles to be overcome and in one moment of crisis they had been the path to safety. And I had known them at Sedbergh and I learnt to love them, getting on terms with them, fashioning my steps to their steepness and following each false crest until at the pile of stones which marked the top I could rest and look around and wonder. Now I could see how beautiful was the world that we had saved from evil.

I wandered largely alone. My singleness had many components and I preferred to walk by myself. The Lakes were mine; my plate was overfull. Where should I start? Behind the house rose Black Crag, but it was difficult of access, being girded with barbed wire and a barely penetrable forest; so I contented myself with looking at its dark brow and starting elsewhere. The Langdale Pikes did well. They lift proudly up from the valley bottom of Mickelden and impose more than their height warrants and they have a splendid shape. I walked up Mill Gill, not a very exciting approach, and glancing at the crags of Pavey Ark arrived at Harrison Stickle and peered down at the sudden drop of Gimmer Crags where brave men climb. On a later occasion I climbed in mid winter with snow up to my thighs and breathed heavily. It was a place to return to and never to exhaust; it is a fine grandstand.

To the west lay Bow Fell and this I climbed, a rare twosome, with a retired Indian Army colonel my parents had known. "Don't let's talk", he said, wise advice for those needing to save their breath. We went up The Band to the shattered fragments at its summit and across Crinkle Crags which spread like giant fractured dentures to the south and then down one of the gills to Oxendale. We were weary but exhilarated and not exhausted; that is what the Lakes offer.

"Have you been up..?" There were some peaks you had to conquer, the places where you met other people answering the same question. Helvellyn. I went up from Wythburn on its western shoulder, where coaches empty their loads of climbers. It is a dreary route, a blind trudge, staring into a hillside that offers few vistas. So the following day I tried again from the East from Patterdale where many years afterwards my son was married. And of course Striding Edge. I do not like heights but I found this no trouble at all; there is little verticality, though the last scramble is on uncertain rocks. And I discovered what all hill walkers know: if you want to enjoy yourself make for the ridges.

And of course there is Scafall Pike. There are three routes and I tried them all. The best is undoubtedly from Borrowdale and the Corridor Route where all the way the great heights keep you company. The sweatiest is from Langdale and up Rossett Gill which offers you little but rocks, and the quickest from Wastwater, which is just a steep trudge, but you do have as an accompaniment the gigantic frown of Great Gable. I spent a week at the head of Wastwater with my nephew and we managed this between the showers. On one occasion I started from Langdale and arranged to meet a colleague who had started from Borrowdale. The meeting place was Esk Hause, where many high ridges meet, and remarkably we were only five minutes out.

But the advantage of being a dweller rather than a visitor is that you can climb less well known and so less frequented peaks. Some like the Fairfield Horseshoe are only slightly less famous but they elude many. Many have climbed Coniston Old Man; fewer have continued along the ridge as I did on one enchanted day to Brim Fell, Swirl How and Grey Friar and that outrider that can be seen from so many places: Wetherlam. Many mount the Langdale Pikes; fewer have tried the other side of the valley and Pike o'Blisco. One summer my parents had to vacate the Hawkshead house and stay at Troutbeck village which lies to the north of Windermere. From here I took a route which I had entirely to myself: up to Thornthwaite Crag and High Street, a remarkable plateau along which the Romans had marched and whose course can be plotted to Penrith and where there was once a race course; and on to Kidsty Pike.

This is a detached massif, and you have to have time to explore it. Time was what I had. And on the occasion when I sat at the top of St

Sunday Crag and gazed at Ullswater I saw no one. After each walk my car was waiting to take me back to the house where I told my parents where I had been and the joy my journey had given me. My father gently shared my delight; my mother was not really attuned to the hills. "Not another book about the Lake District?" she once exclaimed testily.

In 1955 something happened to the Lake District that took it by surprise. Wainwright brought out the first of his guidebooks, on The Eastern Fells. They followed in steady succession, the footprints of a man who went on walking: 1957 The Far Eastern Fells, 1958 The Central Fells, 1960 The Southern Fells, 1962 The Northern Fells, 1964 The North Western Fells, 1966 The Western Fells. He wrote in the last book, "It has been a long and lonely way", but he preferred its loneliness to a companion who might alloy his delight and it gave him time to record with a matchless pen every hill in that lovely land. His drawings are magically meticulous and his words sing his delight and reflect his inner feelings with a force that you have no right to expect from a guidebook. Some of his work is clearly out of date, and some weary of his fearless strictures and wonder why his fortune went to animals. But to me and countless others who have trudged those hills they are incomparable. They are here by me as I write. I was in these places because of the East. It was an unexpected harvest.

While I roamed my nephew Alan worked. I saw him grow up in the hills, first as a small boy wholly devoted to fishing, and then as an Oxford undergraduate and finally as a serious academic. In a shed at the bottom of our garden he toiled at a D.Phil that was going to launch into academia a mind whose tireless curiosity was to discover new truths and change settled ideas. Witchcraft in seventeenth century Essex was perhaps an unlikely eye-opener but that is what it was. He was to turn some accepted historical ideas upside down and become a Fellow of the British Academy in his forties. The first serious bits were put together in that shed in the garden while my father gardened, tilling the soil that he had waited so many years to turn over, and my mother, seeking an outlet for a more exciting life than was now her lot, turned to the racecourse and expended much energy and too many assets on trying to guess who was going to win. My guess, I sometimes thought, might have been as good as hers, but I was never brave enough to say so. My two nieces were not attuned to books but to life. They helped me to feel avuncular and when I grew too pompous they laughed, sometimes at my jokes, which they knew by heart, and sometimes gently at myself. And they gave me the idea of children.

One day, hoping to give my care for them a larger dimension, I took them to Morecombe to see a pantomime. I cannot recall which one it was – with pantomimes this is of no great importance. But I do remember that it was a foul day with rain scudding along the promenade and that the theatre appeared to be empty except for us and a coach party from Wigan, to whom the cast, suitably primed, directed many of their remarks. I was glad to see the end of it, but unfortunately the children were not and implored me to take them to the next performance. Arguing furiously we struggled to the car and made our way back to the hills. It was fun of a kind.

There was a shifting of scenes. Iris and Mac, on retirement from the East, seemingly finding the Lake District rather suburban, moved to the Outer Hebrides and bought a croft on North Uist. There I believe they found happiness until Mac died tragically; a heart attack while he was mending the roof and Iris away in Glasgow learning Gaelic, their worlds still not entirely coalescing.

My parents anyway had to move south in 1964 to a more accessible home, to a house that I bought for them, one of those acts of generosity that prove highly profitable. It was a comfortable building in a faceless neighbourhood a short distance away from Broadmoor Prison, and within limited boundaries they seemed content and were to have eight more years together, the Raj fading in sandy wastes. Lives shot through with colour and movement ended in a kind of dull peace. My father gardened until he could no longer move and my mother endeavoured to hold back tedium by a pursuit of horses so furious that we grew anxious, knowing that we could do nothing to abate her zeal. It was a partnership of two very different people that had overcome much. It had been a complex lifetime.

My mother was widowed for fourteen years, and in those years she was tended with unceasing care, latterly near Cambridge, by the daughter she had so seriously misdirected, a sort of final irony (were there too many?). Her ebullience was moderated only briefly by a collision with a motor car. She spent some time in Addenbrookes Hospital and there in her ward she held court dispensing her own brand of charm and frankness, and before she left she held a kind of prize giving for all those who had helped her: the nurses got mugs, the consultant a glass vase. We knew she was on the mend when she muttered, as she emerged from her operation, "Who won the two thirty?" Her life was one of overcoming, pushing obstacles and sometimes people aside. She was not one to be disregarded, and we never did. She left this life cherishing memories and summoning up a parade of those who, in a life as colourful as most who had crossed her path, seldom forgot her.

My parents had left the hills, but I was to return to them again and walk over them; this time to share their delight in a way that surpassed my wildest dreams.

15.
Another

To be forty six and unmarried is to invite a host of thoughts, which the reader will now be mulling over.

Being unattached had enabled me to take part in Christian youth work in the school holidays which was difficult for a married man, and this had yielded a rich harvest. But there was an incompleteness that it was becoming increasingly difficult to cope with. I had looked after other people's children for over ten years. I could share some of the burdens of the job with house tutors, but the sharing I wanted was a life and there was something a good deal better than other people's children – my own. And someone to love.

The Haileybury I came to in 1947, as I have described, was a bachelor's haven and most of the housemasters were unmarried, which today sounds quite odd. Year by year the scene changed and by 1966 I was the only unmarried housemaster, a fact that the Master rather tactlessly mentioned in his Speech Day oration. I was the odd man out, and this must have had some effect on parents considering a house for their sons. I was not a "confirmed bachelor" and I longed to prove it.

Miracles do happen; my life's work with the young had proved that. I was hoping it would happen to me. And it did. To say that I met Rachel in a snowdrift would be to exaggerate an already remarkable chain of events, but it was in Davos at a skiing party that she had only joined at the last moment that I suddenly realised that my dream might at last be coming true. As I write this, world leaders are meeting at that splendid mountain resort to try to plot the world's prosperity. I was plotting the course of my emotions and seeing where they were leading me.

One thing, as they say, led to another. A colleague at Haileybury, who was privy to my plot, helped to arrange a party to which Rachel, *among others,* was invited. There was a mingling which I hoped was anonymous. A boarding school is a public place and it was not easy to disguise one's manoeuvres. I hoped that I had succeeded, but the word spread around, "Is it true that RJ has got a bird?" There was an air of expectancy and suppressed disbelief; surely he was too far gone. Every courtship has its defining moments. "You must meet my people", said Rachel, an amber light which promised to turn to green.

It was Speech Day. I said goodbye to the last parents, dashed to my car and drove furiously to Euston. There was serious traffic. Would I make it? The possibility of missing the train in which Rachel was waiting for me was too awful to contemplate. I left my car in the nearest street at a time when you could do that sort of thing and we leapt on to the train. It was a train that travelled on the same line that I used all those years I had been at Sedbergh and as the stations flashed by a part of my past was re-enacted. We alighted at Crewe where the person I hoped would be my father-in-law was waiting to drive us some miles to his Cheshire home. I had crossed the Rubicon; was Rachel willing to accompany me?

I met her parents and realised that the miracle had many dimensions.

We walked along the canal that ran through the valley below her splendid house. She turned to me and said, "There are nineteen years between us." I must say this shook me a bit, and my future father-in-law when I told him my intentions said, "It's a pity you can't turn the clock back." Which was a fair comment but I recollect that Empire builders flexed their muscles in their long bachelor years and then, finding themselves incomplete, dug quite deep into the cradle to find the love that had eluded them and could bring not only a new kind of joy but also children, a creation of a wholly new kind.

To propose I took Rachel in the school holidays into the boys' dormitory, that vast shed where fifty boys slept, and I said "Would you like to share this with me?"; because of course a boarding school is a whole life. Those iron bedsteads were a poor substitute for an arbour of roses or the pale reflection of the moon, but it seemed to me very much to the point. We announced our engagement on the sixth of September 1967 and planned the wedding for the thirtieth of December. This was hurried and maybe inconsiderate; but teachers have certain constraints on when they can take a break, and the thought of waiting until the Easter holidays was something I could not contemplate; I had waited long enough. Rachel visited the school and was aware that she was under massive scrutiny. Whom had Sir chosen? Rachel was working on a PhD in clinical pathology. "Is it true that RJ is marrying a nuclear physicist?" My colleagues and the parents of my boys showed their delight in different ways, and the Master could know that he was about to have a full hand.

The road to Hell, they say, is paved with good intentions. Perhaps the opposite is true: the way to heaven may have an obstacle or two to contend with. That autumn the country was struck by the biggest epidemic of Foot and Mouth disease for very many years. Cheshire, where our wedding was to take place, was one of the two most seriously affected counties. There were immediate repercussions. Quite a few invited guests said they were very sorry, but they could not enter an infected area. Rachel's parents felt it was necessary to move the reception from their own lovely house to a nearby hotel.

There was worse to come. We had planned our honeymoon in Ireland with all the hotels booked. And then the Irish government said that no one from Britain could land; so the dream of so many years went up literally in smoke, the smoke that hovered over the piles of slaughtered cattle. Where should we go? We booked into the Bulkeley Arms in Beaumaris on Anglesey. We set out. Our wedding night was spent in a nearby hotel, our joy somewhat muted by a dawn disturbed by the sound of a helicopter in the garden, part of the apparatus for monitoring the Foot and Mouth situation. We crossed the Menai Straits Bridge which was reeking with chemicals and above it was the discouraging notice, "Is your journey necessary?" On Anglesey we were not allowed to walk on the grass, and chose the seashore. We were very happy, but could be excused for being disappointed.

The Road From Mandalay

After the honeymoon we drove back to Rachel's home to pick up the presents and drive south. That day a fearful snow storm blew. The snow was so deep that we almost got benighted on one hill and the motorway was down to one lane. After many hours we reached Haileybury. A colleague had very kindly lit a fire. We unloaded the car and found how weary we were. I thought: things can only get better.

Fortunately they did – triumphantly. The transformation matched the dream. The boys arrived and their parents, all curious to see who she was, the one who had captured an ageing bachelor – if that is the right way round to put it. I was not nervous. With the untarnished confidence of a new husband I knew they would like what they saw, and with the arrogance that many years and a family have given me I discovered I was right. And the joy was complete on the next Speech Day when Rachel and I could together offer hospitality and I could show to all and sundry that I was complete. That day has something of a feel of a second honeymoon. I retired to bed not worn but soaring.

"Do you want children?" That is a very reasonable question to put to one who wants you. My "yes" was, I think, the most confident statement I have ever made; and being the age I was I knew that there was no time to be lost. We lost none at all. Clare was born one night in October. I witnessed the birth and then drove back to school. I tip-toed into the dormitory and posted on the house notice board the news of what had happened that night. I wished I could have been there to observe the reactions of the boys as they tottered sleepily to their washing, and indeed how they retailed the news to their parents. My colleagues, having witnessed one miracle, shared their delight in another. Each summer the house posed for a photograph. In 1968 for the first time a lady appeared, and then in 1969 a baby. Things were getting under way.

But one child does not make a family; there was more to come. Lizzie arrived very quickly and in unusual circumstances. It was a home birth, a procedure much friendlier than being born in hospital as if the mother was ill, but requiring gynaecological conditions to be just right and the timely arrival of the midwife. The second condition was in hazard. Lizzie is one of life's activists, and she showed it from the start. Rachel woke me to say that labour had started and we telephoned the mid-wife. After less than two hours of labour Lizzie was being born and there was just me and an elderly Australian nurse to cope. In Australia, I believe, all deliveries are in hospital and she did not know what to do. Drama had reached me quite late in life. At that moment I heard steps on the stairs, a sound whose welcome was only matched in my experience by the sound of Dakotas bringing us our food in Burma. The mid-wife went into action more quickly than I suppose she usually did and we could draw breath and rejoice. So in 1971 two children appeared in the house photograph.

For us all was well, and the tale was complete when Jonathan appeared in circumstances altogether more normal, in hospital and giving decent notice of his arrival. We had thought that two years was the best gap; he appeared on Lizzie's second birthday. I had waited many years for completeness, and this statistical miracle was, I suppose, the icing on the cake, a decoration further enriched when many years later Jonathan became head boy of Haileybury. Little did I guess... But I have learnt not to guess too much; just to wait and see what happens and in circumstances like these to give thanks.

The Road From Mandalay

There was in fact a hazard. Not long after Jonathan arrived a large slab of plaster fell from the ceiling just round the corner from where he and Rachel were lying. I was on the games field at the time and a prefect came and said, "Sir, a bit of roof has fallen in, but all is well." The bursar came and inspected with ill ease the imperfections of one of his buildings. (Buildings have indeed their hazards. I was invigilating an exam one day in the main school hall, when I saw to my horror a piece of moulding detach itself from its fastenings and fall crashing to the floor, demolishing the desk that lay in its path. Miraculously no one was sitting there; there were few entrants for that exam. I assembled the unnerved candidates in the centre of the hall, free of all mouldings and called for help, a difficult task as I was the only invigilator. The bursar arrived and gasped. This was something new. We had a strange tale to tell to the Examination Board.)

The wonder continued. To climb is a joy; to take up the hills those you have generated is something special, for which I had waited long. I had to wait a little longer until they were ready. And so to Sedbergh, the hills that had given me some of my happiest days. The return brought to me a contentment that I can still sense; the hills giving their unchanging welcome. Did I ever think this was going to happen? Some of the first ascents were not wholly willing; going up Crook required continuous persuasion. But as the years went by the peaks came very willingly and we have a gallery of pictures of cairns that I had reached those years ago now mounted by my family: Winder, The Calf, Cautley Spout, Black Force. And there were the Lakes. Back to square one, but in company. The Langdale Pikes offered no problems; our young were growing up.

There was a particularly satisfying ascent of Scafell from Eskdale by Cam Spout and up a gully to Fox's Tarn and across scree to the summit. The weather was not good, so we felt we had overcome. At the top the visibility was almost nil. It is not a good top in these conditions; if you lose direction you can either go over the edge or end up in the wrong valley. Jonathan took out his compass and mobilising a skill gained at his scout troop guided us safely down to our car. It was a good day together.

Our horizons widened. There were higher places in Scotland and we talked about Monroes, the mountains that ambitious walkers 'bag'. We did not count our score but were glad to have reached a few: Ben Hope in the far north, one of the Ben Mores on which we overtook a youth group on the verge of mutiny; and on one ambitious day three near Pitlochry. By this time our strength patterns were changing. The encouraged were now the encouragers. My children were strong but I was no longer defying the years, and on that day by Pitlochry my son had to persuade me that I was not as weary as I thought I was. Marrying late was beginning to exact its price, but it was a small price to pay. The doing together was what mattered.

We looked further for our hills and found many. Europe beckoned, but in its time. I refused to take small children on long drives to foreign places when all they wanted was a good stretch of sand; and this we found in Norfolk in the scorching mid seventies. But when the time was ripe we checked our passports and set off. The wait was marvellously rewarded. An organisation called Alpine Holidays said they had flats to let in Haute Savoie in the village of Le Grand Bournand. It was a miraculous blind date. From our balcony we gazed in wonder at the ring of high places and in the sun that always shone we walked many miles. Then, happy to be tired we recalled each day and became one in a new way. I looked round at what Rachel and I had created and gave thanks to the one who had created us all.

The years transform. Our children set off from home and we watched, as they did more things than I had ever done at that age. They entered on a rite of passage denied to me, the 'gap year', drawing breath before life's learning started in earnest. Clare flew to Ethiopia by Aeroflot, surely one of life's false economies, hoping to arrive. She did, though arriving at Moscow Airport the day a German landed a light plane in Red Square found her in an atmosphere of crisis, and from Ethiopia she travelled the length of Africa. Jonathan, travelling across central Asia, had his passport stolen in Kazakhstan. He flew to Moscow for fresh documents, his flight financed by a British business man who saw his plight and simply handed him the money. He got a new passport but not the Pakistan visa he needed; he had planned to return by the Karakoram Highway from China to Pakistan. But he managed a Chinese visa and travelled to Beijing, three days in a hard seat coach and there got a standby seat on Polish Airlines. Lizzie was given a year's commission in the Army and at Her Majesty's expense saw Germany and Sardinia, sailing in the Baltic and playing rounders in Berlin.

And Rachel and me? We followed them with wonder, thankful for a generation unafraid of enterprise and a world that despite all its worries was still open. Remembering the thirties and their limited and uncertain horizons I could believe that not all was despair. And when having travelled they 'went up', as they say, two to Oxford, my cup was beginning to fill. Rachel and I watched and then embarked on our own rite of passage: ourselves 'neat' and undiluted by children and discovering who we really were. And our travels took on a new dimension; we could journey on our own. The Lakes were now ours and we went to new places; a day on the Mosedale Horseshoe and a brisk walk up Blencathra told us that we were still in good working order. There was a sombre moment. We were on the side of Harter Fell one day when we met a man who said, "Don't come this way. Someone has just died". He had been engaged in a cross country competition. A stretcher party arrived and we directed them to where the man lay. We walked on, just a little less buoyant.

It was time to celebrate. I retired finally in 1991, at seventy, and we went to Brittany, rejoicing that it was in term time, and two years later to remember twenty five years together we tasted the magic of Madeira, the gardener's paradise. We walked along paths like none other and though my left hip was clearly approaching the end of its shelf life there were many moments of wonder. I showed a friend a photo I had taken on a walk. "Is this the Himalayas?" he asked. Reeds Hotel gives few clues to the towering land that lies behind it.

My past nudged in. We travelled to Ethiopia, where Rachel had family connections. Our host said, "Here is someone you might like to meet." It was an Ethiopian who had served under Wingate. This strange remarkable man under whom I had served in Burma had helped to raise the tribes against the Italians in the war and had managed with tactics suited to this wild country and in his own particular way to help bring about their downfall. With the aid of an interpreter I talked with this warrior and we exchanged thoughts about our common commander. In a curious way Wingate has left his trail round the world.

And with the past came the East again. 1995 saw us in Pakistan visiting our elder daughter, the news of whose birth I had posted in the dormitory at Haileybury twenty seven years before. She was now a civil engineer and engaged in a vast project to reorganise the irrigation on the left bank of the River Indus, mending a system that the British had created many years before. For me it was another return journey and I was delighted that the words I had been forced to learn in the war still made sense and I could read the graceful coils of the Persian script, Urdu Redivivus.

Clare fashioned the holiday for us. Emirates took us in some style to Dubai, where the shopping area gave us a close imitation of Aladdin's Cave and then to Karachi, a troubled city we were glad to leave, and by road to Hyderabad where Clare worked, in an office with dozens of male Pakistanis, a dusty place where few would choose to live. We flew to Peshawar in a plane of a newly formed airline. It looked old and had seen service elsewhere, all the instructions being in Spanish, and we were glad to arrive. In Peshawar thousands of refugees huddled in encampments, refugees from the horrors of Afghanistan. Where did their future lie? Clare, who seemed to have contacts everywhere, arranged for a trip through the tribal areas to Kohat, once a British military outpost. We passed through a settlement where arms were manufactured, were advised not to linger and had to hurry back because nightfall would bring extra hazards. It was a fascinating glimpse into an area that the British had never really made up their mind how to control. It was the area where the Indian Army did its fighting. The change from there to the jungle was a significant one.

At Islamabad through another contact of Clare's we climbed into a plane for a flight that can have few equals, and which requires perfect weather, *through* the mountains with Nanga Parbat far above us, to Gilgit, once a remote military outpost. And then it was up the Karakoram Highway, an engineering wonder, driving a road through the mountains to China, fashioned by Pakistan and China as a strategic affront to India. Hundreds died to make it. We saw why as we drove along the edge of precipices and across raging torrents. We stopped about fifty miles from the Chinese border at 10,000 feet, and spent one of the coldest nights I can ever remember, a cold soon dispelled as the blazing sun rose and showed us a mountain wonderland.

We returned to Gilgit and awaited our return flight. We were unpleasantly surprised. We heard our plane seats being given to others, which I believe was standard practice. There was only one other way south; by road. There followed an eighteen hour bus journey, with us sitting in the front because that is where ladies had to sit. We were glad we went that way. It was a remarkable experience, and, although some of the precipices were unsettling and we had to change a wheel at one of the stops and from time to time the bus would stop and the other travellers got out and attuned their mats to Mecca for brief worship and towards the end the driver appeared almost to fall asleep, it gave the holiday a new dimension. We arrived at Rawalpindi at about 2 am, and Flashmans Hotel took us in without a murmur. My father had helped to administer this town in the 1930's and we entered the Anglican church to re-enter the Raj, mock gothic and with memorials to the many British who died far from home, and at many different ages. How often Pindi had appeared in my parents' conversation. And here it all was, and by it the Grand Trunk Road which almost smelt of Kipling. To come back with another was a remembering of a special kind.

But with the remembering came a change. We did not come as rulers but as friends and we conversed easily. I said I had fought in the war, and they thought I meant the war against India, an enmity echoed in every newspaper leading article and in every blocked border crossing.

I showed Rachel my past, and it was disappearing. It was a marvellous way to say farewell.

Is joy infectious? Some ageing bachelor friends, seeing our union and seeing that all things are possible, took courage and took wives. We have learnt that it is not wise to think that we can fashion our future, but to be willing to be surprised by joy.

16.
Surprised by Joy

It was January 1944. It was India. We had alighted from our train after a six day journey from our training area in central India and were preparing to march towards the concentration area before launching on Wingate's second long range penetration operation into Burma. It was a march of one hundred and twenty miles. On the first night in the hills Jack Masters, the Brigade Major, turned to me and made an unexpected request: that every evening I should read a passage from the New Testament. And so I read the splendid verses from Paul's letter to the Galatians, "The fruit of the Spirit is love, joy, peace, patience, kindness, goodness, faithfulness, gentleness and self-control." And each night I read and men who declared no faith listened to me.

How come that I was doing this? They thought that I had something which might help us if death was near. They were correct. It is a faith that the English are curiously embarrassed to talk about, an embarrassment that other faiths and other peoples do not seem to share. But as it has governed my life, and as it is my life that occupies these pages, and I have given hints to it earlier, it cannot be left out. It was as a boy by a skating rink high up in the Swiss Alps in 1937 that I found faith, a simple act of trust based not on fantasy or wishful thinking but on a God who had showed himself and in incontrovertible words had shown the way to life. Was this an escape for a boy cut off for long periods from the closest human relationships? I think not. The Christian faith, as I found, was not an escape; it was a challenge and those who profess it know that it is as difficult as swimming against the current. It is as difficult as Peter found it in a moment of peril when asked, "Are you one of them?" He was courting serious trouble; we just face embarrassment.

In the holidays my faith was nourished and sustained by a remarkable organisation dedicated to building up brick by brick a personal faith in Christ. It is evangelical, a word that used to amuse but now disturbs. Those who draw back from it in distaste are either alarmed or upset to realise that it is now the powerhouse of the Church of England. Its certainties they cannot stomach, thinking them naïve and ascribing to it that most misunderstood of all words, *fundamentalist*. The arrogance of some of its practitioners they rightly abhor. Its theology they largely suspect, I think, because their trust in the Scriptures is moderated by scholarly misgivings. and they are affronted when the words 'born again' slip off the tongue so readily, cheapening into a slick password what are the most revolutionary words ever spoken. Black and white are to them suspect shades. The world after all is grey. And the worship that some evangelicals indulge in seems to them to be embarrassingly extrovert and damaging to the dignity of their God. Yet having pitted all they can against these wild ones they see something remarkably vibrant and confident and in a world that seems to have lost its way they may wonder if the truth may be there, and they see that their scholarship can now be taken seriously; and they see full churches.

Oxford University is a very superior talking shop. Fuelled by coffee and strong opinions you can talk the night through and pretend that you have changed the world. I had a chance to share my faith without inhibitions and to identify where I stood. This was then firmly in the Oxford Inter Collegiate Christian Union, the evangelical flagship. Those who could met to pray each day and at weekends gathered to hear the Bible being expounded and Christ preached. Many laughed at us, but they could not gainsay our fervour. Even the clever who curled their lips saw something worth acknowledging.

But on looking back I see some chinks in what we thought was the armour of God. Evangelicals were then in a kind of ghetto. They were small in number and determined to withstand the pressures of a world whose values seemed a threat to their faith. They must withstand that world lest it endanger what they believed. 'The world' had a deep theological meaning; it meant where God did not reign.

So we must flee it. This meant avoiding plays and films and dances and many kinds of book and alcohol; and mixing with girls with care. And I felt that it was not right to join the Oxford Union to avoid a taint with what might corrupt. In effect it cut me off from quite a few areas of university activity. When people say, "Did you enjoy your time at Oxford"? I have to remember not only the unusual time in history that it was with the war on and the war just finished, but also the restraints I put on myself. Today these restraints seem absurd, indeed laughable, and the coming of television certainly made a nonsense of our strictures on films, but then they signalled total commitment. The question is: if the values underlying this commitment are misplaced do they lose their force? In short; were we heroes of faith or ridiculously misled? Growing confidence has enabled evangelicals to dismantle some of the defences that they put up against an unbelieving world and to climb out of the ghetto. They hope that the bathwater has gone out but not the baby.

But there was zeal and this is a commodity not lightly discarded. I arrived at Haileybury ready to teach both what I knew and what I believed. They had to come in that order, but I hoped that the one could infuse the other. I had come to a believing school. The chapel stood imposingly in the main quadrangle, towering over the other buildings, and here we worshipped: sleepily at nine o'clock each morning and more consciously twice on Sunday. And once a year many boys went forward to be confirmed, much of the preparation being in the hands of housemasters who felt more or less comfortable in this role. Scripture was placed firmly in the teaching programme. To summarise, we were a Christian school.

This framework instructed the boys in the faith and in the worship patterns of the Church of England, but it was not signally designed to instil zeal for this faith or personal commitment; that in the opinion of some was to bring excessive pressure on one's pupils. But once a year we invaded their hearts. This was the Lent Mission in which a speaker was invited to come for several days to expound the Christian faith and invite response from the boys. Each evening they were offered the chance to come and listen, and if they wished to have an interview with the missioner. The impact of these talks varied with the quality of the speaker, but they always aroused interest.

In 1966 remarkable things happened. The speaker was the Reverend David MacInnes, a very gifted proclaimer of the Gospel. And he set the school alight. Eh? I repeat: he set the school alight, unearthing a huge hunger for the truth. My house prefects, in whom I had not detected any great religious zeal, came to me and asked if I could suggest a way in which they could hold Bible studies. I contained my surprise and made suggestions.

Many sought David's counsel and I believe found faith. The Christian Union which met under my auspices found itself crowded; and many were eager to go further in their faith by attending the Christian houseparty that I had helped to run for many years. Something had happened to the school which delighted some but perplexed others: what was going on? Was this zeal healthy? There was that word that sat so uneasily in the minds of the mainstream of the Church of England – emotion. The fact that I appeared to be sane helped matters and the boys affected seemed to have been strengthened.

The revival – for that is what I was bold enough to describe – continued unabated. In 1974 the Lent missioner was the Reverend David Watson, that most remarkable and charismatic figure of modern times who held spellbound all who listened to him - he had filled the Albert Hall - and he did it without histrionics, just a compelling and totally focussed conviction. The boys flocked to hear him. He had interviews with 135, and he believed that 61 found faith. I have the names in front of me as I write. The Sunday meetings, gatherings for Bible study that I had been presiding over for some years, became so crowded that they filled two large rooms in the flat which I now shared with my wife and we had to install a relay. I watched amazed as the movement of the spirit continued, as it did for many years.

But was this a passing emotional phase, the zeal of youth? On the 11th of May 1996 about seventy old boys met at Haileybury for a Christian reunion, a day of remembrance and thanks. We met in the school chapel and sang and remembered those days of epiphany and heard testimonies from those who told of their coming to faith and we lunched and prayed and talked to each other and wondered if any school had witnessed anything like this. Many others wrote and said they were sorry they could not come. Their faith had stood the test of time in many places and in many callings. And one wrote in terms which warmed my wife and myself in moments of doubt. 'The Rhodes Jameses, whose ministry seems to have had such a profound significance over the years for so many of us.' 'Over the years.' It was for real.

17.
Into open country

When you marry late, the future needs rearranging. It was 1981.

In the independent sector teachers are usually required to retire at sixty. Two reasons are given for this, one more likely than the other: by that age teaching at a boarding school leaves a person worn out; and teachers at the top of the salary scale are very expensive. The school needs fresh and cheaper staff. They gave me a fine farewell and said things designed to warm and encourage. I had given and received much.

I was in fact ready to go, conscious that I had indeed run out of steam. Boarding schools have an unusual *cursus honorum*. When you give up your boarding house you become just a member of the teaching staff and the drop is considerable in both status and pay. My friends quoted to me what was said of Britain, "You have lost an empire and have not yet found a role." I found it a kind of vacuum; much less worry but a considerable loss of identity. Fortunately there were only four years of it and I left the place that had been my life for thirty four years with thanks and without regret.

And my children? They were eight, ten and twelve. The unusual age range in my family brought some amusing misunderstandings. On one occasion someone turned to Rachel and said of Clare, "She looks just like Granddad", and on another occasion, "Your father-in-law doesn't seem to be able to control the children." I took a somewhat mischievous delight in people's puzzlement as they tried to guess our relationships. But of course behind the fun there were some problems. Retirement does not usually bring with it a young family, and a teacher's pension, unassisted for five years by a state pension, is in serious need of reinforcement. I must continue to work. Rachel and I first put ourselves on the market as a couple and offered ourselves in a number of directions. The replies were sympathetic but yielded no jobs. So we then took what might reasonably be called a step of faith. We would go to Cambridge. It was a place we had got to know a little, being not far from Haileybury, and despite not being Oxford it was clearly a place where a lot of learning went on; and learners need teachers.

There was also a chance coincidence. The MP for Cambridge was my much younger brother Robert whose arrival had so surprised me in 1933. He held the seat for sixteen years until resigning at the election of 1992. So when I said who I was it tended to mean something. The baby I had pushed round Kensington Gardens, the small boy I had punted down the Thames and sailed across the Broads had gained a distinction so far removed from the limited horizons of a very ordinary family that we could only watch and wonder. A clerk of the House of Commons, Fellow of All Souls College, Oxford, Head of the

Institute for the Study of International Institutions at Sussex University, Assistant to Kurt Waldheim, Secretary General of the United Nations ("I am working for a Nazi") and elected for Cambridge at a by-election in 1976. All that and a string of books about men and politics and editing the speeches of Winston Churchill. My own role in all this was a rather humble one, "Are you any relation to …?" Fame by proxy has its limitations. We said a very sad goodbye to him in 1999 at the chapel of the House of Commons, a farewell to one who had reached far beyond us and achieved more than we could have imagined. He went much too soon.

There was a further connection with Cambridge: MR James – Montague Rhodes James – was a relation, the second cousin of my grandfather. To the general public he was known as our greatest ghost story writer. To the academic world he was a renowned Provost of Kings and an antiquarian who dug deep into the past and knew more about stained glass windows than most. He went on to be Provost of Eton, but Cambridge was his first love.

In October 2006 Rachel and I went to what could be called a kind of family occasion. We went to the 12th century Leper Chapel in north east Cambridge, and there we saw enacted under a Norman arch with guttering candles a splendid rendition of two of M R James's stories – *Canon Alberic's Scrapbook* and *The Mezzotint*; academia playing with our imaginations. It was a virtuoso performance. We clapped and returned to a city where the present was pressing in, the city we had decided was where our future lay.

At Haileybury we were in tied housing and we had to get out by the first of August 1981. We drove to Cambridge and, after a quick reconnaissance and some help from a colleague who had moved there, found a house. I had a house that I had bought for my parents and that would have to be sold. A problem: the awkward gap between selling and buying, every mover's nightmare. We were saved by an act of extreme generosity of a friend of ours who forwarded to us the money for the new house and said he would wait for repayment when we had sold ours. I took the cheque to the bank and the cashier drew a deep breath. This might qualify as a miracle; it was.

Would the miracle continue? It did. The start was a defining one: crossing the great educational divide into the public sector. It was a new world. I was given a fill-in part-time post for two terms at a comprehensive school just north of Cambridge while a teacher took her maternity leave. The entrance into this sector was a trifle droll. I was an untrained teacher, having never taken the training course and so I was put on probation for four years. The probationary period was usually two years, but this was a part time job. I received a duplicated hand-out telling me of my Union rights, a document which started with the words, "As this is your first teaching appointment." It was a good laugh. The job was an easy one, sixth form economics, and I discovered that sixth forms in comprehensives were quite small, many having left at sixteen. They listened to what I had to say and when they were examined they were successful. I had been put in at the shallow end, well within my depth.

The two terms finished. Where next? Where, indeed? What followed was a kind of educational fruit salad. I hawked my services to anyone who could offer me a job, and many did. The public sector had another arena, the sixth form college, an institution not wholly clear about its identity – what did 'college' mean? A through-put of two years to receive, identify, charge with knowledge and send out with the best qualifications that they could manage; for a teacher with academic aspirations it was a great place to be. There are two such in Cambridge, at Long Road and Hills Road and I taught part time economics at both. The latter was and maybe still is an academic powerhouse for which people queue up to enter containing many children of university staff, and I found myself challenged and stretched, not always knowing the answers to the questions they threw at me.

In other ways it was another world. A boy and a girl in my class were said to be living together. I took a party to London to visit the Bank of England and the money market. This couple missed the bus and caught up with us later. "I'm terribly sorry. We overslept." It was also new for me to have pupils arriving by bus, some from quite far off places. On one occasion a couple were late; lateness was a continuing problem. What made them different was their excuse. "We have just effected a citizen's arrest. We saw someone grabbing a woman's handbag, so we chased him and took him along to the police." I judged that truth was stranger than fiction and congratulated them.

Those were good places to be - later my two daughters went to each of them - but they did not quite bring home the bacon and I looked elsewhere to fill in the gaps. My search took me to the academic undergrowth, the world of tutorial colleges, private institutions that for a significant price coached people to the edges of their ability and gave to those who had failed at school or for whom school had been abhorrent the chance to reach the qualifications they wanted; or, to cut a long story short, A Level.

Some had failed this magic talisman and wanted to have another shot; others preferred to call these places their school, having fled what was usually the private sector. They do not like to be called 'crammers' and for most of them in 1981 this was a misnomer; the market was competitive enough for them to seek a wider remit and many called themselves independent sixth form colleges.

When I searched for jobs there were still some odd corners. In one the lady running the establishment prowled round the gaunt building in which she operated to make sure everyone was working; they had to do it all on the spot. In another I taught in the basement and in the next room a mad chef raged, I never discovered why, and the teachers had to record the amount of work they had marked. It was a busy life. One year I was teaching at four different places and bicycling between them. Servitude? No, a deep satisfaction that teaching was still fun, that the wolf was far away from the door and that retirement was something to laugh at.

In fact after a bit my hectic schedule subsided and I found a full time job at a tutorial college with a difference. It offered small classes, but much else: boarding, a full programme of sports and other outside activities and a pastoral network unusual for this kind of organisation; there was a caring necessary to remind the pupils that freedom needed a framework. I taught there full time for six years, and when I retired they made me astonishingly their Patron. This was at seventy, when my son had just left school. It was an autumn to my teaching life that I could never have imagined. It was also highly profitable. I discovered that I could draw my full teacher's pension while teaching full time and after sixty five no national insurance.

To this I added some years of examining at O Level Economics, the scripts coming from overseas from many different parts of the world, including a set from Harare Central Prison. There was little pleasure in this; it was purely a money-raising enterprise, though some of the overseas schools were so awful that at times there was little to mark. And you got a nice free lunch at a London hotel as you sought to agree on the standards of the marking. I earned far more than I did at Haileybury, which gave me a certain satisfaction, and this was teaching without all the other cares that came with boarding schools. I could just teach. It was a new lease of life.

The teaching stopped, but I believed that there was still much to learn and as I thought that longevity was as much a function of the mind as of the body. I did not want to bequeath to Rachel too long a widowhood and anyway learning was fun, I set my mind to it. There is in Cambridge an institution tailor-made for me: The University of the Third Age, which is like no other. Here oldies teach each other in a very large variety of classes. At present there are about two thousand members and about two hundred classes. We gather, some in classrooms hired by the organisation but mostly in people's houses and week by week we find out things we never knew before; and once a week if we so wish we can attend a central lecture and listen to an expert speaker on almost anything. Experts are not too hard to come by in a place like Cambridge. At the moment I am in a group studying Wittgenstein but with only fair success; I cannot grasp what he means by 'understanding.' The incomprehensions of 1946 are still with me. To resolve them now would be remarkable. I tend to take comfort from Browning, "Man's reach must exceed his grasp, or what's the heaven for?" These much repeated words must have comforted many.

What do you *do* in Cambridge? I am asked; but not very often. And when I wonder what sort of place it is I wander down King's Parade. And there I see buildings that people have come from all over the world to see. And I see the people. They have come to Cambridge not only to see its beauty but also to share its learning and to learn its language and our world is suddenly full of people from many places trying to finish their PhD's or attending one of the many language schools.

Many of them are Japanese, and for me that rings a complex bell. They have the special kind of charm and graciousness of their nation; and some have special agendas. One young Japanese man Mr R Matsui came to me and said, "We young Japanese want to say sorry for all our grandfathers did to you during the war. How do we set about it?" I was moved and took thought. I wrote to the local Burma Star POW Society – large numbers of the Cambridgeshire Regiment were taken prisoner by the Japanese. The secretary wrote back curtly: the only people who should apologise were the ones who committed the atrocities.

My young friend was undeterred. He set up a gathering to discuss the issue. I was joined by two others, who had both been Burma POW's. We met in Darwin College before a small audience of Japanese and people engaged in Japanese studies. We talked about our experiences and said it was time to forget our enmities. Unresolved hatreds, we argued, harmed the haters as much as the hated. We opened the meeting to questions, and these lasted an hour. We all learnt much.

I was in fact engaged in a reconciliation project. Some of us who had fought in Burma set up an organisation we called The Burma Campaign

Fellowship Group. Its purpose was to meet with the Japanese we had fought against and make friends. As the chairman says, "BCFG is firmly committed to the view that the Japanese are a people with whom reconciliation is greatly needed, and it is absurd to let distant events however painful at the time, cloud our present day perspectives." The organisation was not specifically Christian, but its ethos surely was. We met each year and dined together and met Japanese warriors and also members of the Japanese Embassy.

On 17 August 1995, the Sunday nearest to the day that we celebrated fifty years after VJ Day we held a service in Westminster Abbey and invited the Japanese. It was the only gathering that they were invited to attend. At the same time another service of a very different kind was going on in St Paul's Cathedral attended by the Queen and Prince Philip in which past animosities were paraded and described in the Press as 'bitter'. They looked back with barely disguised hatred. We had an act of reconciliation, and garlands were laid on the unknown warrior's tomb, prayers were said and the Dean of Westminster, Michael Mayne, preached words of peace. The contrast was stark and regrettable.

We continued to meet our foes. In 1996 I received a letter from an English teacher working in the Gyosei International School in Japonica Lane, Milton Keynes, a boarding school for the children of Japanese working in this country. "Would you be prepared to visit our school to participate in a seminar-type event on the subject of World War Two and the issues surrounding reconciliation in particular. Of course I do not know your views on these matters and would invite you regardless of whether you feel inclined towards reconciliation or not, since it is just as important for my students to realise why some British people will never forgive their country as it is for them to realise why others have done".

On 26 November we drove first to Bletchley Park to see where in the war the great cipher breaking operation had taken place with particular interest in the Japanese section and then to the school. With me was Alan Eliott, a BCFG member who had been a prisoner on the notorious railway, and his wife. We introduced ourselves and talked about reconciliation and forgiveness and answered some hesitant but challenging questions. The following year a larger party returned to an extended seminar. There were only ten students there, their English assisted by Miss Tomoyo Nakao who was researching on British POW's at Essex University. It was a small happening, but we believed that we had done something real.

In Cambridge the story continued. In 1996 on 11 November something moving happened. Among the many Japanese in the city was Mrs Nobuko Kosuge, the wife of a Japanese research student. She was an authority on wartime problems having translated a book on the Tokyo war crimes trials and written a book of her own. She wanted to make a gesture on behalf of her people. Dressed in kimono and obi she knelt at the War Memorial and asked forgiveness for what her people had done. One ex POW went up to her and said he had vowed never to speak to a Japanese person until then. And in the words of the local paper, "We had to prise them away from each other."

Events have a habit of telescoping. Yesterday I was explaining all this to some young at a local youth centre. I joined what I thought was a rather rough and tumble collection, but when I spoke of war and what I had seen of it and how we needed to forgive I was aware of many eyes riveted to my words. They knew little and when they were told they were gripped. They questioned me on many things, not to catch me out but to resolve questions that had been hiding in their minds. It was encouraging to think that they wanted a dose of reality. And today arrived a book giving the most comprehensive account yet of the Japanese prison camps. There is a lot to forgive.

The learning was all about us. A pastor from South Korea came to me and asked me if I could help him help him with his PhD in theology. The title *The eschatological hermeneutics of John Calvin and Wolfhart Pannenberg*. You smile. I know little about the subject though I learnt quite a bit as we proceeded. My job was to sort out his English which was in fact rather good. He was successful and he gave me the first bound copy of his thesis with the generous inscription, "Hemingway once said, 'Having a great mentor is indeed a great blessing'. Thank for being just that for me". He lunched my wife and me after the ceremony, a gathering of people from many lands. There was a girl from Indonesia researching orang-utans in Sumatra whom we met through a local hospitality scheme. And a newly married Thai couple, both doing further degrees who used us as their base and referred to us movingly as 'Our dear papa and mama in England.' As I write they are in the USA and Thailand searching facts. The world is full of unanchored academics.

Every so often you get a big surprise. Some years ago some people from Germany spent a night with us on their way to the wedding of a mutual friend. They came from Dresden, a place with a loaded name. Hesitantly I asked, "What do you think of the Dresden raid?" The answer was astonishing. "We deserved it. It was the exact anniversary of a terrible persecution of the Jews there." They added that the day before the raid a pastor said that he had had a vision. All must flee the city, because on the morrow the city would be destroyed. It seems that the citizens of Dresden paid little heed to the warnings.

In such a setting it has not been difficult to continue to think. I do not play golf, nor do I garden and I must find other means to keep my joints in good working order but I treasure the continuing ability to make sense of things in a world where there is too much nonsense. In Cambridge there is sense of many kinds. On 28 February 1953 Francis Crick, flushed with the double helix, burst into the Eagle Inn and announced to what must have been a startled gathering, "We have found the secret of life." Whenever I hear this story, I feel like retorting, "Has God heard about this?" It is the old awkward interface between How? and Why? It is the Cavendish Laboratory looking across to Kings College Chapel and wondering what they have in common. Is pure mind just that?

Fortunately the soul is well represented in Cambridge and there are as many avenues to God as in most other places. It is a kind of ecclesiastical supermarket and you can shop around to find the church that suits you and you try to sing with conviction, "The Church's one foundation." And ponder what weight that foundation has to bear.

I searched. The evangelical is ill at ease in the deep rituals of Little St Mary's and does not find in Great St Mary's the cutting edge that he perhaps rather narrowly desires. There remain a clutch of churches where the gospel takes centre stage and where many young foregather: Holy Trinity, where Charles Simeon carried out his great ministry in the nineteenth century, and St Andrew the Great, a resurrected church in the city centre whose congregation had outgrown the Round Church and had moved. Students come to these churches in large numbers to be instructed in the faith and to be encouraged to extend it through the activities of the University Christian Union. They are not afraid to be zealous.

And if you are an evangelical who is looking for a more relaxed liturgical style and a family feel St Barnabas may beckon. This is where I stopped, struck by a pastor, the Reverend Dennis Lennon, a man of genius, much friendliness where everyone is taken as they are and a place where children matter. I found myself surrounded by a throng of the very young and facing new liturgical challenges rather late in life in a cultural setting that reminds me how old I am: guitars in full fling but with words that matter. In a life committed to the young perhaps this is an appropriate autumn, though the strain of accommodating to the young and the way they approach God has increased as the years have gone by. Am I willing to be deafened by truth? I am beginning to wonder. But I am encouraged to discover that they are willing to hear what I say as I preach and explain to them that our faith is not just for Christmas but for life.

And it is for all. I found myself in the women's section of a high security prison, the place where Myra Hindley expired, a dark land of towering fences where a myriad doors are locked and unlocked everyday and there seem few people around; a cold quiet. The inmates were mostly Afro-Caribbean and mostly drug carriers and many of them were Christian believers who had lost their way. Paradoxically I found an unusual freedom in speaking my faith and challenging them to return to theirs. We sang hymns that they chose and most of them knew and we took refreshments and chatted and I heard many kinds of despair and regret. Leaving I felt empty but hoped I had filled others. They needed filling. Some years ago I had embarked on a study on the theory of punishment. Arriving at rather a cul-de sac I handed over my work to a young man who was working on a Master's degree. From my study one fact emerged on which all seemed to agree: that prison achieves very little.

At the other end of the scale: on some Sundays I have had a distinguished listener. Professor Stephen Hawking came to our church from time to time. On one occasion I had to preach on Wisdom and so I was anxious about what he made of it. He growled his general agreement. But on another occasion when I spoke from a savage part of the Old Testament he was reasonably furious. When I was first surprised by joy I never imagined that such challenges would come my way. I hope there will be some more. In Cambridge you cannot stop thinking.

18.
Back to battle

In the early spring of 1995 I received a phone call. "This is the BBC". There can be few sentences that generate such interest, and excitement, unsettling only if you have something to hide.

I had received the same message in 1978, followed by the magic information, "We liked your script." So much so that I gave a talk on Radio Three on Paul Scott, to commemorate the first anniversary of his death. He was the novelist who brought the Raj to life in an unforgettable way in his *Raj Quartet,* novels which were turned into one of the finest television series ever made under the heading *The Jewel in the Crown.* I tried to show how closely his words mirrored what I and many others had experienced over the years which I have described in the pages of this book. It was broadcast in term time, and although it was at an hour when most lights should have been out clearly many boys had listened and next morning they greeted me with commendatory grins. It was fame of a pleasant kind.

In 1995 the script was more complex and even more exciting. "This is Mark Fielder. I would like to come over to you and talk." He had been given my name because I had written a book on one rather unusual part of the Burma war. We talked and then he said, "Would you like to come to Burma to help make a film of the campaign to celebrate fifty years after VJ Day?" Hoping I had heard aright – it was beyond all that I had expected – I gave an instant and loud Yes, and awaited further instructions, of which there had to be many. Passport, visa, blood groups, clothing, "Forget the Armani, travel light. The weather will be extremely hot". (It was; over 100 degrees.). We were being very efficiently shepherded by the charming PA, Jessica Powell. The filming schedule arrived, with the names of the party. Mark Fielder was the producer, a specialist in military programmes, quietly professional, and the presenter the matchless Charles Wheeler, scarcely younger than the 'veterans' having seen some of the war, but still at his age with a perceptiveness and integrity that few can equal. The cameraman was the burly and splendidly reliable Mike Fox and the sound recordist Bob Webber. And the veterans? There were three of us. Bruce Kinloch had been in the 3rd Gurkhas and I met him at the regimental centre on his return from the Burma front in 1942; he had just won the Military Cross. John Hill was from the Berkshire Regiment. He had had a relentlessly fierce campaign as a company commander and had won the Military Cross by the Irrawaddy. Beside these two warriors I seemed rather a lay figure.

We were due to meet at Terminal Four at Heathrow on the evening of the fourth of April, but the operation very nearly didn't get off the ground. Mark Fielder was told that he could not go; he was *persona non grata*. Five years earlier he had written an article for The Guardian which contained "uncomplimentary references to the military government." Charles Wheeler said that he would not go with any other producer, but relented and said he was willing to work under the researcher and assistant producer, Tuppence Stone; a second best, but possible. It was a bad start. This crisis set off some frantic diplomacy with the British Ambassador in Rangoon, the Burmese Ambassador in London and several other intermediaries. Peace was declared and Mark arrived a little breathless at Terminal Four for Flight BA 9.

Charles had work to do. He had no first hand knowledge of the Burma campaign, and he had to learn fast. He took a copy of my book *Chindit* and during the eleven and a half hour flight to Bangkok he read furiously. The speed at which he digested what I wrote was remarkable. At Bangkok we waited for two and a half hours. I chatted with Charles and he showed me something of the skill of his profession; he listened closely. At Rangoon we were met by our researcher, Tuppence, who had spent three weeks with our Burmese 'fixer', Jamieson, planning and travelling along the route we wished to take, and then to Baiyoke Kandawgyi Hotel, Hotel on the Lake "There is no other hotel with a view like this in the world". There, after an excellent meal and much talk, we retired to bedrooms so comprehensively air conditioned that we had to pile on blankets. It was a nightfall that I could never have dreamt of.

A day in Rangoon. Bruce went to the docks and before the cameras recalled the shambles that there had been in 1942; shambles was the defining word of that year when we were thrown out of Burma at a speed which must have surprised the Japanese and landed us with one of the longest retreats in history, a campaign that has been described as 'a hell of a licking.' John and I, whose tales lay elsewhere, visited that marvellous Buddhist pile, the Schwedagon Pagoda. I had seen in our home paintings by my grandfather of the great building, but now I could see for myself.

On the following day we drove twenty miles out of Rangoon to the great British War Cemetery at Htaukkyant. Here was the price of victory. There were the graves of 6368 of the fallen, and on huge plaques the names of 26,380 who were never found. I saw the grave of Jim Blaker who won the Victoria Cross about a mile from my HQ and of one of my sergeants who had taken the wrong turning when withdrawing from a very tight spot. The bodies had been retrieved from remote places and one can wonder at the huge achievements of the War Graves Commission. While the camera rolled, Bruce observed the names of those who had died in the action where he won his MC but who were never found, and John hovered round the graves of many of his men - they had taken a terrible pounding. Mike Fox climbed up to the top of the stone memorial and from a delicate perch swung his camera to take in a lovely garden with memories not easy to digest. His pictures were used appropriately as the dying shots of the film.

The next day we flew north. We were due to leave our hotel at 0430, and I nearly didn't make it. My alarm was due to sound at 0400, but I heard nothing. And then I heard a fearful pounding at my door and surfaced; it was 0415. At 0425 I joined the others who were beginning to wonder. We reached the airport just before 0500. It was a scrum, but Jessica, the perfect PA, had food ready and we took off at 0650. We were meant to fly straight to Mandalay, but the head of state was visiting that city and it would not do to clash with him. So we stopped for an hour and a half at Pagan, a wonder city of over 5000 temples and monuments, where my parents had spent some of their honeymoon; sadly there was no chance to see its wonders. We arrived at Mandalay, my birthplace at 0945 and drove to the Emerald Land Inn.

Two features command Mandalay; Fort Dufferin, a huge area with walls so massive that they withstood point blank battering by medium artillery and the Hill which rises precipitously to the north east. Fortunately for us the Japanese evacuated the Fort before we could attempt to storm it. The Hill was captured by a night assault by a battalion of the 4th Gurkhas, but it had to be cleared out and we took the cameras up for John to describe the mopping up process. This was effective and brutal. Japanese caught in a tunnel were flushed out by pouring in fuel and setting light to it. Those who escaped the flames rushed out and were shot or flung themselves down the hillside. John explained this to Charles, and I wondered if viewers would find it too distressing. I don't think they did; the screen has hardened us to almost anything.

We had time in Mandalay and took a taxi. I tried to locate my past, calling in at the church where I thought I had been baptised. I spoke with the Burmese pastor but he was unable get access to the records. It did not look right. There was one church where John had found a Japanese officer praying during the recapture. What did he do with him? I cannot remember, which is perhaps just as well. I took photographs of the Irrawaddy and the Fort and compared them with pictures painted by a grandfather that are now in my sitting room; the resemblance is uncanny. It was a wandering that gathered in so much of my family. That evening there was Thai and lentil soup and much drinking. We would turn to Jessica ask, "Can the BBC afford another round?" The BBC could.

We took off at 1152 for a three quarter hour journey to Myitkina. This was in the extreme north where my own battle took place. I tried to take a picture of the airport. "No", said our minder. "Yes", said Jessica as she distracted the officials. At the terminal, not much more than a hut, Mike Fox turned to me and knowing my religious leanings said, "Richard, here is someone you might like to meet." It was the Bishop of Myitkina, who pastored about 10,000 Christians in very wild country, a diocese which had to contend not only with the scorn of Buddhists but also their own kind embroiled in a fierce theological controversy. The bishop was going to Lambeth. What solace would he find there?

We sat outside the airport and lunched, and waited. There was a setback. The head of state, whose progress we seemed to have been following, was in Myitkina and so there must be no filming. Mark was undismayed. We drove a few miles north to what looked like jungle and filmed. I made my way through the undergrowth in a parody of the sweaty stumblings of those distant years describing the heat and thirst but also the strange safety that thick jungle sometimes gave one and the unwillingness of the Japanese always to follow us; and that sweet sound, a Dakota about to drop what we needed. And then the only funny bit of the film. When the weather turned back the planes and we had no food, we were forced to eat some of our mules. "I do not recommend mule steak," I said to Charles, "it is impenetrable". Charles did his best to keep a straight face, but at the press showing there was loud laughter.

Richard Rhodes James

And to complete the unreality of the situation we repaired to a Chinese restaurant for a splendid meal at which Mark proposed a toast to the three of us and Jamieson, a very friendly and helpful interpreter. We also had a 'minder' who said nothing and was just a presence. I hope he enjoyed it.

Next day there was a setback. Mark was unwell and spent most of the day in bed. Tuppence took over and tried her hand at directing us. We walked by the Irrawaddy and told tales about that defining river. Wingate's force had crossed it in 1943 to their cost – they found themselves trapped – and my own brigade had made a mess of crossing it in 1944 because we could not get our mules to swim. Now it looked beautiful. I also tried to locate the airstrip that we flew out of after five months in enemy territory, but sadly we were halted at a military checkpoint and told to go no further. The soldier, a Christian, told us that the head of state was visiting. It was that man again.

Next day we started early. A private train was going to carry us down the spine of Burma and we could film at our leisure. Reveille at 0500. Our train was due at 0600 but there had been a derailment and we did not leave Myitkina until 0720. The first stop was Mogaung which a Chindit brigade had captured after a ferocious battle and two VC's in July 1944. Its capture was first attributed to the Chinese. The brigade commander, the supreme warier Mike Calvert, signalled, "Chinese take Mogaung. We take umbrage". A query is said to have come from the Americans. "Umbrage? Where is that?" It was sobering to look at the site of other people's gallantry. I was there just after its capture; a very different sight.

At 3 pm we reached Namkin, a place of no importance except that a few miles away in woods so dense that we could not reach was the hill where my brigade had been surrounded and pounded for three weeks and from which we escaped either by the exhaustion of our enemy or by a miracle, or perhaps a bit of both, and in which we had to leave our badly wounded behind. I sat by a stream and told my story. It had an ending so stark that I had to choose my words carefully; we had to shoot many of our wounded to prevent them falling into enemy hands. I do not know what the viewers made of this; the Sunday papers made quite a lot. Those were my last words.

That evening Tuppence surprisingly proposed my toast; whether because she had a regard for me or because my words had gone home I do not know. In either case I was gratified.

The train continued slowly on its way, stopping at our behest and also to allow other trains to pass; we were effectively jamming up the railway system. "Stop", I said, "this is a bridge we blew", and we did, as we did at other places which Mike Fox thought showed promise, Mark suggesting gently. At the stations Burma's lovely people stared at us and there were some shy smiles. Always we harboured a deep regret that a lovely land and such lovely people should be so misused by their government. There were some ironic comparisons. The British had not allowed the Burmese to govern themselves, but it was a deprivation of the politest kind, only tempered by force if their subjects had other ideas, and they had used the Burmese economy to further their own interests. The Burmese had been given the freedom they yearned. They were now free – to be oppressed by their own and to see their economy ruined.

We stopped at Shwebo, which lay to the north west of Mandalay. It was an important place in the campaign as the British forces debouched on to the central plain to prepare for the crossing of the Irrawaddy. We spent a comfortable night in the train and next day, Good Friday we drove to Kyaukmyuang, a very pleasant village by the great river. This was one of the main crossing places and John told the story as they chugged across. My brother Bill had crossed very near here. Opposed crossings are a challenge, but the Japanese could not defend everywhere and as John explained all went well; the test came later, and it was a severe one, as the Japanese reacted and tried to push us back into the river.

There followed a very bumpy 2¾ hour bus journey to Mandalay. As we went through the city we were showered with water. The water festival, an important celebration, was in full swing; a grandstand had been erected from which to see the fun. It was good to see the people doing what they might call their own thing without let or hindrance. My other self meditated on the Cross; and I joined the others for a more earthly encounter with good food and drink.

15th April. Breakfast at 0610. Bruce was unwell. D. and V. and a very bad night. If you take veterans with you their health is a hazard. He went to the airport in a car. On arriving at Rangoon we found that the water festival was reaching its climax and there was fun and games in which they tried to involve us. When we could not dodge the water we submitted to it as best we could, hoping to add to the delight of people short of joy. It took us over an hour to reach our hotel.

Easter Day. Our last day's filming and a rendez vous with disaster. We drove north east and breakfasted at Pegu, where in 1945 the last

Japanese were engaged. Our objective was the Sittang River. Here on the 23rd of February 1942 disaster struck. The 17th Indian Division had been retreating towards Rangoon and reached the Sittang. The Japanese were close behind and it was vital that they were denied the crossing of the river. By a series of misjudgements the bridge was blown with two brigades on the wrong side; they were trapped. It was the turning point in the campaign, leaving Rangoon open to the enemy. Here Bruce comes into the picture. After attempting to defend his position by the bridge he swam a thousand yards across the river, found some boats and made five crossings ferrying men over. He had recovered and was now strong enough to tell the story of his truly remarkable effort which got him his MC. It was our last filming and the first to appear in the finished film. The language he used was that of an angry warrior.

That evening we took drinks with the British Ambassador and his wife. She, a glamorous foreign lady, gossiped without restraint. He spoke with a frankness that surprised and delighted us. It must be a difficult posting.

The filming was over, but the veterans had to be delivered back in good order. We were given a business class lounge at Mandalay Airport and a rest-room for the five hour wait at Bangkok. We took off at 2300 and after a flight of 12 hours 40 minutes were back at Terminal Four. We said our goodbyes and hoped that what we had said would make sense when it was transmitted.

It made sense. Mark Fielder and his editor had taken our fleeting memories and attached to Mike Fox's expert images and Bob Webber's crystal clear sounds they came to life. The media assembled and watched. I was moved by seeing places and recalling events that over the years I had to keep reminding myself had actually happened. The programme when it was transmitted on VJ Day drew the attention of many to a war which we thought that too few knew about. Were they surprised by what they saw?

This, I believed, would be my last glimpse of that land of war where I had begun. But I was proved wrong in an unexpected way.

19.
Full circle

In November 2005 something remarkable happened.

A number of people went halfway round the world to pay homage to my grandfather. This is to cut a long story quite short and to bend the truth gently in my direction. How gently will emerge. What will also emerge is an ending to a story neater than I could have imagined.

On the ninth of November about fifty met at Terminal Three at Heathrow. They were warriors bent on returning to where they had fought, and remembering; and there were some wives, though some warriors had sadly lost theirs and were having to remember by themselves, wishing they could have shared their past. A few had been born in Maymyo and were taking the opportunity to return to their birthplace. And there were some young. What were they doing there?

They came as carers to help old men; all of these were in their eighties, and they were sponsored by a remarkable enterprise. Someone somewhere had a good idea. Many were eager to return to where their war had taken them; but not all could afford it. Enter the National

Lottery Fund. With the war sixty years ago and with men wondering whether they would ever make the journey here was a place where money could be well spent. So there came what was rather grandly titled "The Heroes Return", a scheme to fund the return of veterans, spouses and carers. I was in an unusual position, my spouse being young enough to be a carer, but I was given a beefy young man to stand by and carry a bag and generally encourage. The arrangements were in the hands of what must be one of the world's most worthy travel companies: Remembrance Travel, whose sole object was to take people to where they or their relatives had fought. It was one arm of the great body that sustains warriors, the Royal British Legion.

We met at 1830 hours at the Thai International Desk, looking round at the other warriors and wondering what their stories were. It was Flight TG 917 to Bangkok. There were no direct flights to Burma. Rangoon Airport cannot take jumbos and other countries would anyway be unwilling to fly direct, as the traffic might not justify it and views on that country might make airlines unwilling to have direct contact.

Old men prepared to be spoilt, welcomed by lovely ladies who took us in that Thai cabin straight to the East, though an East significantly different to the one in which we fought, and plied with food that we were content to call very good. And we tried to sleep. We had learnt to sleep in strange places. But that was too long ago. We had to relearn and few succeeded. The silk-clad ladies offered us drinks, and we took them eagerly. And eleven and a half hours passed and we flew into the eastern day and our past.

Transit is a hurrying to a new place, a hurrying and another waiting. And Flight TG 305, an Airbus of an early vintage, to Yangon, which we were told was not a new name, but a new pronunciation of the old name. And so to the Inya Lake Hotel, a hotel trying to look like a palace and almost succeeding. We had arrived. We were processed. We awaited orders.

Early next morning on the 11th of November, having had little time to shed our journey, we set off for a Service of Remembrance at the great British War Cemetary at Htaukkyant, remembering sixty years of peace. It was a mighty gathering. The representatives of twenty one embassies laid wreaths. I returned to the grave of one of my sergeants and a fellow officer. One was a simple soldier who had taken a wrong turning, the other a decorated warrior killed when leading his men in a dangerous place. I showed them to Rachel; it was her nearest glimpse of my war. We wandered in the blazing sunshine and took pictures of each other, rather conscious of our medals. It was a splendidly managed occasion, and perhaps the last. Sixty years is enough; we are growing old.

But where does my grandfather come in? I must explain. A two hour drive from Mandalay lies the hill station of Maymyo. Its name has been changed, for obvious reasons. The name was taken from a British Army officer, Colonel May, who was posted to the hill station in 1887 to suppress a rebellion which flared up after the annexation of Upper Burma to India. (The way Britain annexed Burma does not bear very close examination). It is now called Pyin U-Lwin. But to me that name means nothing. Maymyo was where my parents were married in 1918 and where my brother Bill was born in 1919; and where my grandfather Rodway Swinhoe lived and worked, as I explained in my first chapter. My parents were married at All Saints Church where my grandfather worshipped.

After he died, which was in 1927, two splendid stained glass windows each approximately 10 feet by 3 feet and divided into five separate panels were installed in his memory. They are extremely fine examples of Pre-Raphaelite stained glass and are believed to have come from either a William Morris or Burne-Jones studio. And they were erected in honour of my grandfather.

In January 2004 Brigadier Van Orton and his wife visited the church hoping to see the windows. What they saw was a sorry sight. Their condition was such that without urgent repairs they were likely to collapse. The figure of £8000 was put forward and an appeal made. The speed with which the money was raised says all sorts of things about the British which readers may turn over in their minds. Was it nostalgia for our colonial past; the wish to remember a good man; the love of a fine piece of art; a hope that this church will continue to worship God in the beauty of holiness? Perhaps a bit of all of this.

Who was to restore the windows? It was David Knowles CBE, one of the great restorers of our day, who had already restored glass in Westminster Abbey and St Albans Cathedral and in 2003 he had repaired windows in Holy Trinity Cathedral, Yangon. He agreed to mend the Maymyo windows at cost. This was typical of the man who came with us, a person willing to give himself without stint and greeting every circumstance (and taking old men round Burma there were many) with enormous good cheer. He was also a commanding figure in international veterans organisations. It was good to know him.

The Road From Mandalay

The project was sanctioned by the Most Reverend Samuel San Si Htay, Archbishop of Burma and the work started in February 2005.

So why had many of us come to Burma? To attend a service of dedication of the repairs to the church, the main one my grandfather's windows. Two of our coaches were named somewhat enigmatically Windows 1 and Windows 2. That was why they had come.

We had first to get to Maymyo. We flew from Yangon to Mandalay by a strikingly improved domestic airline, Air Mandalay, to what must be one of the most remarkable airports in the world. It has only recently been completed and is many miles from Mandalay. It has a huge runway, said to be one of the longest in the world and an almost palatial terminal. All it lacked was aeroplanes. The day we arrived there were seven movements and the day we left eight. This was either a white elephant built at the whim of the generals or a very optimistic look into the future. It was weird.

The drive to Maymyo required skill. It twisted up the mountainside giving us backward glimpses of a land beset with pagodas and a feeling of expectation as we approached the object of our pilgrimage. We were also feeling a fresher air. The British knew where to escape the heat, and it was a very British place. The Park View Hotel, which had few pretensions but some comfort, received us and we awaited the day. The windows were drawing near.

The Service of Dedication and Remembrance took place on November 13th. It was a beautifully shaped act of worship. The Rt Rev Mya Than, the Bishop of Mandalay, presided. Prayers were said by Canon Robert Teare, from the diocese of Winchester, a diocese that has Burma on its heart. A special prayer for the windows, written by the Bishop of Manchester, was said by Brigadier Colin Van Orton, the chairman of the project. "Heavenly Father, who in creating the world gave us the brilliance of light and the brightness of colour we offer to you our praise for the restoration of these windows and for the talents that have enhanced their beauty…"

The lesson was read by the British Ambassador, Ms Vicky Bowman. She was one of the surprises of our visit, a single 37 year old lady, more sprightly perhaps than diplomats usually are, and one who had an uninhibited friendliness that was very attractive. She had already two days before opened her splendid embassy gardens to us and I had tried to get alongside as many Burmese as I could and found myself talking to some journalists and wondering what they were allowed to discuss. I left them with the rather enigmatic remark, "The truth is what matters." Ms Bowman was fluent in Burmese which must have eased her position, but the government, infuriated by a political opponent who could only be referred to as The Lady, must have had complex thoughts about this other lady.

"After the Service the congregation is requested to gather in the Garden of Remembrance for a commemorative photograph." We did, and many cameras clicked. Viscount John Slim, the son of the incomparable Bill, the famed commander of the Fourteenth Army, was there, as he always was when Burma veterans gathered, and an old and heavily decorated Gurkha who had operated behind enemy lines; we had been rededicating a memorial to the 10th Gurkhas. I identified myself as a relative of the man whose windows we were honouring and was thrust into a row of warriors and clerics, still wondering, as I continued to do, why people had come so far to see the memorial to my grandfather. In the blazing sun we mingled and were glad to be there. It was a Sunday like no other.

The rest of the day was ours and we wandered. Maymyo still had the feel and smell of a colonial town and I realised how much my family must have enjoyed it. The house where my grandfather lived, Park View, is no more. There is a mulberry plantation on the garden and a silk factory nearby. Next door is a development which will one day be a government-sponsored Ethnic Village. The top military brass live in Maymyo and there is an elite military training establishment. But there are still the magnificent Botanic Gardens that my grandfather had helped to establish, based on Kew, and many were enjoying them. We added to their number, gazing at a beauty that seemed miles from the turmoils of this land and a piece of the Raj of which surely they could not be ashamed. That evening after our meal we had an informal party, and the ambassador joined in, becoming one of us.

The following morning we left. I had seen some of my family beginnings. There were two others to come. My father had come to Burma on secondment from the Indian Army to monitor movements of Chinese on the China-India border in the area of Lashio in 1915. Lashio was where two roads met: the original Burma Road starting from Rangoon, the scene of savage fighting between the Japanese and the Chinese in 1942 and that other remarkable road stretching from Assam that the Americans hued out in the war and which remains as a tribute to the unconquerable will of a nation that when it sets its mind to something sees it through. It was in this direction that we got on the train at Maymyo, a little extra that our travel company had arranged for us. The Burma government was gradually loosening restrictions and although Lashio was still out we could make for one of the engineering wonders of Burma, the Gokteik Viaduct. Tourists could go there and wonder.

We went slowly as all Burmese trains do, but we were in no hurry and were content to see the land slip by, and watch the Burmese working their land, a people striving to get from that land enough to make up for all the constraints that their country faced. And then the trees closed in and there was jungle bearing echoes of our past. We climbed to nearly 4000 feet and then started the slow descent to the gorge, crawling round the contours and hooting at every turn. And there it was, a stunning structure described by one travel writer as "a monster of silver geometry in all the ragged rock and jungle". It was built by an American firm, completed in 1903 and spans a 990 foot river gorge. It had been an objective for the first Chindit operation in 1943 but proved too far. Anyway, it would have needed a mass of explosives to dent it. The train crawled across it and we peered down to a depth that we cannot have seen before. We could go no further than the next station, but it had been a marvel.

Our coach, Windows One, was waiting for us and drove us back. That is poorly described. It was in fact a most remarkable piece of driving on a road that twisted and turned, first plunging into the gorge and then struggling up the other side, each corner so sharp that the coach had to stop in order to realign itself. This was another triumph of construction.

There was one final bit of my past to tidy up: my birthplace, Mandalay. I had visited it ten years before, film-making. This was a final goodbye. We arrived late at the Mandalay Hill Resort Hotel, a mammoth building, a vast intrusion into the trees that skirted the hill. Rachel said it was a blot on the landscape, and I was inclined to agree. But old men are glad to rest and be pampered, and our bedroom gave us a dazzling view of Mandalay Hill which the Gurkhas conquered in a night assault. That evening there was a gala dinner by the pool, to celebrate a remarkable collection of warriors; other parties had joined us, drawn skilfully together by the organisers of Remembrance Travel. We exchanged each others' pasts and were glad to be there. It was surely our last visit. Lord Slim gathered the veterans on to the stage by the pool and said good things about us and about the need to remember much – about the past and the needs of those who had served and those who still serve. The other diners applauded us. Being a veteran is a strange business. Those who applaud us and the medals we wear assume that we have been brave. We could tell them of fear and an unwillingness to die. But we agreed that it was a rough place in which to serve.

In the morning when I was writing these words a relative rang up and said, "There is a talk going on about Burma." Hurriedly I switched on. It was a tale about the suffering of the people of Burma, and I wondered what those who oppressed their people so cruelly thought of those of us who now used their land to remember how we had freed it. Our remembrance was a very comfortable one. The people we freed, and who greeted us with such charm and affection, were now in chains. We had a splendid dinner and perhaps did not think of them enough. We hoped that they were really glad to see us. Their smiles suggested that they were.

We had a day in Mandalay, driving out to see the reaches of the Irrawaddy, stretches of water surrounded by pagodas and in the evening we mounted Mandalay Hill where pagodas and temples competed for space in a kind of frenzy of devotion – though perhaps frenzy is not a word that Buddhists would be happy with. The huge Buddhas who reclined there invited us to share their ease. And as the sun set we gazed down on a lovely land.

As we left the following morning, I said to the guide, "I would like to see the church where I was baptised." Our guide was a man of wide culture who had travelled to many countries and was able to tell us much that we needed to know, which he did wisely and with good humour. He said, "Certainly" and we drew up at St Mary's Church. This was it. I went inside and posed by the font. This was my beginning. It was good to be there, if only for a brief moment. It was an important look at where I had begun.

So back to Yangon, a dinner by the pool and after an extra trip up the west coast to Akyab, renamed Sittwe, sampling a part of Burma which had been the objective of singularly frustrating campaigns, some aborted, others expensively unachieved in the Arakan, that muddy cul-de-sac where Bangladesh now lies, we mounted our jumbo at Bangkok, sought sleep again without success and returned to an England that looked suddenly very grey. Heathrow in November at 0630 hours cannot smile. We said goodbye to each other, an uncomfortable exchange as we were trying to locate our baggage on the carousel. We hoped but did not expect to meet again. We certainly did not expect to see again the places where we had been so long ago, in my case a whole life.

My past was complete. Or was it?

There was a last shadow. In the days before I left England my brother Bill had become very ill and the end seemed near. Should I cancel my trip? The family said, "No. Go ahead." They wanted me to visit our beginnings. I was uneasy. We gave details of our movements and awaited news. On the 19th of November we received a call in our hotel bedroom in Yangon from my son that Bill had died on the previous day, and the funeral would be on the 24th. I was greatly relieved; not because he had died but because I would be able to attend his funeral.

We were due back on the 21st. On the 23rd we drove 200 miles to Dorset, a considerable endeavour, and on the following day we gathered in a lovely church in Dorchester. The family had come together from many places, one daughter from Edinburgh and another from Australia. It was an important gathering. My sister Iris was too frail to attend, her mind as active as ever but a body that could do little.

Over the years, to the Raj families who had given me shelter, death came too soon too often: three suicides, death by dysentery, by drowning, by streptococcal infection, by submarine, by cancer. They had all been touched. But Bill's going was different. At eighty six his time had come, a brave quiet ending to a life in which he had overcome much and had a steady regard for others; limited horizons amply reached.

I gave the address, piecing together Bill's life and recalling much that I have described in these pages. I had to measure my words carefully. I could praise Bill, which was no problem, particularly his remarkable skill at games, but I could not say all about a rather tangled childhood and the deprivations that Bill and I both felt that led to his determination that he would give to his own family the care he himself had lacked. In other words I could not describe in detail every bend in the road. But on looking back I could see amid all the regrets a contentment that we had found families whom we did not have to leave far away. No one would repeat our past.

It was not a bad way to say goodbye, to the land where I had started, and to the one who had shared its memories in war and to an East that had always been a distant backdrop.

The road from Mandalay had come full circle.

20.
And finally

The East had one more statement to make. On 3rd February 1806 twenty three students began the first term at the East India College in Hertford Castle. On 4th February 2006 a large body of people gathered at Haileybury to which the college moved in 1809 to celebrate those two hundred years. I returned to the place where for thirty four years I had taught the young and there were the buildings that had housed the men who had ruled the strange empire that had taken generations of my family.

We started in the Chapel, noting as we entered the memorial to the forty who had died in the Indian Mutiny. The young had, sometimes reluctantly, been told to be upright rulers and to show a Christian way forward, and they had largely governed by these principles. The Raj had not a little goodness in its ways.

The Bishop of London preached. This dignitary had been the visitor of the college, his last visit being a hundred and fifty years ago.

The present bishop crafted his words beautifully, recalling those two hundred years, urging us to grasp the principles that lay behind the training of those young men and, with a forthrightness that to today's ears delivered a slight shock, challenged us to follow Christ. We could not help listening.

Then we ate, in some style, trying to remember who we all were. We looked round the buildings, some new and grand designed to improve in order to attract, some of them now housing girls. But on the outside many were just as they had always been, where the future rulers of India had slept and worked and caroused. And there were documents to plot the sequence of events that had brought all this about.

Had it been worthwhile, the striving of these worthy young men? That is perhaps a ridiculous question for a very complex issue, and argument continues to rage. What I saw was what it cost, and this is what I have tried to describe here. Bringing up today's young in yesterday's buildings made me think. Would they have done better, and could they have stood it? It is easy to mock at the Raj and how British we all were and how unwilling we were to mingle with those we governed; we were unwilling as it were to remove the veil. As a child of the Raj, may I put it differently. We saw it as a huge endeavour at a huge cost, which today those in India often regard in a better light than those on our shores who are pleased to bear the guilt of those who stood the strain.

I grew up in an age when we hoped we knew where we were going and were proved spectacularly wrong. Today we know that we don't know where we are going, certain in our uncertainties. I tried, as I taught, to point the direction in which certainty could be found, and to share a joy that came my way.

I left Haileybury that afternoon mindful of the past, to return to this present world, and to believe that today is what matters. The road has been a fascinating one. Its origin was Mandalay; its terminus I await, thankful for what I have learnt, the people whom I have met and who have enriched me and for the ultimate encouragement that there is hope.

Postscript

There is one last milestone. On the 13th of February 2007 Iris died and we laid her to rest on the 20th; the last sibling. Long widowed she had given our mother faithful care over her last few years and then, freed, she had moved from place to place, her body increasingly frail but a mind that was always seeking new experiences. In 1993 she returned to India for the first time in thirty years and made five further trips, twice to Kalimpong, once to South India and twice to Assam, latterly on a Zimmer frame.

It was a complex mind-set. The country she loved. What gave her a bitterness that never really left her was how the British had ruled, and what that rule had cost her. Her thoughts come unrestrained in her last book, *Daughters of the Empire,* which was published recently, a tale of ladies caught up in the tangles of the Raj and her own life spelled out with an honesty that makes at times heart-breaking reading.

At the crematorium near Wolverhampton we said goodbye to one who had the fierce and intemperate candour to voice the regrets of so many who went east and wished that it could have been otherwise.

I believe that the family past has at last been laid to rest.

About the Author

Richard Rhodes James was born in Mandalay in 1921, one of five children of an Indian Army officer. He was educated at Sedbergh School and The Queen's College, Oxford. In the war he served in Burma with the Chindits and was mentioned in despatches. He taught for 44 years, chiefly at Haileybury where he ran a boarding house for 21 years. He moved to Cambridge where he finished his teaching and where he continues to learn. He has contributed to The Times and a number of magazines. He is married and has three children and six grandchildren

Printed in the United Kingdom
by Lightning Source UK Ltd.
124812UK00002B/43-147/A